The Christian Counselor's Commentary

The Gospel of Luke

Jay E. Adams

Institute for Nouthetic Studies, a ministry of Mid-America Baptist Theological Seminary, 5640 Airline Road, Arlington, TN 38002
mabts.edu / nouthetic.org / INSBookstore.com

The Gospel of Luke: The Christian Counselor's Commentary
by Jay E. Adams
Copyright © 2025 by the Institute for Nouthetic Studies,
© 1998 by Jay E. Adams

ISBN: 978-1-949737-95-0 (Paper)
ISBN: 978-1-949737-96-7 (eBook)
Old ISBN: 0-889032-09-3

Editor: Donn R. Arms

Library of Congress Cataloging-in-Publication Data
Names: Adams, Jay E., 1929-2020
Title: *The Gospel of Luke:*
The Christian Counselor's Commentary
by Jay E. Adams
Description: Arlington, TN: Institute for Nouthetic Studies, 2025
Identifiers: ISBN 978-1-949737-95-0 (paper) | OCLC: 40531356
Classification: LCC BS2341.2 .A33 | DDC 225.7

All rights reserved. No part of this publication may be reproduced, stored in a retrieval system, or transmitted in any form or by any means – electronic, mechanical, photocopy, recording, or any other – except for brief quotations in printed reviews, without prior permission of the publisher.

Published in the United States of America

CHAPTER 1

1 Since a number of persons have undertaken the task of compiling an account of the events that have most certainly taken place in our midst
2 just as they were handed down to us by those who from the outset became eyewitnesses and ministers of the Word,

---

The Gospel of Luke is unique in several ways. For one, the introduction to the book is unlike any other in the New Testament. It has the look of the educated writer of the day. It is the sort of document that one might expect from the hand of a scholar who was trained in the schools as a physician. And it is addressed to a person of prominence (the **excellent Theophilus**). Moreover, Luke wants the reader to know that he has carefully investigated the sources for his information and has found them **reliable**. Luke was concerned about the way in which others had written about the ministry of Jesus Christ and so determined to do so in a more correct manner (he does not refer to the other canonical writers). In addition, since Matthew had a tendency to group many of his materials under headings (within the broad sequence of events), John wrote about other aspects of Jesus' ministry, and Mark failed to include much material that was available, Luke wished to set forth what had transpired in a fuller, **chronological order**. Luke's concern for women, his interest in medicine and healing, his understanding of the preaching of the Gospel by the apostle Paul all went together to give a tone that is different from other Gospels. While we see little of him in action in the book of Acts (he appears largely as Paul's companion) one can imagine that it was he who did much of the counseling of new converts. There is a compassion about his writings that no student conversant with them can fail to recognize; it simply seeps out.

In these first four verses, you find a periodic sentence, composed in the grand style. Luke's vocabulary is clearly the literary *koine* rather than the everyday, man-on-the-street variety, in which much of the rest of the New Testament is written. After the preface, however, the style changes as Luke closely follows his sources. Yet, even in this (unlike other writers) he is never simply the Jew writing Greek—even when his sources are quite Jewish.

The accounts that one reads of what happened, including conversations, etc., doubtless come from firsthand sources (**eyewitnesses**). Luke, for instance, could know about the encounter between Gabriel and Mary from Mary herself. As a contemporary of the apostles, though younger

3 it seemed good for me too, because I had thoroughly investigated everything from its beginning, to write an orderly account for you, most excellent Theophilus,
4 so that you might know the reliability of the facts in which you have been instructed.

---

than most, Luke was able to hear the stories of eyewitnesses. That he was able to take down notes from such witnesses and others precisely (as he did in reproducing the speeches and sermons of Paul in Acts) is apparent. Physicians were taught shorthand in order to take exact notes. When he speaks of that which happened **in our midst** (v. 1), clearly, he refers to those things that happened among *Christians*, but not necessarily including himself as an eyewitness. He means that he was *now* part of the body that (before his conversion) had been privy to the happenings he reports. There were people like James, the Lord's brother, Mark and Mnason, an early disciple (Acts 21:16), as well as others from whom Luke could have easily drawn much material. Then there were written sources as well (v. 1). And according to the verb used in verse 3, we know that Luke thoroughly studied (**investigated everything**) that had taken place from the **beginning**. That is to say, from the arrival of John the Baptist on the scene, the beginning of the Gospel story. In an accurate way he detailed all the data that he found **reliable**.

Theophilus had learned the gospel and, perhaps, much Christian truth. That he did not have the complete record of the ministry of Jesus, however, seems apparent. This is what, in God's providence, Luke provides him—and us!

For the counselor, there are insights into human nature. Touches such as, **while they still disbelieved out of joy and amazement** (24:41), help the counselor to understand the reactions of persons to unusual events. As we go along you will see that, *par excellence,* Luke is the counselor's Gospel writer. Indeed, he has been called a psychologist (in the older sense of the word) by Carpenter, A.T. Robertson and others. So, without further discussion, let us move along to the Gospel as such.

Luke begins with the story of the birth of John the Baptist, citing the time when this took place as **in the days of King Herod of Judea** (v. 5). Luke's concern for exactness comes out in this way as you will see again and again throughout the book. Counselors ought to be as careful about times and dates as well as facts when speaking with counselees. There is much that may hang upon exactness, and counselors who are not careful

5 In the days of King Herod of Judea there was a priest named Zechariah who belonged to Abijah's division of the priesthood, whose wife Elizabeth was a descendant of the daughters of Aaron.

6 And they both were righteous in God's sight, living blamelessly according to all of the Lord's commandments and ordinances.

---

will find themselves in trouble sooner or later. The counselor who misquotes, the one who gets his facts and dates wrong, may not only make false assumptions about the data he gathers (and so misdirect his counselees) but will also find that his counselees lose confidence in him. The concern for accuracy that Luke claims, and that his writings demonstrate, is a trait you ought to develop. If you have been careless about such things, you will fail as a counselor.

Luke introduces us to **Zechariah**. He tells us that he was a **priest** of **Abijah's division** (the eighth; cf. I Chronicles 24:10). The priesthood was divided into twenty-four divisions. Each served according to **lot** (v. 9). Because of the number of priests, which were reckoned at about 20,000 at this time, a man would only serve in the capacity here outlined once in his life. Is it remarkable that, out of so many, Zechariah just "happened" to be on duty at that very time? Certainly not. His lack of a child, his prayer for one and his righteous life all were part of what God had ordained to lead to the events that were to transpire. Things don't *just happen*. They happen in God's providence in just the ways that He wants them to happen. It is not that your counselee is merely one out of 20,000 (or more) either. Whatever it is that God has for him will take place precisely as it should. God arranges all circumstances in His way. Teach counselees to praise Him for that and to trust in His omniscient wisdom.

The accuracy that appears in Luke's statements about Zechariah continues in his identification of his wife, **Elizabeth**, who was also in the priestly line of Aaron (v. 5). Now comments are made about both. They were **righteous in God's sight**. That was an uncommon thing at this time. Most of the people of Israel—including the religious leaders—were self-centered, self-righteous and contemptible in the sight of God. Here were two among those **righteous** few who looked for God's Messiah in saving faith, rather than trusting in their own self-righteousness (cf. Romans 10:1-3). When Luke says that they lived **blamelessly according to all of the Lord's commandments and ordinances** (v. 6), he was describing how they observed the Old Testament laws of sacrifice that looked forward to a coming Savior and lived by God's power according to the com-

> 7 But they had no children because Elizabeth was barren, and both were getting old.

mandments of His Word. The expression **blamelessly** does not mean that they were perfect (sinless), but that when they sinned, they carefully followed the Old Testament method for dealing with sins.

People today who come for counsel often have wrong ideas about sin. Not only do some think that there is no hope for those who are not sinless, but there are those who believe that if one sins he loses his salvation. Both ideas are false. In this age, as well as in the Old Testament era, God not only made provision for our salvation, but also for sin committed after conversion. One must confess his sins and forsake them. He must grow by grace. He must ask for Fatherly forgiveness and grant it to others (Matthew 6:12, 14). What Luke means, then, is that they were faithful believers.

But, Luke goes on to observe, **they had no children because Elizabeth was barren, and both were getting old** (v. 7). It is important to know these facts to understand the miracle that followed. But it is also of value to deal with counselees according to the side implications of these two verses. It is possible that Christians today, who are truly doing the things that God commands them, may not have children. Too often the counselor will hear the question from such persons, "Do you think that God is punishing us for something? Is that why we can't have children?" Well, of course, a nouthetic counselor will investigate by gathering the relevant data whether the counselees have done something wrong that they think might have been the basis for such a punishment. If so, he will help them deal with the sin. But he will also point out that to be childless is not necessarily the result of God's punishment. Indeed, he will want to be sure that the couple to whom he is talking has not "manufactured" some sin or other as an explanation for the condition, when that is not the fact at all. Here, and in the case of the man born blind (John 9), this situation was decreed by God in order that He might manifest His work in them. Not in a miraculous way, but in some fashion, God may be doing something similar in the childless counselees who inquire about their problem. He will want to help them discover some purpose which may not have occurred to them. Even if that is not possible at this point, a counselor will want to eliminate the idea that childlessness cannot accompany an exemplary life before God. I know of no other passage that presents this fact in so powerful a manner.

Luke 1

8 Now while he was serving as priest before God when it was his division's turn to be on duty,
9 according to the custom of the priesthood it was his lot to enter the Lord's temple and burn incense.
10 And at the hour of incense, there was a group of people praying outside.
11 Then an angel from the Lord appeared to him, standing on the right of the incense altar.
12 When he saw him, Zechariah was upset and terrified.

Verses 8 through 10 indicate that the event that follows happened at the time when Zechariah had entered the holy place to **burn incense** as a fragrant offering before God in conjunction with a daily sacrifice. (Such sacrifices were offered morning and evening every day.) This **incense** was emblematic of the prayers of the saints. The incense was burned in a fire pan (censer) within the holy place while a group of **people** (who were also divided into 24 courses for the purpose) representing the whole of Israel, **prayed** without.

That God interrupts even righteous worship (as He did here) in order to impress not only Zechariah, but the people as a whole (who would go back and spread the news) is instructive. Sometimes people seem so caught up in forms of worship that they (themselves) have devised so as to think that any change would be sacrilegious. If even a ceremony, such as this one, that was divinely ordained could be momentarily set aside for a message from God, surely something man-made can be for a good purpose. Super-strict believers at times may be concerned (indeed, worked up) over matters of this nature. God has the right to interrupt His own ordinances for His good reasons. So do we.

In the holy place, the angel Gabriel **appeared to** Zechariah. He stood **at the right of the incense altar** (v. 11). Even though he was a **righteous** person Zechariah was **upset and terrified**. It was a holy place in which this happened; not everyone was allowed to enter. It was a dramatic moment for Zechariah—a moment for which he had waited a long time. Now, on top of all of that, an angel had appeared; no wonder he reacted as he did! Moreover, as we noted before, he was righteous by faith in a coming Redeemer to which the sacrifice before him pointed, but that did not mean that he was sinless. As a matter of fact, in just a few more verses we shall see the sin of unbelief outcropping.

The response of sinful man to a visitation of the supernatural is invariably fear. Again and again when they appear to men, the first word

13 But the angel said to him,
       Don't be afraid, Zechariah; your prayer was heard and your wife Elizabeth will give birth to a son, and you must call his name John.
14   Then you will be glad and joyful and many will rejoice over his birth.
15   He will be great in the Lord's eyes.
       He will never drink wine and strong drink,
       but he will be filled with the Holy Spirit from his mother's womb.

---

of angels is, "**Don't be afraid**" (v. 13). In the garden of Eden, before the fall, there was no fear in the relation of Adam to God. The two talked freely, naturally, in the cool of the day. But since the fall, men (as sinners) fear the presence of God. This is a good response, given the fix that we all are in. When you bring a counselee into a proper relationship with God in a counseling session—which is the purpose of the session—something of that same sort of fear ought to be present. When one is in that condition, he is in a mode to hear and properly respond (even though he may vacillate, as Zechariah did).

For some time Zechariah had prayed for a child. Perhaps by now, however, he had given up praying, resigned to the idea that God's answer was "no." But the angel says that the prayer (offered so long ago) at last would be answered affirmatively. How often have counselees wanted instant answers to their prayers! That is not always God's way. In His time, for His purposes, He often postpones the answer to our prayers. Patience is one of the virtues that a believer must cultivate. Here, at long last, God was going to give this couple what they had longed for, for so long!

The angel is specific: he says, "**Elizabeth will give birth to a son, and you must call his name John**" (v. 13). Then he describes the effects of the birth: "**You will be glad and joyful and many will rejoice over his birth**" (v. 14). He is predicting not only the joy of having a child at last but also what gladness this child would bring to his people through his proclamation of the message that the Lamb of God was coming. Doubtless, Zechariah heard these words without understanding much of their import at the time.

The angel continued, telling this father-to-be what sort of man John would be. The Lord would consider him **great** (v. 15). He would be like a Nazarite, never drinking **wine** or **strong drink**. And he would be **filled with the Holy Spirit from his mother's womb**. That word surely must

Luke 1

16 He will turn many of Israel's sons to the Lord their God,
17 and he will go before Him with Elijah's spirit and power
to turn the fathers' hearts to the children and
those who disobey to the righteous way of thinking
in order to prepare a people for the Lord.
18 Then Zechariah said to the angel, "How can I know this is going to happen? I am old and my wife is getting up in years."

---

have been enigmatical to Zechariah. Nevertheless, he remembered it and passed it on (perhaps through others) to Luke. **Gabriel** went on. In the words at the very end of Malachi (and of the Old Testament Scriptures) he described his mission as that which was prophesied about the Elijah to come (v. 16, 17). John, by his preaching and by his baptism of repentance, would **turn the hearts** of the **fathers** and the **children** to one another. That is to say, in this land barren of faith, many would once again turn in repentance to the faith of the **fathers**. Indeed, he now says explicitly that John would **go before** the coming Savior in a manner like **Elijah** of old. In other words, he would fulfill Malachi's prophecy. And in doing so, he would fulfill Isaiah's prophecy of the one who would **prepare a people for the Lord** as well. The **spirit** of Elijah was the spirit (attitude) of the reformer, who would spare none, and who would right all wrongs. The **power** of Elijah would be in his preaching (not in miracles, because John did no miracle; John 10:41). God would use this voice crying in the wilderness in a powerful way to stir a whole nation.

This word must have overwhelmed Zechariah. He was a man versed in the Old Testament. Certainly he understood now the import of the angel's word. But he had difficulty in believing it. Consequently, he questions the angel. He wants assurance (v. 18). He is like so many who when God says something doubt, and ask for some sign. Today God will give no more signs. Jesus said "An evil and adulterous generation seeks a sign" (for more on this see my book *The Christian's Guide to Guidance*). Zechariah protests that he and his wife are too old for this to happen. But the angel tells him who he is, **Gabriel, the one who stands in God's presence.** He is not only an angel, but one of the foremost angels; one privileged to stand before God in order to carry out his bidding. He reproves him by telling him that what he has come to do is to **announce good news** to him. Why would he disbelieve such a message? But, if a sign is what he wants, he will give one: **You will be speechless and won't be able to talk until the day these things happen** (vv. 19, 20). That is both a sign and a punishment. The sort of sign God gave was chosen because Zecha-

Christian Counselor's Commentary

> 19 The angel replied,
>   I am Gabriel, the one who stands in God's presence; I was sent to speak to you and to announce this good news to you.
> 20   Now, you are going to be speechless and won't be able to talk until the day that these things happen, because you didn't believe my words, which will be fulfilled in their own time.
> **21** The people were expecting Zechariah, and they were wondering about his delay in the temple.
> 22 But when he came out and couldn't speak to them, they realized that he had seen a vision in the temple, because he kept making signs to them but remained speechless.
> 23 When the days of his service had been completed, he went home.

---

riah didn't believe the angel. In God's time the prediction that accompanied it would certainly come to pass, Gabriel assured him.

Sometimes, as in this instance, unbelief complicates matters for us. When God says something in the Bible, we should believe Him and not doubt. While He will not give us a sign as He did on this occasion, we may be brought into situations that are not altogether pleasant in order to bring about that which God has in mind. The sign, becoming public, served not only as a sign to Zechariah, but (in God's good providence) to the people waiting outside as well (vv. 21, 22). So indeed by grace, God's punishment of His erring child turned Zechariah's sin into a blessing for the people waiting here and for others throughout the nine months to come (cf. Romans 5:20). In a sense, through it, John's work of preparing a people for the coming of the Messiah had already begun! Your sinning counselees who doubt their salvation may take a measure of comfort in the fact that a righteous priest like Zechariah could express disbelief.

After all of this Zechariah **went home** (v. 23). After the excitement there comes the time for reflection. Doubtless, there was plenty for this couple and their friends to think about over the next few months. God sometimes allows counselees time to consider their thoughts and words and actions before bringing to fruition the many things that He wants them to do and experience. These times of waiting can be important in preparing them for what He has in store for them. Many counselees must be told that delay is often God's way, and be taught to take advantage of the time He provides rather than wasting it on frivolous or unrelated matters. God does not operate on Eastern Standard Time (II Peter 3:8).

Verses 24 and 25 describe the beginning of the fulfillment of the angel's prediction and mention that Elizabeth's **disgrace** because of **bar-**

Luke 1

24 Some time later his wife Elizabeth became pregnant and went into seclusion for five months.

25 She said, "This is what the Lord has done for me; He has looked upon me with favor to take away my disgrace before people."

26 Now in the sixth month the angel Gabriel was sent from God to a Galilean city called Nazareth

27 to a virgin who was engaged to a man named Joseph, who was from David's family; and the virgin's name was Mary.

---

renness (as it was considered to be in that community) at last had been removed. There was nothing more unusual to relate about the birth of John; Elizabeth's pregnancy, thereafter, was treated in the normal fashion of the times. But there could not help but be great anticipation by all who knew about the episode in the temple as John's birth drew near.

Gabriel (his name means "God's strong man") was busy. He next appears to **Mary** in the **Galilean city** of **Nazareth** (note again Luke's concern for detail: **in the sixth month** [of Elizabeth's pregnancy] v. 26). Carefully, Luke describes Mary's status: 1) she was a **virgin**; 2) she was **engaged** to **Joseph**; 3) her husband-to-be was in **David's** line. All of these facts were important to the fulfillment of Old Testament prophecy. Moreover, the virgin birth was essential to the incarnation. If Jesus had been born by the natural process, He too would have been a sinner like the rest of us. And beyond that all-important fact, neither would He have been the God-man. He would have been but another purely human sinner. As it was, the divine and the human came together each contributing that which would produce a Divine-human being Who, because of the intimate presence of the Holy Spirit (canceling out sin), would be sinless and, therefore, able to die in the place of guilty sinners.

Once again we see God working out every aspect of this birth according to His plans and purposes. Counselees with notions of "luck" and "chance" must be shown how there is no such thing. God is in absolute control of all that happens. Even though it may seem at times that things are out of His control, that never is true. Time, patience and trust (as noted above) are all essential to discovering how He works providentially in life. God is ordering affairs just as they ought to be ordered so that His purposes will be achieved. This record of the virgin birth of Christ and all that follows shows this in the clearest light.

When Gabriel told Mary that she was to be **greatly favored** (v. 28), this teen-age girl had no idea how great the favor of God was to be. She was to become the mother of the Lord Jesus Christ! Verse 29 once more

Christian Counselor's Commentary

> 28 He went to her and said, "Greeting. You are greatly favored; the Lord is with you."
> 29 But she was deeply upset at these words and wondered what sort of greeting this might be.
> 30 Then the angel said to her,
>   Don't be afraid, Mary; you have found favor with God.
> 31 Now you will conceive a Child in your womb and give birth to a Son, and you must call His name Jesus.
> 32 He will be great and will be called the Son of the Most High, and the Lord God will give Him His father David's throne,
> 33 and He will reign over Jacob's house forever, and of His empire there will be no end.

---

records her response—deep concern, fear and confusion. Gabriel reassures her, "**Don't be afraid, Mary**." God, he says, has determined to show His grace (favor) toward you (not because there was anything special about her, but because out of His mighty mercy He had deigned to do so).

When your counselee receives some favor from God, he should not be proud about it. God's grace is always undeserved favor. He should be grateful, not only giving thanks with his lips but also by the response of his life. Mary, doubtless, was one out of many other devout Hebrew girls who, for His own reasons, God chose to be the recipient of this very special favor. Surely, throughout the days ahead, as she **pondered** all that Gabriel was to say, she would have much to thank God for.

Gabriel gets right down to business. I like the way the angels who appear from time to time in the Scriptures carry out their tasks. They are messengers (that is the meaning of the word "angel") who don't delay, don't talk all around the subject, don't dilly-dally. Having reassured her that all was well, Gabriel tells her what she needs to know. His message? "You will **conceive a child** Who, when born, will turn out to be a **Son**, and you **must call His name Jesus**" ("Yahweh Saves"; v. 31). In addition, he says, "Jesus will be **great and will be called the Son of the Most High**. John would be called **great** also, but he would not be the **Son of God** Almighty; Jesus would, therefore, be greater than John (something John, himself, continually stressed). Also, He would be the Messiah. That is to say, He would be the Promised One Who would reign forever on **David's throne** according to Old Testament prophecy" (see Psalm 2; Daniel 2, 7, etc.; vv. 32, 33). This was a lot for a young girl to take in. She wants to know how this could be since she was still a **virgin** (v. 34). That

Luke 1

34 But Mary said to the angel, "How can this happen, since I haven't known any man?"
35 The angel said to her,
>   The Holy Spirit will come upon you and the power of the Most High will overshadow you, so that your Holy Child will be called God's Son.
36   There is your relative Elizabeth, who also is going to have a son in her old age, and she is in her sixth month, even though she has been called barren.
37   Nothing is ever impossible with God.

38 Mary said, "Here I am, the Lord's handmaid; let your word take place." Then the angel left her.

---

was a good question. It did not evidence disbelief (as did Zechariah's response) but merely puzzlement. The angel, who appears quite willing to answer, explains that the **Holy Spirit** will effect this in order that the child might become the holy Son of God (v. 35). And as an added assurance, he refers to **barren Elizabeth's** pregnancy in her old age (something that apart from God's miraculous working would not have been possible) and utters these powerful words: **Nothing is ever impossible with God** (vv. 36, 37).

Those last words, though through them you should not promise counselees miracles (nevertheless), are great words to use in countering a counselee's disbelief about the outcome of some complex situation. Promises of the Bible may be buttressed by this assurance. Though the counselee can see no way out of his dilemma, you may assure him that I Corinthians 10:13 has not been erased from the pages of Scripture. How God may extricate him, and when, may not be apparent at the moment, but the promise remains. And you may say to him, "Nothing is impossible with God. Believe that and, in His time, you will see His grace manifested." In one sense, it is an exciting venture to look forward to the way in which God will carry out the promises in His written Word. If He told us ahead of time the ways and means that He would employ, the denouement would be a ho-hum experience. Instead, He invites us to trust Him, obey His Word and watch for the outcome. Disbelief destroys that adventure.

Mary's response (v. 38) differs radically from Zechariah's. It is the response of faith and obedience. It is the response that you want to hear from your counselees, once having helped them to understand God's will for them in the situation. You want to hear them say such things as, "If the

39 So during those days Mary got ready and hurried to a town in the Judean hills,
40 and went into Zechariah's house and greeted Elizabeth.
41 When Elizabeth heard Mary's greeting, the baby jumped in her womb, and Elizabeth was filled with the Holy Spirit.
42 And she exclaimed in a loud voice,
> Blessed are you among women, and blessed is the fruit of your womb.
43 Why is it that my Lord's mother should come to me?
44 Just as soon as the sound of your greeting reached my ears, the baby in my womb jumped for joy.
45 Blessed is the one who believed that what the Lord told her would be fulfilled.

Lord says that I must go and seek forgiveness, so be it," or "Since God requires me to be a submissive wife, I will learn how," or "I recognize that I have been blameshifting; I will begin to assume the responsibility for my actions from now on as God requires." These, and dozens of responses of a similar sort, often exhibit the breakthrough point in a counseling session. You too, like Gabriel, may leave a counselee who has reached this place (v. 38^b) with the certainty that if the counselee truly follows through as he has said he will, you will have accomplished your mission. In the future, things will take a turn for the better.

Next Luke relates the encounter of Mary and Elizabeth (vv. 39-56). It is altogether appropriate for this meeting to have taken place. What happened on this occasion is remarkable. When **Mary** heard Gabriel's message, she packed up her things and hurried from the North to the Judean hills near Hebron where her cousin Elizabeth was living (vv. 39, 40). Upon hearing of what had happened, the unborn infant John **leaped** in **Elizabeth's womb** (v. 41), and Elizabeth, herself, was **filled with the Holy Spirit**. What occurred is beyond our ability to understand. But that there was some acknowledgment by John of the fact that Mary was bearing the Messiah (as well as by Elizabeth) is certain. How this could be is uncertain, but with God it is possible. That John **jumped for joy** is Elizabeth's explanation (vv. 42-45).

That there are events and happenings that we shall never understand this side of glory (and perhaps not even then) is likely. We must leave them where we find them, remembering Deuteronomy 29:29. Far be it from me to attempt an explanation.

Elizabeth proclaims Mary's **blessedness** (happiness); she will bear

Luke 1

46 Then Mary said,
    My soul greatly honors the Lord
47   and my spirit rejoices in God my Savior,
48   because He has looked upon His handmaiden in her humble position.
    From now on, all generations will call me blessed,
49   because the Mighty One has done great things for me, and His Name is holy.

---

the Lord of glory. Twice the word blessed appears in verse 42 and once in verse 45. Elizabeth, overjoyed at her own long-awaited pregnancy, as a humble believer, is able to see beyond herself to the greater miracle that would take place in Mary's life. Many counselees are so taken up with themselves and what is happening in their lives that they have a hard time obeying the command to "rejoice with those who rejoice" (Romans 12:15). Here is a great example of doing just that. Counselees must be able to share in the blessings of others that are beyond their own interest. If this meeting had taken place in the self-centered atmosphere of many a home, you would have a record of how Elizabeth was so taken up with her own miraculous baby that Mary would not have been able to get a word in "sledgewise!" When the **Holy Spirit fills** the heart of a believer, he rarely focuses on himself and his own concerns. It is always others (and the Lord in particular) upon which he concentrates. A study of this in the New Testament would be instructive for you and for some of your counselees. Indeed, Elizabeth was so excited at Mary's news that she shouted (as the word in v. 42 indicates). Counselor, when is the last time that you stood up and shouted at some good news that your counselee has told you? It is not beneath your dignity to do so!

In response to this wonderful greeting by Elizabeth, Mary now breaks out into poetry (vv. 46-55). In this magnificent piece we read about her humble gratitude for what God has done in choosing her for the task of carrying and giving birth to the Messiah (vv. 46-49). There is no pride in what she says. She does not exalt herself; she does not gloat over Elizabeth, taking something away from the latter's joy. No, precisely not that. What she does is give God glory and thanks. She sounds amazed and grateful. There is too much self-aggrandizement among believers in our time. When something good takes place in their lives they are all too ready to claim credit for it rather than to thank God for His goodness and mercy to them. Often, these are the same persons who will assure you they are not responsible for the bad things they do; that is always someone

50   **His mercy is for generations upon generations of those who fear Him**.
51   He did mighty acts by His arm:
      He scattered those who in the thoughts of their hearts were proud,
52   He pulled down powerful rulers from their thrones and raised up humble ones;
53   **He filled the hungry with good things and sent the rich away empty**.
54   He helped His servant Israel because He remembered His mercy
55   to Abraham and to his seed forever.
56 So Mary stayed with her about three months, and then returned to her home.

---

else's fault. Counselors will have to struggle with these sinful tendencies in their counselees all the time. They should not be overlooked. Here are two faithful women—Elizabeth and Mary—who become models for all women today.

Mary looks forward and backward in her praise of God (vv. 49-55). She acknowledges that the mercy of God has extended from the far distant past into her time and beyond (v. 49). This, she affirms, is the same mercy that in the past was experienced by those who were delivered from the proud and wicked by the poor whom He fed, by the humble raised up in the place of the powerful, and by Israel and Abraham. She understands that all of them were looking forward to that of which she is now to become so intimate a part—the birth of the Redeemer. And she sees her continuity with them in the God Whose mercy and goodness is for all generations.

How important it is to recite the goodness of God in ages past when counseling. To refer to God's goodness to Abraham, to Jacob, *et al*. It is important to help counselees recognize their continuity with the saints of the Scriptures in that they, too, are a part of the great community of saints with whom God has made covenant. He not only is the God of Abraham, Isaac and Jacob but the God of your counselee as well!

Wouldn't you like to have been a fly on the wall listening to Mary and Elizabeth over the next three months in which they talked as they awaited John's birth? (cf. v. 56). That must have been some time together!

As we move next to the birth of John keep considering verses 57 through 66, especially, but also the verses that follow. Women all seem to rejoice over the birth of a child. This must have been the situation with Elizabeth and her friends, relatives and neighbors because of her long

Luke 1

57 Now when the time came for Elizabeth to have her baby, she gave birth to a son.
58 Her neighbors and her relatives heard that the Lord had shown great mercy toward her and they rejoiced with her.
59 On the eighth day they came to circumcise the child, and they were calling him by his father Zechariah's name,
60 when his mother said, "No; instead he must be called John."
61 They said to her, "But there isn't anybody in your family who has that name."
62 So they made signs to his father, asking what he wanted to call him.
63 He asked for a tablet and wrote: "His name is John." And they were all surprised at this.
64 Then all of a sudden his mouth was opened, and his tongue was freed and he spoke, praising God.
65 And fear came over all their neighbors. And all who lived in the whole Judean hill country talked about these facts,
66 and all who heard laid them up in their hearts, saying, "What is this child going to be?" Indeed, the Lord's hand was with him.

---

period of barrenness (cf. vv. 57, 58). John was born. All seemed perfectly normal up until then. But, eight days later, when it was time to name him at his circumcision, a couple of unexpected things happened. First, as the crowd of well-wishers began to call him by Zechariah's name, John's mother protested, "**No; instead he must be called John**" (v. 60). This was confusing; no one in his immediate family had been named John, so why would he be? According to the patterns of name-giving in the community it didn't make sense. "His mother must have made some mistake," they thought. "We'll ask his father." But Zechariah agreed with her, writing on a tablet (since he couldn't talk) **His name is John** (v. 63). This surprised everyone.

As soon as Zechariah had done this, he could speak again. This time there came from his repentant lips not the words of doubt and disbelief that had led to his sign-punishment but words of praise (v. 64). All of these strange happenings were the beginning of the stirring of the people that John had come to effect. It led to **fear**, questioning, wonder about John's future mission (vv. 65, 66). His ministry had already begun in a very real sense.

It is amazing how little things like standing pat for something that God has required (here the name to be given to John) can have such large repercussions. Counselees ought to be urged to obey all that God requires of them. That includes what they might otherwise sluff off as inconse-

67 But his father Zechariah was filled with the Holy Spirit and prophesied, saying,
68   Blessed be the Lord God of Israel
     because He cared and brought about redemption for His people,
69   and raised up a horn of salvation for us
     by the house of His servant David,
70   just as He said through the mouth of His holy prophets long ago,
71   **so that we might be rescued from our enemies**
     and from the hand of all these who hate us,
72   to show the mercy promised to our fathers
     and to remember His holy covenant,
73   the oath that He swore to our father Abraham,

---

quential. This is not legalism (as some might protest); Elizabeth and Zechariah obeyed *all* God required of them. And that (even apart from the miracle of the latter's tongue being loosed in the act) was the beginning of the stirring John had come to bring about among the people (note the words, **Indeed, the Lord's hand was with him**; v. 66). So too, obedience in little things often leads to larger opportunities to serve God. Sloppy counselees, disorganized and undisciplined in their ways, will often skip right over what they consider unimportant requirements by the Lord. Nothing God commands is unimportant.

Now, Zechariah's tongue being freed, he takes the opportunity to praise God in words (vv. 67-79). Like the other poetic speeches in this chapter this one was impelled by the Spirit of God (v. 67). Indeed, it is called **prophecy**. It is that because Zechariah has been given wisdom by the Spirit to predict that in these happenings with his wife and with Mary a new era has begun. It is an era instituted by God sending salvation to His people in Jesus Christ (vv. 68, 69). And, he sees it as the fulfillment of the many Old Testament prophecies that have predicted the coming of David's Son, the Savior (vv. 69ff.). This he describes in terms of **salvation** from all one's enemies. He understands that the Abrahamic covenant given so many years before was finally being fulfilled. And he knew that his son, John, would be the new Elijah who would fulfill the predictions of Isaiah and Malachi. What a tremendous amount of truth had flooded into his doubting mind since the visit of Gabriel in the temple!

Sometimes it takes some happening—illness, or whatever—to bring us to our senses. How wonderful that what seems like tragedy many times is but the blessing of God Who is teaching us His Word. Surely, John had spent much time during the last nine months devouring the Old Testament

Luke 1

74	delivering us out of the hand of our enemies,
	making it possible for us to serve Him fearlessly
75	in holiness and righteousness before Him all our days.
76	And you, child, will be called the prophet of the Most High,
	because you will go **before the Lord to prepare His way**,
77	to give knowledge of salvation to His people
	by the forgiveness of their sins,
78	through the tender mercy of our God
	by which the rising sun will beam on us from on high,
79	**to make things visible to those who sit in darkness and the shadow of death**,
	to guide our feet into the way of peace.
80	The child grew and became strong in spirit, and was in the wilderness until the day of his appearance to Israel.

---

trying to understand what was happening; it comes out here in his words. But God had to shut his mouth, retire him from other things and give him a special portion of His Spirit in order to bring him to this understanding. Tell counselees that the times when God slows us down, often thwarting our purposes and bringing us into serious consideration of His sovereign ways are for our blessing. Urge them to take advantage of them by digging into His Word.

Christian Counselor's Commentary

CHAPTER 2

1 Now in those days a decree went forth from Caesar Augustus that a census of the whole Roman Empire was to be taken.
2 (This was the first census taken while Quirinius was governor of Syria.)
3 So everybody went to be enrolled, each to his own city.

Probably the best known and loved account of the birth of Jesus Christ is found in this chapter. Once again, in its historical detail it is precisely worded so as to place the event in time and space. Such care for accuracy does not fit a fable. The virgin birth, if a myth, would not occur in such a setting. This accuracy of detail, denoting research of the most minute sort, is consonant with truth, not with myth. Counselors can be grateful for such an account (vv. 1, 2).

According to verse 3 the method by which people were enrolled (at least in Palestine) was by returning to one's native city. We shall see in this decree, and in much of what follows, the providence of God at work, fulfilling the Old Testament prophecies. Jesus was to be born in Bethlehem; Mary and Joseph lived in Nazareth. In this way the birth would take place according to the prophecy, even though God's providence might inconvenience many people. You must make it clear to your counselees, whenever it is appropriate, that because God is in total control of His universe, history is not some happenstance, but the outworking of His purposes. If He wishes to, He may even move great populations of people to bring about His sovereign will. What is happening to them, therefore, is something that an Almighty God is controlling. Though it may occasion hardship—as it did for Mary and Joseph and others—it will truly work out for good to those who love Him (Romans 8:28). The fact that what happens in life is not some unfortunate slip in God's universe, but part of an ongoing, divine program, should relieve the minds of troubled counselees.

Obviously **Joseph** going up to **David's city**, **Bethlehem** ("house of bread, where the Bread of life was to be born), links Jesus with all of the Old Testament prophecies concerning the line of David and the promised Messiah Who would appear. God is working many things in multiple ways in order to bring about His will.

Mary went along—probably because of her pregnancy (v. 4). Joseph would not want to be apart from her at such a time. While in Bethlehem,

Luke 2

4 Joseph also went up from Galilee, from the city of Nazareth to Judea, to David's city, Bethlehem, because he was from David's house and family,
5 to be enrolled with Mary his wife, who was pregnant.
6 Now it happened that while they were there the time came for her to have her child,
7 and she gave birth to her first-born Son, and wrapped Him in strips of cloth and laid Him in a manger, because there wasn't any place for them in the inn.

---

therefore, she delivered Jesus, her first-born son (vv. 5-7). As was the custom, she wrapped Him in strips of cloth which were torn into lengths. Because of the crowded conditions caused by the enrollment, there was no place for them to stay in the inn, so (in one place or another—in a house where animals were allowed on the first floor or in the cave-stable to which many point) Jesus was cradled in a manger (eating trough) when He was born. The lowly conditions of Christ's birth were an appropriate beginning for a life of humiliation and exceptional enough that these conditions were mentioned as a **sign** to the **shepherds** (vv. 12, 16). Jesus' background was not among the schools, nor was it in the courts of royalty. It was a humble, carpenter's upbringing that from the beginning offered no special advantages. Those counselees who claim that their childhood has so disadvantaged them that they are not able to excel need to be reminded of the facts of Jesus' birth and childhood. Such lack might disadvantage one, but if dealt with properly, it can be overcome by turning the liabilities into assets.

Sometimes, when I point out such things, people think that I am being harsh or cruel, that exhortations are always forthcoming, but little compassion. What they misunderstand is this—there is an exuberance about the things of the Lord that not only overcomes difficulties but turns them into blessings. Every exhortation from God is a cause for hope. God never urges His children to do anything that He is unwilling to give them the wisdom and strength to accomplish if they will only turn to His Word and avail themselves of the power of His Spirit. To exhort is not to be cruel or harsh; it is of the essence of kindness. Counseling should not strike notes of despair, unmitigated tragedy or sloppy compassion; rather, it should be as upbeat as possible. If hope does not exude from the counselor at every turn (while taking the effects of sin seriously) it will not ordinarily be generated by the counselee himself. The birth (and subsequent life) of Jesus Christ is hope-engendering.

Christian Counselor's Commentary

> 8 In the vicinity there were shepherds living in the fields, keeping watch over their flocks by night.
> 9 And an angel from the Lord came upon them, and the Lord's glory shone around them, and they became deeply afraid.
> 10 But the angel said to them,
> > Don't be afraid. Listen, I am announcing to you good news of great joy that will be for all the people,

Now we come to **shepherds** (vv. 8-20). Once more, shepherds being among the poorest lower class, the lowly nature of the Savior's birth is emphasized. While **Caesar Augustus** was reveling in the finery of his Roman palace, that night in a field outside of Jerusalem shepherds **were keeping watch over their flocks** (v. 8). It was to them (not to Caesar—or even Herod) that the **angels** appeared to announce the birth. First, one **angel** (probably Gabriel who is elsewhere so prominent in Luke's narrative) appeared in **glory**. A brilliant light **shone** around the shepherds, who were startled and filled with **fear** at his sudden appearance. Once more, the angel found it necessary to assure them that there was no need to be afraid (vv. 9, 10).

I have spoken before about the fact that upon outbreakings of the supernatural sinful man's reaction always seems to be fear. It might be interesting to know how often fear is also what wells up within counselees who face the Lord in counseling sessions, as you bring them face to face with Him in the Scriptures. Have you ever noticed how many counselees will do everything that they can to move away from the clear requirements of the Bible even when they are presented to them as Jesus' commands? Of course, this may often be because they don't want to meet His requirements. But, in other cases, could it be that there is a certain **fear** about having to face the Lord Himself in the Word? Watch for this; in such cases, assure counselees that there is no need to fear Him and His message to them (v. 10).

Here, the angel was bringing to them **good news of great joy that will be for all people**. Whenever the Lord Jesus (Who here is the subject of that joyful good news) requires anything of His children it is always (in the long run) in order to bring **great joy**. That is because everything that He does for them is an outgrowth of His saving grace manifested on the cross. Because He died, counselees may overcome their sins. Because He died, they may solve their problems. Because He died, they may fulfill His will. Everything stems from the great joy of the birth of the Savior Who came to die. That is why I said before that in counseling, while

Luke 2

11 because to you there is born today in David's city a Savior, Who is Christ the Lord.
12 This will be a sign for you: you will find the Baby bound in strips of cloth, lying in a manger.
13 Suddenly there was with the angel a group of the heavenly host, praising God and saying,
14 Glory to God in the highest,
    and on earth peace among those persons toward whom He is showing goodwill.

---

always acknowledging the misery of sin, a counselee must be helped to see beyond that to the **great joy** of triumphing over it in Christ. The note of joy in the angel's voice as he announced the birth of Christ and the glory that shone around, captures the spirit in which counseling ought to be done.

This **great joy** announced by the angel was to **be for all people**. From the beginning, it was clear that Jesus had come to die not for Jews alone, but for His own out of all tongues and peoples and languages and nations. That the announcement came to lowly shepherds also makes it clear that He would become a **Savior** of people from all classes as well. There is no counselee, therefore, who may plead that his status is too lowly for him to achieve what God commands of him. Keep that fact in mind. It is amazing what excuses counselees invent to try to escape their responsibilities!

Here the shepherds are told that Jesus is a Savior, that He is Messiah, that He is Yahweh (the Jehovah of the Old Testament). Those are astounding truths—a veritable mouthful of theology packed in a brief statement! And given to uneducated shepherds. Your counselee, no matter what his background may be, can learn the vital truths of Christian teaching. The poorest saint, the least educated one, can become wise in the truths of the Bible. Don't hesitate to teach theology to every counselee; but be sure that you explain it in words that are intelligible—not in the jargon of the schools. Why do all counselees need theology? Because having the right theological understanding of God, men and things leads to right living (cf. Titus 1:1). All righteousness is living according to correct theology.

The shepherds are given a **sign**. The baby will be found in a **manger**, wrapped in poor swaddling clothes (strips of **cloth**). **Suddenly**, an army (**host**) of angels was with the angel, **praising God and saying** (singing?), "**Glory to God in the highest**." Here, they were singing God's praises for what He was doing in bringing Jesus into the human race to redeem men.

Christian Counselor's Commentary

> 15 When the angels went away from them into the sky, the shepherds said to one another, "Let's go to Bethlehem to see this thing that has happened, that the Lord has made known to us."
> 16 So they went in a hurry and found both Mary and Joseph, and the Baby lying in a manger.
> 17 But when they saw it, they told about the words that had been spoken to them concerning this Child,
> 18 and all those who heard were amazed at those things that the shepherds told them,
> 19 but Mary kept all these things, reflecting on them in her heart.

God is addressed as the One Who dwells in the **highest** places. All that that means is not clear, but it does signify that He is above all His creation. It probably is a way of distinguishing Him from that creation as the Creator and the Sovereign Preserver of it.

In contrast, on this **earth**, a small part of that creation, this One Who is so high above it all has deigned to stoop to care for sinful human beings on a small planet in that creation. By the birth of Jesus Christ He is bringing **peace** to those to whom He is showing His **goodwill** (grace; v. 14). This peace, however, is not the peace for which men look. It is individualized peace that comes into the hearts and lives of those to whom He brings salvation. It is peace *with* God; then peace *from* God (cf. Romans 5:1; Philippians 4). Christians have found peace with God in justification; it is not that, however, but the peace that passes all understanding that they are seeking in counseling. Jesus came to bring both. The announcement here should be a great encouragement to all who are troubled at heart (cf. John 14:1). If Jesus came to bring peace to all toward whom He is showing His good will, then His children (who are those included in that designation) should know that they may have such **peace**. Troubled counselees, who claim otherwise, may be referred to this birth announcement in order to contradict their glum, non-christian doubts. **Joy** is possible because **peace** is available. God, at His birth, announces that peace is the object of His coming. How, then, can one deny the possibility of attaining it? If there is no peace in a counselee's heart, that is *his* fault, not God's.

In verse 15 we see that the shepherds obey the injunction of the angel and find exactly what he told them they would (v. 16). Consequently, they too praise God and rejoice (v. 20). When they arrived, they told Mary and others present what the angel said. This was the source of great amazement to those who heard. And Mary, who had already experienced so many wonders in her life, took them to heart and reflected on them

Luke 2

20 The shepherds went back, glorifying and praising God for all they had heard and seen, as it had been told them.

21 Now when the eighth day had come and it was time to circumcise Him, he was called Jesus, the name given by the angel before He was conceived in the womb.

(vv. 17-19).

That word **reflected** is important. It has in it the idea of throwing things together in order to compare and systematize (make sense of) them. She was beginning to put two and two together (as we say). Every counselee should reflect on God's truth in relation to himself. It is not enough for him to be guided by a counselor (who has done all of the reflection for him). He should be taught to think, meditate, apply and implement truth. If you have done it all without engaging the counselee's mind, you have helped him little. He may get out of the immediate difficulty by following your directions, but he will not be able to emerge from future ones. He should be taught to **reflect** on what God has said so as to *understand* it. Mary is a good guide in this.

Having covered the birth of Jesus, Luke now moves on to show how He was identified with sinful men by his **circumcision** (vv. 21-24). Just as in John's baptism of Jesus, in spite of the hesitancy of John, here Jesus was made subject to the rite of circumcision. **Circumcision** outwardly, was a sign of the righteousness that one had by faith (Romans 4:11). Obviously, a child of eight days could not exercise faith. When he grew up, however, the sign of circumcision was to be a **sign** to him that he was expected to exercise faith in the coming Messiah, by which he would be declared righteous. It was a sign of the replacement of his sin with the **righteousness** of Jesus Christ (Colossians 2:11-14). In symbol, the old was stripped away and replaced by the new. Christ not only died in our place, He also was circumcised for us!

Again, a name is emphasized (v. 21), the Name, Jesus. The gospel song reads, "There is something about that Name . . ." This verse tells us what: that "something" is: the Name **Jesus** ("Yahweh saves") indicates what He came to do—save men from sin and its consequences. Point out to a counselee that every time he hears the word **Jesus** it ought to remind him of the fact that Jesus came to deal with all the problems that sin has brought into his life. The very name Jesus, therefore, ought to encourage and comfort him.

Verses 22 through 24 have to do with **purification**. Birth was cere-

Christian Counselor's Commentary

> 22 When the time of their purification according to Moses' law was over, they took Him up to Jerusalem to present Him to the Lord
> 23 (as it is written in the Lord's law, **Every male who opens the womb shall be called holy to the Lord**),
> 24 and to offer a sacrifice according to the requirement in the Lord's law: **A pair of turtledoves or two young pigeons**.
> 25 Now at Jerusalem there was a man named Simeon, who was a righteous and devout person who was expecting the consolation of Israel, and the Holy Spirit was on him.
> 26 It was revealed to him by the Holy Spirit that he would not see death before he would see the Lord's Christ.

monially defiling (though, in fact, Jesus' birth could not have been). Again, the identification of Jesus with sinners is apparent. The mother of a child was ceremonially unclean for forty days following the birth of a son. Jesus was **presented** in the temple because Jesus, Who was conceived **under the law**, had to be redeemed at the price of five shekels (Numbers 18:15, 16; Exodus 13:2). The **sacrifice** of the **turtledoves or pigeons** indicated that the one sacrificing was poor and could not afford a lamb.

Five times in this chapter, Luke uses the word **law**—more often than in the rest of the gospel. Why? Because Luke wishes to make clear that Jesus was entirely subject to the law as He, a Jew, was supposed to be (Gal. 4:4). There was nothing deficient in the identification of Himself with the Jews or with sinners. Though not Himself a sinner, He takes the sinner's place.

Now Luke relates the story of what happened when Jesus was presented in the temple (vv. 25-35). **Simeon, who was a righteous and devout person** (i.e., a faithful, godly Israelite) was present. We are told that he was **expecting the consolation of Israel** (that is, the help Israel would receive at Messiah's coming; v. 25). Prior to this time, it had been **revealed** to him in response to his inquiry about the matter (the verb implies such) that He would not die before he saw the Messiah (v. 26). Literally, "in the Spirit" (v. 27), **he came into the temple to do according to custom.** It was the custom to bring the child to a rabbi to bless it and pray for it (v. 28). Simeon then said, "**Now, sovereign Lord, let your servant depart in peace according to Your Word.**" That is, let me now die since Your Word that I would remain alive until Christ's advent has been fulfilled. The death of Simeon would be a **peaceful** one now that he had the joy of holding and blessing the Lord's Christ. Though counselees will

Luke 2

27 Now he came led by the Spirit into the temple, and when His parents brought in the Child Jesus to do for Him as the custom of the law provides,
28 he took Him in his arms and blessed God and said,
29 Now, sovereign Lord, let Your slave depart
in peace according to Your Word,
30 because my eyes have seen Your salvation
31 that you prepared in the presence of all peoples
32 **to be a Light for revelation to the Gentiles**,
and to be a glory for Your people Israel.
33 And His father and His mother were amazed at the things that were being said about Him.
34 Simeon blessed them and said to his mother Mary,
Now this Child is destined for the fall and rising again of many in Israel, and for a sign that is spoken against
35 (and a sword will pierce through your own soul too), so that the thoughts of many hearts may be revealed.

---

not have special revelations of the Spirit, yet whenever the promises of the written Word of God are fulfilled in their lives they, too, should have **peace** that grows out of having experienced the fulfillment of those promises.

Once more the promise of **salvation** to **all people**, which includes the **gentiles**, is reiterated (vv. 30-32). All these things, heaped up one on top of the other, **amazed** Mary and Joseph (His adoptive father; v. 33).

But now, a new note is struck. All would not be joy and gladness about this Child. Some would **fall** (that is, stumble and fall) because of Christ. They would fall in unbelief. Others who were prostrate in sin would be raised out of it through faith. In other words, there would be two responses: one positive, one negative. And throughout His ministry there would be those who spoke against Him. His life would be one of misrepresentation, opposition and trial. It would not be easy. And Mary, herself, would feel deep grief—like **a sword passing through her soul**—at the crucifixion (vv. 34, 35). Thus a realism about the event was introduced that, so far, amidst all the jubilation, had not been sounded. Mary needed to know what would happen so that she would be prepared. While it is not spelled out in detail, the crucifixion would bring sorrow of the keenest sort.

There is another factor of importance. Simeon makes it plain that **the thoughts of many hearts will be revealed**. That is to say, their innermost intentions, plans and beliefs will be brought to the fore by the coming of

Christian Counselor's Commentary

> 36 Now there was a prophetess, Anna, a daughter of Phanuel, from the tribe of Asher, who was quite old; and she had lived with her husband for seven years after their marriage,
> 37 and as a widow until she was eighty-four. She didn't leave the temple, but worshiped night and day, fasting and praying.
> 38 At that very time she came up to them and gave thanks to God and spoke about Him to everybody who was expecting the redemption of Jerusalem.

---

the Lord. The Pharisee and Sadducee is included in this prophecy. Their hypocrisy will be exposed. The fickleness of the populace—concerned only about material benefits—will be made known. The Lord Jesus is in the business of exposing the things that lie hidden. He still does so. By His Word, in counseling sessions (as well as elsewhere), He often brings counselees to see what is hidden in their hearts. That is one reason why the Scriptures are absolutely essential in counseling (cf. Hebrews 4).

Counselees must never be assured that their lives will be one unending stream of joy and happiness. That is impossible in a world of sin. Sin brings misery—even to One Who was sinless Himself. How much more so when, in addition to the sin of others, one must face the tragedies occasioned by his own sin! Yet all that is said about joy is still true. There is no doubt about that. And, the deep truth that the believer may have joy in the midst of trials (cf. James 1) must not be lost. The balance between the two must, therefore, always be maintained by counselors. They must recognize the pain and suffering of sinners (with which they certainly should identify in their counseling) but also, at the same time, hold out the hope of victory and gladness that there is in Christ. It is not easy to hold the two in proper balance at all times. Yet every counselor must strive to do so in his dealings with counselees.

The story of **Anna**, the **prophetess**, follows (vv. 36-38). Again, notice the precise detail in this short episode. Here was a woman who lived in the **temple**, doubtless, helping out in every way she could. There she also engaged in a ministry of **prayer** and **fasting**. She also recognized the Child-Messiah, **thanked** God for Him and **spoke** about Him to all of those she knew were faithfully awaiting His coming. What you see in all of these incidents is that God's true saints are used to confirm the events of the birth and to begin to make known the coming of the Lord. God especially rewards His own in grace by giving them insight into His ways and by bringing them into special contact with His Son. That still happens through His Word. Christians who remain faithful will understand what

Luke 2

39 When they had completed everything according to the Lord's law, they returned to their own city, Nazareth in Galilee.

40 The Boy grew and became strong; He was filled with wisdom, and God's grace was upon Him.

41 Now His parents went to Jerusalem every year at the feast of the Passover.

42 And when He was twelve years old, they went up according to the custom of the feast.

43 Then when the feast days were over, as they were returning, the Boy Jesus stayed in Jerusalem, but His parents didn't know it.

44 Supposing that He was in the group of travelers, they went a day's journey and looked for Him among their relatives and acquaintances.

45 But when they didn't find Him, they returned to Jerusalem to look for Him.

46 After three days they found Him sitting in the temple in the midst of the teachers, listening to them and asking them questions.

---

others do not.

Having done all that was required of them, Joseph, Mary and Jesus returned to Nazareth. Then we read that Jesus grew and became strong. His humanity is thereby emphasized. He was filled with wisdom (again, He had to learn), and God poured out His grace (favor) on Him (vv. 39, 40).

One more pre-ministry event is cited: the episode in the temple (vv. 41-52). This incident is indicative of the early concern of Jesus for truth and wisdom, and how assiduously He had acquired it. There can be no doubt about the fact that a child can know much, if he will only apply himself to the study of Scripture. In counseling believers, don't neglect to teach truth to youngsters; they too need to see that the Word of God is the standard for living.

At the age of twelve, Jesus seems to have gone up for the Passover (perhaps for the first time). At this age a Jewish boy became *A Son of the Law*, a designation that required him to keep all of the requirements of the law on his own (one of which was to go up to Jerusalem to observe the Passover). On this occasion, the parents left Him behind as they returned to Nazareth, though they didn't realize it. They thought He was with some of their relatives in the returning caravan. After a time, when they couldn't find Him (though they looked up and down for Him), they returned to Jerusalem to seek Him. After three days from when they had lost track of Him, they discovered Him in the temple **in the midst of the teachers**. He

Christian Counselor's Commentary

47 And everybody who heard Him was amazed at His understanding and His answers.
48 When they saw Him, they were astounded, and His mother said to Him, "Son, why have you treated us this way? You see that your father and I have been anxiously looking for you."
49 He replied, "Why did you have to look for Me? Didn't you know that I had to be in My Father's house?"
50 But they didn't understand this word that He spoke to them.
51 Then He went down with them and came to Nazareth and was subject to them. And His mother carefully kept all these incidents in her heart.
52 Jesus grew in wisdom and in stature, and in favor with God and people.

---

was **listening and asking questions**. It appears that He was also offering His point of view as well (v. 47). His questions and His answers amazed those who were listening. They could not believe that one so young could have such **understanding**. Mary rebukes Him (thinking of how worried she and Joseph had been; v. 48). But Jesus refused to take the blame she wanted to place on Him. They knew Him. They knew how deeply He was concerned about God's truth. "Why, then," He asks, "**did you have to look for Me? Didn't you know that I had to be in My Father's house?**" The question is penetrating. It also made it clear to Mary that there should have been no concern on her part; He was only doing what was to be expected of Him (knowing Him as she did). It is interesting that the Lord Jesus refused to be blamed for that which He did not do. The wrong was theirs; He would accept no responsibility for it. Counselees, all too often ready to make peace by accepting blame that they shouldn't, must be told that this is not acceptable. It is every bit as much a lie to do so as to tell an out-and-out lie.

Mary probably knew He was right, but on the other hand, there was so much more behind all of this than she was able to fathom (v. 50). She and Joseph simply **didn't understand**.

He **went down** to Nazareth with them ("up" on the map; down so far as topography is concerned) **and was subject to them**. He had not yet come to the point where He had left their authority. He was still living in their home and was willingly **subject** (see comments on John 2:4 for information on when that relationship changed). Mary continued to accumulate these data in her heart (Luke, doubtless, heard about them from her). So, all we have about the next 18 years of Jesus' life is what we read in verse 52. He continued to **grow in wisdom** and in physical **stature** and **in favor with God and people**.

Chapter 3

1 In the fifteenth year of Tiberius Caesar's reign, when Pontius Pilate was governing Judea, while Herod was ruling as tetrarch of Galilee, his brother Philip was ruling as tetrarch of the region of Ituraea and Trachonitis, and Lysanias was ruling as tetrarch of Abilene,
2 in the high priesthood of Annas and Caiaphas, God's Word came to Zechariah's son John in the desert.
3 He went into the whole Jordan region, preaching a baptism of repentance for the forgiveness of sins.

Once more, placing events in precise order, detailing times and places (vv. 1, 2), Luke continues. Having dealt with the harbingers of the birth of John and Jesus, and the actual birth episodes themselves, he now turns to the beginnings of their ministries. There is much to learn for counseling from this point forward in the book.

Note that John's ministry began with **God's Word** coming to **John** (v. 2). The ministry in which he engaged was not some fluke of his own; he was called by God. No one should take on the ministry of the Word otherwise. There are all too many, strictly on their own, apart from authorization by God or His church, and usually without adequate training, who have taken it on themselves to tell the church how to counsel. These "ministries" are subject to no one. They have no church behind them and are operating strictly under a board, the composition of which they themselves have determined. That is not how things are to be done in Christ's service. He ordained the church, and He calls and ordains men through it. John was of a priestly family and, presumably, had been ordained to the priesthood. One of the many duties of the priest was to teach the people (cf. Deuteronomy 24:8). Here, John takes up that legitimate duty as the call of God through His Word which, as it did with reference to the prophets, **came** to him.

So, obedient to God's Word, John went up and down the region of the **Jordan** valley **preaching a baptism of repentance** (v. 3). That is to say, he preached "Be baptized in order to demonstrate your repentance from sin." John, unlike many today, believed that people needed to repent. There is abroad a teaching that it is unnecessary to repent once one has become a Christian (for details, see my book *A Theology of Counseling*). That is quite wrong. Repentance means "a change of mind." Certainly, when one departs from sin, it is because he first has a change of mind.

Christian Counselor's Commentary

> 4   As it is written in the book of Isaiah the prophet,
>   **The voice of someone shouting in the desert:
>   "Get the Lord's road ready; make His paths straight.**
> 5   **Every rut must be filled in and every bump must be flattened,
>   the crooked places must be straightened,
>   and the rough places must be smoothed out,**
> 6   **and all flesh will see God's salvation."**

Prior to that he thought he could get away with it, that God didn't care, or some other erroneous concept. Such thinking requires a change of mind. Every counselor, therefore, is in the business of calling counselees to repent. That doesn't mean he has to use the word "repent" all of the time; what he is interested in is a counselee coming to see things God's way rather than his own way (cf. Isaiah 55:8, 9). He wants him to recognize his wrong thoughts and to replace them with right thoughts (about God, himself and others).

The Old Testament word for repent is *shub*. This interesting term means "to turn." It pictures the result of the rethinking process: one turns from his ways to God's because he has turned from his thinking to God's thoughts. Together, the Greek and Hebrew terms mean, *a change of mind leading to a change of life*. If that isn't what counselors are in the business of helping people do, then I don't know what it is! Together with those who preach the Word, they minister that same Word for the same purposes.

The **forgiveness of sins** mentioned in verse 3 did not come from obedience to the command to be baptized. No, it came from the repentance. One saw that the sacrifices and offerings that he made could never take away sin, and he came to understand that faith in the coming Redeemer Whom they prefigured was what would save. This was a fundamental change of thought for the ritualistic Jew of the day. Water baptism was the sign that one recognized his need of cleansing—that he could not please God by empty ordinances devoid of faith in what they symbolized. That is why John emphasized that Jesus is **God's Lamb Who takes away the sin of the world**.

Luke shows that John was not some self-styled prophet. No, he was the one predicted in Isaiah 40:3 and 4, which he proceeds to quote. As the apostle John in the first chapter of his Gospel made clear, John the Baptist was not the Word (that was the Messiah); rather, as Isaiah said, he was but a **voice**. He was in the **desert**, as we see here, and he was preparing the Lord's way by smoothing out the road He would travel. When oriental

Luke 3

7 This, then, is what he said to the crowds that came out to be baptized by him,

> You brood of vipers! Who warned you to flee from the coming wrath?

---

monarchs traveled, they sent the pick and shovel crews ahead to see to such matters. They preceded him and prepared the road for him. That, precisely, was John's task. He was a human bulldozer. His job was to so prepare hearts that those to whom the Lord Jesus would speak would be ready to hear. He was to stir up a nation that for 400 years had lain fallow. He was to convince people that they needed a Savior so that they would turn to God's Lamb in faith. This, we shall see, he accomplished.

Counselors, as a part of their work, also have this task. They must speak of sin, and make ready a people who will turn to the Lord's ways from their own. People today—even God's people—too often have lives that are like rough, impassable roads. They are filled with the potholes of iniquity, the ruts of sin. They have heaped up the bumps of pride and hills of self-centeredness. These must be cut down if the Lord Jesus is to ride comfortably into their lives. Counselors must fill in the gullies, smooth off the bumps. In other words, they must so wield the picks and shovels of Scripture that they smooth out roads.

How did John do this? What was his message? Well, having cried out as a voice in the **desert** (emblematic of a people who were dried up and barren spiritually) that people must repent for the forgiveness of sins, John then preached to those who came for baptism. In effect, he said, "It is not enough to go through another ritual; you must believe what I preach and that must change your lives." John's preaching was blunt, rough, powerful. He called the people the **offspring of vipers** (v. 7), and asked **who** had **warned** them (lit., "tipped them off") to **flee from the coming wrath**? John was a prophet in a time of need. Less than forty years hence the wrath of God would come upon the people of Israel in the terrible destruction of 70 AD. This was an event that was far more devastating and far more significant than many Christians have understood. It meant the end of the Old Testament era, the destruction not only of a temple and a city but of a people as well (cf. I Thessalonians 2:14-16).

Counselors, too, must make it clear to their counselees that it is not enough to go through the motions of repentance (*doing* things that God requires); repentance must be genuine, from the heart (Romans 6:17). Heart-motivated action, taken in order to please God (not to obtain some

8	Bear fruits that are appropriate to repentance, and don't begin saying to yourselves, "We have Abraham as our father." Let me tell you that God can raise up children for Abraham from these stones.
9	The axe is already laid at the root of the trees; so then, every tree that doesn't produce good fruit will be cut down and thrown into the fire.

---

personal boon), is what he called for. That is what he meant when he spoke of bearing **fruits that are appropriate to repentance** (v. 8). The counselor may not read another's heart. He may not even challenge his repentance when he "says" he repents (as we shall see when we come to Luke 17:4). However, he can urge genuine repentance and decide whether he may treat that repentance as genuine after the counselee has had opportunity to produce **fruit**. We may look for fruit to determine whether there is genuine repentance; it is **appropriate** for a repentant person to bear fruit—especially, when he has had the cultivation of truly biblical counseling. If, after some time of such effort expended on a counselee, a counselor doesn't see the appropriate fruit, he may begin to question the repentance. But to grow fruit takes time and effort.

John was a good counselor; he knew the sort of thing that his listeners would say in justification of their lack of genuineness. They would plead the fact that they were part of the covenant people: **We have Abraham as our father**. That is to say (in modern lingo) "We are Christians; members of the church." Formal membership either in the covenant community then, or in the church today, means nothing if there is nothing more to it than that. They are doing God no favor by it. He doesn't need them; He could **raise up children for Abraham from stones**. To formally do as God requires, but not mean it from the heart, is nothing: indeed, worse than nothing. Urge the importance of genuine repentance that leads to a genuine change of life upon every counselee who needs to hear it.

But that isn't all John said. He stressed the urgency of their repentance: **the axe is already laid at the root of the trees**. What does that mean? Just this: that as one lays the edge of the axe at the spot he wants to strike just before raising it to do so, God's judgment is already aimed at Jerusalem and all of those who do not genuinely repent. He is about to strike! Often counselees must be warned that if they persist in sin and do not repent they may not have much longer to do so. The time will come when it is too late (cf. I Corinthians 11:30-32).

Luke 3

10 And the crowds asked him, "What, then, should we do?"
11 In reply he told them, "Whoever has two coats must share with the one who doesn't have any, and whoever has food must do likewise."
12 Then the tax collectors also came to be baptized, and they said to him, "Teacher, what should we do?"
13 He said to them, "Don't collect any more than you are supposed to."

So his message was **produce good fruit**. *Good* fruit is fruit that is acceptable to God. It is Holy Spirit produced (cf. Galatians 5). All those trees that produce bad fruit (their own works) will be **cut down** and destroyed.

This sort of preaching got results (v. 10). People were concerned. They asked, **"What, then, should we do?"** It was the right response. That is the same question raised in Acts 2:37. It is the response that every counselor wants to hear. When spoken from the heart, it means "Tell me what God wants me to do." John gave several examples in reply. First, to the crowds in general he said, "**share** what you have with others in need. If they need clothing and you have more than you need, give the one who needs it one of your **coats**. If it is **food** he needs, do the same with it" (v. 11). Clothing was scarce and costly in those days. So he was hitting hard when he gave this example. One of the ways in which one may make a functional judgment about a counselee is by watching to see whether he is willing to help others in need. While that isn't the only fruit to look for, it is always one. And if he is willing to put himself out for another in ways that cost him, that may be (in many cases) a good sign.

His other responses were more specific. To the tax collectors he said, **"Don't collect any more than you are supposed to"** (vv. 12, 13). Tax collectors of that day were despised (so much so that they were put out of the synagog!) for several reasons. First, they were despised for the reason all of us tend to do so—we don't like paying taxes (and therefore, tend to despise those who collect them). But with Jewish tax collectors there was more. They were looked on as collaborators with the hated Roman government, traitors, if you will. And the system for collecting taxes was notoriously corrupt. The tax collector often would demand more than was required so that he might pocket the difference. This was allowed under the Roman farm system, so long as the collectors could get away with it. It was this aspect of the problem upon which John put his finger: **Don't collect any more than you are supposed to.** That was virtually unheard of in a tax collector. It is not wrong to urge counselees to do the right

Christian Counselor's Commentary

14 Some soldiers asked him, "And what should we do?" He told them, "Don't extort money by intimidating or by false accusation, and be satisfied with your pay."

15 Now when the people were in a state of expectation and everybody was wondering in his heart about John, whether he might be the Christ,
16 John responded to this by saying,

> I am baptizing you with water, but Someone Who is mightier than I is coming, the thong of Whose sandals I am not worthy to untie; He will baptize you with the Holy Spirit and with fire.

17 His winnowing shovel is in His hand, ready to completely clear His threshing floor and to gather the wheat into His barn. But He will burn the chaff with inextinguishable fire.

18 So with many other words John encouraged and announced the good news to the people.

---

thing, though difficult, though cutting across all the mores of the day, if it is right before God. Indeed, dare you do less?

To soldiers, in his response, John also hit the crucial spot: **Don't extort money by intimidating or by false accusation, and be satisfied with your pay**. Blackmail, threatened use of force, and the like, were to be eliminated from the thoughts and the practices of soldiers who truly repented. They also ought not to complain about their salaries. Surely, all dishonest activities, any undue pressures a counselee might exert, are all forbidden—and they are to stop complaining! Here are some principles that may afford guidelines for counselors to follow when dealing with repentance. Few things could be more practical. Is your counseling this concrete? Practical? Or is it abstract? John would not settle for stating principles and propositions alone; he insisted that these be worked out in concrete ways. So should you.

But that was not all: **with many other words John encouraged and announced the good news to people**. It is interesting to note that the type of preaching John engaged in Luke **calls encouragement** (here, possibly also "persuasion"). Not too many seem to understand this. *Paraklesis*, the word used in this place, as you can see, includes strong warning, blunt language and direct advice. Those who want to distinguish *nouthesia* from *paraklesis* in order to avoid counseling as John did will find the use of the word here difficult to understand. Indeed, you will seldom find them referring to John at all; he is too unrefined, too rustic for their liking. But Jesus didn't seem to be put off by John. He called him the greatest prophet of all. It was **good news** to tell people that if they repented of their

Luke 3

19 But when Herod the tetrarch was convicted by him about Herodias his brother's wife, and about all the evil things that Herod did,
20 he added this to them all and he locked John up in prison.
21 When all the people were baptized Jesus was baptized too, and as He was praying the sky opened,
22 and the Holy Spirit came down upon Him in a bodily form like a dove, and a voice came from the sky: "You are My dear Son; I am well pleased with You."

---

sins, believed in the Lamb of God as their Savior and did works that were appropriate to repentance, that they would please God.

Next, we come to verses 19 and 20. John's direct preaching got him into trouble (could that be what prissy counselors want to avoid at all cost?). When John told Herod that he had sinned in marrying Herodias, his brother's wife, it displeased her. She eventually was able to have John put to death. But what of **Herod**? He was **convicted** by John's words about this and **about all the evil things that** he did (v. 19). To **convict** is to so prosecute the case against someone that he is proven guilty of the crime of which he was accused. It doesn't have the sort of emotional content that the word has come to have in modern usage (to feel bad), but rather, it simply means that John successfully made his case against Herod. It speaks of what John did, not how Herod received it. It is the counselor's task to bring the Word of God into a case in such a way that it correctly applies to the situation at hand; it is not his task to bring about emotional responses on the part of the counselee.

Added to all his other sins, Herod threw John in prison because he so plainly exposed his sin (v. 20). People who don't receive the Scriptures, refusing to humble themselves before God, usually compound their sin as Herod did. Don't be surprised that counselees who reject biblical teaching will go on to even worse things in the future. Believers, who persist in their sin, may have to be handed over to Satan through church discipline (cf. I Corinthians 5:5, 13. For details, see my book *A Handbook of Church Discipline*). Satan is rough and will treat them far more roughly than the church of Christ, as the man in Corinth found out.

The baptism of Christ is mentioned in verses 21 and 22. There is little detail. Luke simply says that along with others, Jesus **was baptized**. He does say, in addition, that while Jesus was **praying** at this baptism, the **sky opened** and the **Holy Spirit in a bodily form like a dove came down upon Him** and **a voice from the sky** declared, **"You are My dear Son; I am well pleased with You."**

Christian Counselor's Commentary

> 23 Jesus was about thirty years old when He began His ministry. He was the son (as people supposed) of Joseph, the son of Heli,
> 24 the son of Matthat, the son of Levi, the son of Melchi, the son of Jannai, the son of Joseph,
> 25 the son of Mattathias, the son of Amos, the son of Nahum, the son of Esli, the son of Naggi,
> 26 the son of Maath, the son of Mattathias, the son of Semein, the son of Josech, the son of Juda,
> 27 the son of Joanan, the son of Rhesa, the son of Zerubbabel, the son of Shealtiel, the son of Neri,
> 28 the son of Melchi, the son of Addi, the son of Cosam, the son of Elmandam, the son of Er,
> 29 the son of Joshua, the son of Eliezer, the son of Jorim, the son of Matthat, the son of Levi,
> 30 the son of Simeon, the son of Judah, the son of Joseph, the son of Jonam, the son of Eliakim,
> 31 the son of Melea, the son of Menna, the son of Mattatha, the son of Nathan, the son of David,
> 32 the son of Jesse, the son of Obed, the son of Boaz, the son of Salmon, the son of Nashon,

Again, we see Jesus identifying Himself with sinners, though He was the sinless Son of God. God made it clear by His words that Jesus did not need to repent and be baptized for His sins (He had none) by saying that He was **well pleased** with Him. In this sense, Jesus is not our model; we are all sinners who need to repent.

But, notice, as man, Jesus needed the power and wisdom of the **Holy Spirit** who **came down upon Him** prior to taking up His ministry. Every counselor must likewise depend on the Holy Spirit for these things. He is insufficient in himself. How often, failing to use the Spirit's Book, failing to ask Him for power, a counselor has sallied forth into the fray totally unprepared. And to his chagrin, he has discovered that he not only failed to help counselees, but he probably did harm as well. If Jesus needed the Spirit (Whom He received without measure; John 3:34) how much more do *we* need Him in *our* ministries?

Luke tells us that Jesus was about 30 years of age when He took up His ministry. This was the age when a priest began his work. The high priestly work of Christ was about to begin; naturally, He was to be anointed by God for the task, as priests were (Exodus 28:41). The Holy Spirit, coming down in visible form, constituted that anointing.

Now follows the genealogy of Jesus through Joseph, His adoptive

Luke 3

33 the son of Amminadab, the son of Admin, the son of Arni, the son of Hezron, the son of Perez, the son of Judah,
34 the son of Jacob, the son of Isaac, the son of Abraham, the son of Terah, the son of Nahor,
35 the son of Serug, the son of Reu, the son of Peleg, the son of Eber, the son of Shelah,
36 the son of Cainan, the son of Noah, the son of Lamech,
37 the son of Methusaleh, the son of Enoch, the son of Jared, the son of Mahalaleel, the son of Cainan,
38 the son of Enos, the son of Seth, the son of Adam, the son of God.

---

father (vv. 23-38). There is nothing much to comment about in the genealogy. We may note once more Luke's concern for detail. There are all sorts of studies comparing the list in Matthew with that which appears here. It is not the purpose of this commentary to deal with such issues.

CHAPTER 4

1 Jesus, filled with the Holy Spirit, returned from the Jordan and was led by the Spirit into the desert,
2 where for forty days He was tempted by the devil. He didn't eat anything during those days, so when they were over He was hungry.

Prior to the beginning of His ministry, Jesus was subjected to severe testing. The Spirit had come upon Him (as the God-man) at His baptism. Now, **filled with** (dominated by) the **Spirit**, Jesus left the **Jordan** valley and went up into the **desert**. It is of great significance to note that He was **led** into this temptation by the Spirit. But first, consider the expression **filled with (by) the Spirit**. There is much strange teaching abroad about the meaning of this phrase (which occurs frequently in Acts and in other places; e.g., Ephesians 5:18). When you read of someone who is **filled** with joy, **filled** with fear or later in this chapter, **filled with rage**, you understand immediately that the dominant factor in his life is the joy, the fear or the rage. Everything he does is influenced by the joy, the fear or the rage which colors all his activity. It is the factor that determines how he does what he does. So, too, is it with the Spirit. When one is **filled with the Spirit** his life is at every point influenced by Him.

The idea that the **Spirit**, thus influencing Jesus' every action, should **lead** Him into temptation is interesting. In the parallel passage in Matthew the expression is even stronger: the Spirit, we are told, **thrust Him forth** into the desert temptation. "I thought that James said God doesn't tempt anyone," you object. Well, that is true, of course. But according to verse 2, He was not tempted by God, but by the **devil**. The Spirit **led** Him into harms way, but filled Him in such a way that He would overcome the **devil's** strongest **temptations**.

What does that tell you about your counselees? Certainly, it makes it clear that God does not exempt His children from temptation; quite to the contrary. There are times when He leads them into it in order to prepare them for a work in days to come. Moreover, the same Greek word is rightly translated "temptation" and "testing." That is because the very same experience may be viewed from either perspective. From the devil's side, the idea is to tempt the Christian into sinning; from God's side the idea is to strengthen him by enabling him to pass the test successfully. That is what was happening at the beginning of Christ's ministry. Satan wanted to forestall the work of Christ; God, through testing, was strength-

Luke 4

3 Then the devil said to Him, "If You are God's Son, tell this stone to become bread."
4 But Jesus replied, "It is written that **people don't live by bread alone.**"
5 Then the devil led Him up and showed Him all the world's kingdoms in a moment of time,

---

ening Him for it.

In this desert, little or no food was accessible over the 40 day period of testing. And it was at the end of this period of severe fasting, when hunger was strong, that the temptation came. The hunger aspect being stressed in Luke, he goes right to the temptation having to do with it (v. 3). Attempting to throw doubt upon Jesus' status as the Son of God, but at the same time stressing the possibility of what he is about to suggest, the devil says, "**If you are God's Son, tell this stone to become bread.**" The idea was that this would be one way of proving the divine Sonship. That Jesus had the power to do precisely what was suggested is clear, since He multiplied the loaves for the 5,000 later on.

God had a plan and a program for Jesus to follow. All three temptations are ways that the devil suggests to alter it. In each, he suggested an easier way out. The temptation for which we fall is often just that—taking an easier way out. In the long run, naturally, we discover that it was not easier after all. But at the time it is.

Jesus was not interested in working miracles for His own convenience: especially to prove anything to the devil. He replies (here and each time hereafter) with Scripture that is appropriate: "**It is written**" (v. 4). There is a higher principle of life than the sustenance of the physical body; there is a spiritual life that is sustained by God's holy Words. He would satisfy Himself with that!

Again, the importance of knowing the Scripture and of using it in difficult situations, is seen. Counselees who do not read, study and digest the Bible daily will discover that in the hour of trial they fail to bring forth the proper Scriptural answer to the situation. While counselors cannot teach the Bible in any comprehensive manner in counseling sessions, they surely can show how the Bible is practical in meeting every temptation. Incidentally, there is a right kind (as well as a wrong kind) of proof-texting. Many think it is a crude and wrong use of the Bible to set forth a verse in a situation as the answer to any problem it presents. But, clearly, Jesus did just that. However, He used the verses that He quoted quite

Christian Counselor's Commentary

> 6   and said to Him,
>   I will give you all this authority and glory; it has been delivered to me, and I can give it to whomever I want.
> 7   So then, if you will worship me it will all be yours.
> 8   But Jesus replied, "It is written, **You must worship the Lord your God and serve only Him.**"

---

properly. They were not used out of context, with the wrong meaning or in any other way that we might deplore. Yet, He plainly did "proof-text," as it is sometimes disparagingly called. Be careful about condemning things that are not necessarily wrong. Every counselor should know the Bible well enough that he may be able to retrieve and use single verses in the way in which Jesus did.

The next temptation that Luke presents is the temptation to retake control of the **world-kingdom** in some other way than by the cross (vv. 6-8). Did the devil have the **authority** to grant this? If he didn't, it would not have been much of a temptation to offer it. While he surely had no legal right to the world, John tells us that "the whole world lies in the evil one" (I John 5:19) and Paul called him the "prince of the power of the air" (Ephesians 2:2). How is this? When Adam exchanged allegiance to the Father of lights in favor of the father of lies, he surrendered the God-given dominion that had been his. Now, Jesus has come to bind the strong man, to wrest that kingdom back from him and despoil him of all that he has so illegally taken. But when He rose from the dead and gave the great commission saying, "all authority in heaven and in earth is given to Me," as the basis for that worldwide assault on the devil's territory, it was not because He bowed down to the devil that He could do so. No, it was because on the cross He had soundly defeated him. Once more He rejects the easy way (a way that would avoid the cross) saying, "**It is written. Worship**, divine **service**, is restricted to **God alone.**" This powerful "proof-text" says it all. Nothing more was needed to put an end to any such notion. The Scriptures should do the same thing for counselees who are tempted to go the wrong way. Counselors who know what those temptations are likely to be should help counselees prepare for them by reminding them of the appropriate verses that are a response to such temptations. Many such pithy, memorable verses will be found in Proverbs (see the commentary on Proverbs in this series). A person who is tempted to trust in riches might memorize Proverbs 11:28[a]. One who is tempted to strike back at others verbally might memorize Proverbs 15:1,

Luke 4

9 Then he led Him into Jerusalem and set Him on the highest point of the temple and said to Him,
> If you are God's Son, throw yourself down from here;
10 it is written, **He will command His angels to take care of You,**
11 and, **They will lift You up by their hands so that You won't strike Your foot against a stone.**

12 But Jesus replied, "It is said, **You must not tempt the Lord your God.**"

13 When the devil had ended all his temptations, he left Him for a time.

14 Then Jesus returned to Galilee by the Spirit's power, and reports about Him spread over the whole countryside.

15 He taught in their synagogs and everybody honored Him.

---

etc. It would be well for every counselor to know the Proverbs thoroughly. It isn't a bad practice to read a chapter a day each month (perhaps at the beginning of your counseling day).

Finally, there is the "theatrical" temptation: throw yourself down off the temple—the angels will keep you from harm. Once more Jesus refers the devil to God's Word: **It is said,** God will help and preserve His own. But he does not expect them to place themselves at risk unnecessarily; that is **tempting** (testing) **God**. How effectively the Bible is used; how appropriate are its teachings to our life situations! If you do not see it that way, counselor, you have work to do. Perhaps you have been subject to the propaganda that says the Bible is not enough. Jesus never turned to any other help outside of it and He lived a perfect life. Doesn't that tell you something? Verse 13 makes it clear that the devil is no match for the Bible. When he found he was unsuccessful, he left. And that is what your counselee will find happening in his life too whenever he successfully meets temptation with Scripture. One "resists" the devil by the use of the Bible. When he does, the evil one will "flee" from him (James 4:7).

Following the testing period with which God prepared Him for His ministry, we read that Jesus **returned to Galilee**, again **by the Spirit's power** (v. 14). We are given the impression that the Spirit was guiding Him according to a divine program. Presumably, the Spirit also was enabling Him to perform miracles as He went throughout the countryside. During His trip around the northern part of Palestine Jesus also **taught in the synagogs there**. And His teaching was well received: **everybody honored Him** (v. 15). That the bulk of His labors would be in Galilee was foretold by Isaiah (Isaiah 9:1-7; Matthew 4:13-16).

The preceding statements give a general picture of how things were

> 16 Then He went to Nazareth, where He had been brought up, and, as was His custom, He went to the synagog on the Sabbath day and stood up to read.
> 17 The book by Isaiah the prophet was handed to Him. He opened the book and found the place where it was written,
> 18 **The Lord's Spirit is on Me**
> **because He anointed Me to announce the good news to the poor,**
> **He has sent Me to preach release to the captives**
> **and recovery of sight to the blind,**
> **to set free those who are downtrodden**,
> 19 **to preach the Lord's year of favor**.
> 20 Then He closed the book, returned it to the attendant and sat down. The eyes of everybody in the synagog were fixed on Him.
> 21 Then He began to speak to them: "Today this Scripture has been fulfilled in your hearing."
> 22 Everybody spoke well about Him, and they were surprised at what gracious words came from His mouth. They said, "Isn't this Joseph's son?"

proceeding, and they also form a background for the incident in the synagog of Nazareth which follows (vv. 16-30). In this incident that took place in His hometown He met the first human opposition He would experience. That would not be the end of it. Remember, we saw how He would be for the *fall* as well as for the **rising** of many in Israel. He was handed the book of **Isaiah**, from which He selected the passage that He read (vv. 17-19). Jesus then handed the scroll back to the **attendant** who cared for it, **and sat down** (v. 20). The practice of the rabbis was to teach sitting. Preaching became a stand-up affair only when the gospel went into the Mediterranean world where that was the practice (when we come to Acts, we shall see how carefully Luke makes it clear that Paul adapted to that practice). All His friends, neighbors and relatives anxiously awaited His words (cf. v. 20). Here was the home town boy who had made good. What would he say? How would he perform? Those were the things in their minds. He began by saying that the verses He read were fulfilled as He read them (v. 21). They did not understand that He was speaking of Himself and of them. They were **surprised** and **enthralled** by His **gracious words** (v. 22). They could hardly believe that someone who had been raised in a carpenter's home would have such ability. But as in the case of Ezekiel, it was His performance, not the content of what He said, upon which they focused (Ezekiel 33:30-33).

Never allow counselees to become caught up in the accouterments of

Luke 4

23 But He said to them,
    Doubtless you will quote this proverb: "Physician, heal yourself; do here in your home town the same things that we have heard you did at Capernaum."
24 He continued,
    Let Me assure you that no prophet is accepted in his home town.
25 As a matter of fact, I tell you, there were many widows in Israel in the days of Elijah when the sky was shut up for three and a half years and there was a great famine over the whole land.
26 Elijah wasn't sent to any of them but only to a widow in Zarepta, in the land of Sidon.
27 Now there were many lepers in Israel in the time of the prophet Elisha, yet not a single one of them was cleansed, except Naaman the Syrian.

---

counseling—methods, techniques, strategies, etc. Instead, always bring them back to content. That is what Jesus did (vv. 23-27). He spoke in a manner that was calculated to wake them up. He said, You are interested in seeing Me perform miracles here as I have done elsewhere. When I don't because of the superficial manner in which you are treating My words, you will say, "Instead of talking to us about what we should do or not do, why don't you attend to your own problems?" (the meaning of the **proverb, Physician, heal yourself**).

Jesus knew what was in them. There was no true repentance: they were only interested in His performance, not in the saving nature of His message. After all, look at what He was expounding. He was teaching them that He was the Messiah of Old Testament prophecy Who had come to free them from sin (all of the figures of speech used by Isaiah, and quoted by Jesus (vv. 18, 19 taught precisely *that*). Doubtless, He said so in the message, but He noted that they were not hearing the message; instead, they were only concerned with the fact that one from their city had made it big. "Now, if He would only perform some miracles to boot. . . ."

There are times to become so pointed that the counselee cannot misunderstand. If he is interested only in superficial aspects of counseling, and not in the heart of the issue, it may be necessary to do what Jesus did. He not only exposed their failings (v. 23), but went on to mention facts that were calculated to arouse them

What did He do? First, He said that He recognized that **no prophet is accepted in his home town** (v. 24), thereby indicating that they would not

Christian Counselor's Commentary

28   When they heard this they were all filled with rage
29   and rose up and threw Him out of the city, and led Him to the brow of the hill on which their city was built, in order to throw Him over.
30   But He passed through the midst of them and left.
   31   He went down to Capernaum, a city of Galilee. And He taught them every Sabbath.
32   They were surprised at His teaching, because what He said had authority.

---

really hear what He had to say. Next, He reminded them of two Old Testament incidents in which unbelieving Gentiles **accepted** God's prophets Elijah and Elisha when the Jews did not (vv. 25-27). Thereby, He again indicated they were not **accepting** His words. That teaching finally got through to His listeners! **When they heard this** (about *Gentiles* more readily listening to God's truth) **they were all filled with rage** (v. 28). In order to awaken lethargic, superficial counselees, you too may find it necessary to say things that will startle them into thinking. At times, when you do, their response will be no less negative. People got angry with Jesus and they will get angry with you. That is, if you tell them the truth about themselves. You should not expect to have a better record in dealing with people than Jesus. The key is to be sure that their anger was not stirred by something you said or did that was unbiblical.

These people were so angry that they wanted to kill Jesus, but, probably in some miraculous manner (ironically, the only miracle He performed in that place), Jesus **passed through their midst** (v. 30). And, note the sad word at the end: He **left**. When would-be counselees, who do not really want counsel, fail to respond in proper ways, it may be necessary to break off counseling. That is an important principle: you must not cast pearls before pigs.

There was a very different response at **Capernaum.** Here, Jesus was allowed to teach **every Sabbath** in the **synagog** (v. 31). And the people who heard were also **surprised at His teaching**; they recognized that He taught with **authority** (v. 32). Unlike the scribes, what He said was powerful, had the ring of truth to it. Here were people who recognized true teaching when they heard it. They were content-centered, not performance-centered as those at Nazareth had been. The counselor who is careful about what he is doing, will soon be able to distinguish between those who are there for some superficial purpose and those who really desire help from God's Word. And he will respond accordingly.

We now read of an incident that happened one day when He was

Luke 4

33 Now in the synagog was a man who had the spirit of an unclean demon, and he shouted loudly,
34 "Ha! What do You want with us, Jesus of Nazareth? Did You come to destroy us? I know You, who you are—the Holy One from God!"
35 But Jesus rebuked him, saying, "Be quiet!—and come out of him." After the demon had thrown him down in their midst, he left him without hurting him.
36 Everybody was amazed and said to one another, "What sort of word is this? He commands the unclean spirits with authority and power, and they come out!"
37 And reports about Him went forth into every place in the surrounding countryside.

---

teaching in the synagog (vv. 33-37). A man with an **unclean demon** was present who **shouted** at Jesus. What the demon said through him was that he feared Jesus had come to **destroy** them (the demons). And the demon correctly identified Jesus as the promised Messiah—**the Holy One from God** (vv. 33, 34). Recoiling immediately from the presence of the **Holy One**, this **unclean demon** (note the contrast) shows that he has orthodox theology (more so than some of our day who believe neither in demons nor in their destruction). The doom that God pronounced on him and those like him was well known.

Jesus said, "**Be quiet**" (lit, be muzzled), and ordered him to leave the man. In an angry gesture, the demon threw the man down without doing him any serious harm, and left him (vv. 34, 35). Why did Jesus refuse to have Who He was known? Well, there were at least two reasons (perhaps more): testimonials from such a quarter were not welcome; nor was it yet time to be disclosed as the Messiah (the cross must not be hurried until all that Jesus was sent to do had been accomplished).

There are the right times and the right persons who may legitimately proclaim what Jesus does for them in counseling. There are others, who stand outside, who have wrong motives and who don't conform to any sort of biblical program, whose testimony must be rejected. Every counselor knows about the loudmouthed person who proclaims the virtues of Nouthetic counseling, whose life shows nothing of the change that God requires, whose word makes him cringe because it is such a poor testimony. It is necessary, at times, to silence him.

People were amazed at His authority and power and spread His fame all around the area (vv. 36, 37). This was legitimate and Jesus did not silence them.

Christian Counselor's Commentary

38 After Jesus got up and left the synagog He entered into Simon's house. And Simon's mother-in-law was sick with a high fever, and they asked Him to do something for her.
39 So He stood over her and rebuked the fever, and it left her. Then, at once, she got up and served them.
40 Now as the sun was setting, everybody who had any that were sick with various sorts of diseases brought them to Him, and He laid His hands on each of them and healed them.
41 Demons also came out of many persons shouting, "You are God's Son!" But He rebuked them and wouldn't let them speak, because they knew He was the Christ.
42 Now when the day came, He left and went to a lonely place, and the crowds looked for Him and they came to the place where He was and tried to keep Him from leaving them.
43 But He said to them, "I have to announce the good news about God's empire, because I was sent for this reason."
44 And He was preaching in the synagogs of Judea.

After this, Luke relates the healing of Peter's wife's mother. The incident shows the power of Christ to heal sickness. He is thus set forth as the One Who taught with power and authority, cast out demons with power and authority, and healed with power and authority. In three successive examples, these facts are disclosed to the reader. As a sort of summary statement (vv. 40, 41), Luke records multiple healings and exorcisms. There is no need to detail these since Luke has already made his point. Those who questioned could check out the rest if they cared to. But the number of miracles precluded detailed accounts.

Finally, the chapter ends with Jesus departing to preach elsewhere. This time He went south to preach in the synagogs of Judea. He is clear about His ministry (**I have to announce the good news**). One cannot do everything. There are commitments that each counselor has. If he is not careful, he will overcommit himself. Jesus was careful not to let this happen. The preacher ought to be clear: he must preach and teach the Word. If counseling—an important part of his ministry—pulls him away from his full commitment, he must learn to limit it. As here, people will demand otherwise (v. 42), but the counselor must remain firm. Jesus did not heal all; you cannot counsel all either.

Chapter 5

1 Now as the crowd pressed upon Him to hear God's Word and He was standing by the lake Gennesaret,
2 He saw two boats lying by the shore of the lake. The fishermen had left them and were washing their nets.

Clearly, since in the summary statements at the end of Chapter Four Luke tells us that Jesus had gone to Judea, the beginning of this chapter takes us back to the Galilean ministry featuring, this time, the call of His disciples. Luke goes back to take up this additional matter.

In counseling, it is not always bad to go directly to the bottom line, then to go back and see how the counselee got there. That is why we ordinarily ask three basic questions on the Personal Data Inventory (PDI) to begin with (see *The Christian Counselor's Manual* for a sample copy), one of which is "What is your problem (as you see it)?" Having obtained this from the counselee at the outset, going back and seeing what history leads up to it, then reevaluating whether or not he has rightly analyzed it, is always one good way to open and pursue the early sessions. Here, of course, we know that Luke rightly analyzed the situation, not only because of his careful and detailed research, but also because it was conducted under the inspiration of God's Spirit.

In verse 1 there is a remarkable statement: **the crowd pressed upon Him to hear God's Word**. There are times when this still occurs. When God sends a revival of the faith to a country (or section of it), one of the signs of this is people crowding into places where they can **hear God's Word** proclaimed. Too often, these days, when one sees crowds attending preaching it is not to hear God's Word but to hear the preacher's eloquence, to become part of "a caring group" or for some other purpose. The places where **God's Word** is proclaimed faithfully are few and far between, and often attendance is slim. When it comes to counseling, the same is true. Yet, wherever it becomes known that a biblical counselor is helping people, they will come to him in increasing numbers. But, often, they will come merely to attain some goal of theirs—not to **hear** what **God's Word** has to say about their problems. That is why counselors will find it necessary to negotiate their goals. In order to discover those goals, a second question on the P.D.I. asks, "What do you want us to do about it?" (cf. Christ's well-known question, "What wilt thou have Me to do?" KJV). If the answer is less than that which the Bible sets forth, the coun-

3   So He got into one of the boats, which was Simon's, and asked him to put out a little way from the land. Then He sat down and taught the crowds from the boat.
4   When He had finished speaking He said to Simon, "Put out into the deep and let down your nets for a catch."
5   But Simon replied, "Master, we worked hard all night and didn't take a thing. But if You say so, I'll let down the nets."
6   When they did so, they encircled such a large number of fish that their nets began to tear.
7   So they signaled to their partners in the other boat to come help them, and they came and filled both of the boats to the point of sinking.

---

selor needs to explain what, according to **God's Word**, that goal should be. Otherwise counselor and counselee may end up shooting past one another.

Because there were crowds pressing upon Him, Jesus **got into one of the boats** (**Simon** Peter's), asked Simon to **put out a little way** from shore, and then **sat down** and **taught** from the boat. Christ's flexibility in handling every situation is obvious. There is no stereotyped way in which He conducted His teaching. He did what every good teacher does all the time: He adapted to the circumstances. While even within the preaching/teaching milieu there must be flexibility, there must be even more so in counseling. At least the teacher knows (at least in general) what it is that he will be teaching. But the counselor has little knowledge of what might come up in any given session. He will have a general outline of where he would like to go and what he would like to cover in a session, but when further data are uncovered (as they frequently are) they may change all of that. Rigid, mechanically-oriented persons beware! If you would find it difficult to preach from a boat, you certainly are not yet ready to take on much counseling!

Jesus finished teaching for the moment (v. 4), so He turned from the crowds and took an interest in one person, Simon. Preachers who do not have time to minister to single individuals because of their preoccupation with crowds do not emulate their Lord in this.

He next told Simon to row out into deeper waters and let down his net for a catch. Simon is skeptical. He doesn't expect that this is either the time or place to catch fish (v. 5). Yet he goes along with the suggestion. He and those with him took such a large catch that **their nets began to tear** (v. 6), and they had to call for help (v. 7). Simon Peter was a fisherman; he knew immediately that this catch was not a purely natural phe-

Luke 5

8   When Simon Peter saw what had happened, he fell at Jesus' knees and said, "Leave me, Lord; I am a sinful person."
9   He and everybody with him was astonished at the catch of fish they had taken.
10   So too were Zebedee's sons, James and John, who were Simon's partners. Then Jesus said to Simon, "Don't be afraid. From now on you will be catching men alive."
11   Then they brought their boats to the land, left everything and followed Him.
   12   While He was in one of the cities, He came upon a man covered with leprosy who, when he saw Jesus, fell on his face and begged Him, "Lord, if You want to, You can cleanse me!"

---

nomenon. Nothing like this had ever happened to him or anyone he knew. He **fell at Jesus' knees** at the miracle, recognizing his own **sin** in the presence of the Lord (v. 8)

That is one of the goals of biblical counseling: to help counselees to fall at the feet of Jesus. If you always make the counseling session a confrontation between yourself and the counselee, that will rarely happen. But if, as it should be, you make the session an encounter between Jesus and the counselee by presenting God's Word in such a manner that he knows that it is He with Whom he has to do, it will happen more than you might expect.

Everyone was **astonished** at the catch (v. 9), not just Peter. Some of those in the group of fishermen were **James** and **John** (v. 10). Then Jesus told Peter that there was nothing to fear. As a matter of fact, He was going to so transform him that instead of catching fish, he would be **catching men alive** (v. 10). He and some of the others then came to the shore, left their boats and began to **follow** Jesus as disciples (v. 11). Counselors who counsel biblically will discover that now and then, as you minister the Scriptures, people will hear Christ's call to **follow** Him as fishers of men even as these men did on the seashore. That call may even come in the counseling session. That will not happen often but, where the Bible is ministered faithfully, Christ will call through His Word.

Now Luke records an incident with a **leper**. Notice how he covers all the bases, showing Christ superior to every sort of adverse force, as well as over all of nature itself. Verse 12 describes the scene. A man **covered with leprosy fell on his face** begging Jesus to cleanse him. He did not doubt whether Jesus *could* do so; with him it was merely a matter of whether He *would* do it. Jesus **stretched out His hand and touched him.**

Christian Counselor's Commentary

> 13 He stretched out His hand and touched him, saying, "I do want to; be clean!" Instantly the leprosy left him.
> 14 Then He ordered him to tell nobody about this, but only "go and show yourself to the priest and make the offering for your cleansing that Moses commanded for a testimony to them."
> 15 But the word about Him spread abroad all the more, and large crowds came to hear Him, and they were healed of their sicknesses.
> 16 But He withdrew to lonely areas and prayed.

Ordinarily, that would be taboo. Leprosy was a highly communicable disease and for one to touch a leper was to become ceremonially unclean. But Jesus had come to reverse matters. He was not made unclean by the act; no, the leper was cleansed! *Instantly*, we read, **the leprosy left him** (v. 13). That was a miraculous cure! Once more, since crowds had already begun to follow Him, Jesus ordered the man not to tell anyone but the **priest** what had happened. This He did to forestall undo publicity. He would have to appear before the priest for the ceremonial cleansing by which he would be declared clean (v. 14). Yet, through the man, or through the priest, the word leaked out and the crowds seeking help increased. They became so great that Jesus had to hide in order to find time and space to quietly pray (vv. 15, 16). The cleansing power of Jesus Christ is apparent in this incident. The superior power of light over darkness, of truth over error, of life over death, of health over sickness—all of these things immediately come to mind. Jesus is not defiled by the leprosy; the leprosy is cured by His touch. That principle is one to inculcate in counselees: God is stronger than Satan; good is stronger than evil (cf. Romans 12:21). Since that is true, there is no problem that the counselee can present to which Jesus has no solution.

The withdrawal of Jesus from the crowds (v. 16) denoted two facts. First, as Man, He found it impossible to handle more than any one (even *perfect*) human being can. Secondly, Jesus knew the necessity of prayer—even though filled with the Spirit. There is only so much one counselor—or counselee—can do. Just recently I dealt with a counselee who was destroying himself, his family and his witness for the Lord by his unrelenting pursuit of a goal. That was wrong. God has made us to handle only so much and no more.

Moreover, should popularity pursue you, you must be careful. You need to get away from the demanding crowds, keep a tight control over your own schedule and pray.

Now, in verses 17 through 26 we encounter Luke's version of the

Luke 5

17 Now on one of those days as He was teaching there were Pharisees and teachers of the law sitting by, who had come from every village of Galilee and Judea and Jerusalem, and the Lord's power was present for Him to heal.

18 Then men came carrying a paralytic on a stretcher, and they tried to bring him in and lay him before Him.

19 But when they couldn't find a way because of the crowd, they went up on the roof and let him down on his stretcher through the tiles into the midst of the crowd in front of Jesus.

20 So when He saw their faith, He said, "Man, your sins are forgiven you."

21 Then the scribes and Pharisees began to reason, "Who is this person who speaks blasphemies? Who, but God alone, can forgive sins?"

---

healing of the paralytic. As Jesus was teaching in a home, again, there were **crowds** present. But this time, from all over Palestine, among the crowd there were **Pharisees** and theologians (**teachers of the law**; scribes). Presumably, because Jesus' fame had spread abroad (v. 15), they had come to listen to and see what this miracle-working teacher was all about. We also read that **the Lord's power was present for Him to heal**. That is to say, God was doing a powerful work of healing through Him at this time.

Men came carrying a friend on a stretcher in order to receive healing from Jesus. But because of the crowd they couldn't get near him; indeed, they **couldn't find a way** into the house. So they went up on the roof, pulled up some of the tiles over the courtyard and let him down before Jesus on the stretcher. In verse 20, we read **So when He saw their faith, He said, "Man, your sins are forgiven you."** How could Jesus *see* their **faith**? Is faith observable? No. But what He saw was the results of their faith, thus recognizing that they were faith-driven. The lengths to which they went to bring the man to Jesus was evidence of this faith. Faith, as James makes clear, leads to works. Their works *loudly* proclaimed their faith! The prim, precise scribes and Pharisees must have been astounded at the lack of decorum in this meeting. How could Jesus allow such things to happen? And now, to top it off, He has declared that the man's sins are forgiven. How can He be so brazen? Something like this must have been going through their minds. They begin talking among themselves, **"Who is this person who speaks blasphemies? Who, but God alone, can forgive sins?"** (v. 20).

Well, they were right and they were wrong. Their theology was cor-

Christian Counselor's Commentary

> 22 But Jesus, knowing how they were reasoning, responded, Why are you thinking this way in your hearts?
> 23 Which is easier—to say, "Your sins are forgiven," or to say, "Rise and walk"?
> 24 Now, so that you will know that the Son of Man has authority on earth to forgive sins,
> He said to the paralytic, "Get up and pick up your stretcher and go home." Immediately he got up before them, picked up his stretcher and went home, praising God.
> 26 Everybody was seized with astonishment; they praised God, were filled with fear and said, "We have seen bewildering things today."

rect. Only the One against Whom one has sinned can forgive the sinner; that, naturally, was God. And, if Jesus was claiming to be anything less than God, surely He *was* blaspheming. But Jesus *is* God. And He is about to demonstrate to these eagle-eyed heresy-hunters that very fact. Jesus knew how they were thinking and asked them **Why?** (v. 22). Then He put a further question to them: Is it **easier** to forgive his sins or to heal this man? That was a hard question to answer. How would you if a Pharisee? If you said "to forgive sins, because it not possible to see any effects of this and all you have to do to easily deceive us is speak those words," you would be right. If, on the other hand, you answered, "to forgive sins, meaning that *you are really doing so*, that is too hard for any man," you would also be right. They were stuck.

Since they couldn't *see* forgiveness in action, but could see healing, Jesus replied, I'll heal him in order to show you I have the power to do both (God isn't going to lend His miraculous power to one who is a mere pretender and a blasphemer). He told the man to **get up**, and he did (v. 24). The crowd was **seized with astonishment**, and by its silence the record indicates that for the time being Jesus' detractors were too.

There is no better way to advocate and vindicate the truth of biblical counseling than by demonstrating its power. The power of Nouthetic counseling is in the **power of God** to help through the Bible. Anything less than the power of God in operation in the lives of counselees is not biblical counseling. That means that every counselor—including Nouthetic counselors—at times fails to counsel according to God's power. Jesus never failed; you and I do. That is because He never sinned; we do. When counselors depend on their own wisdom, they fail. When they allow others to detract from a purely Biblical understanding of a counselee's problem and God's solution to it, they fail. When they lean on

27 After this He went out and saw a tax collector named Levi sitting at the tax office and said to him, "Follow Me."
28 So he got up and followed Him and left everything behind.
29 Then Levi held a large reception for Him in his house, and there was a large group of tax collectors, and others, reclining at the table.
30 But the Pharisees and their scribes complained to His disciples, saying, "Why do you eat and drink with tax collectors and sinners?"
31 Then Jesus replied, Those who are healthy don't need a doctor; it is those who are sick who do.
32 I haven't come to call righteous people, but sinners to repentance.

---

human promises and fail to seek divine help, they fail. All of us are subject to those frailties as sinners.

The call of Matthew (**Levi**) comes next (vv. 27-32). Jesus told Levi, the tax collector, to follow Him (v. 27). And like the fishermen, he got up and left all behind, and followed Jesus (v. 28). That his repentance and faith in Christ was genuine becomes apparent by what he did thereafter. He threw a **large reception** for Jesus in his house inviting his fellow outcasts to meet Jesus. But the scribes and Pharisees **complained to His disciples** about the fact that Jesus ate with tax collectors and other sinners (v. 30). This is the standard approach of ultra separatists and legalists today. You will run into it in counseling. People who think this way fail to recognize what we were discussing earlier, the greater power of righteousness over evil. They would not touch these spiritual lepers, or have anything to do with them!

Jesus answers the objection. It isn't the **healthy** who need the **physician** but those who are **sick**. He said, "**I haven't come to call righteous people, but sinners to repentance**" (vv. 31, 32). How fitting a remark for all counseling. How often people come for counseling who protest that there is really nothing wrong with them. Their spouses may say otherwise; they grudgingly may admit to some minor problem. But the answer to all such persons is, "Then why come?" No one goes to a doctor unless he thinks he is ill. Nor should one come to a counselor if he thinks he is O.K. And the hope lies in this, that Jesus came to help sinners. Many, like the Pharisees, receive no help because they will not acknowledge their sin. Others, who have no qualms in doing so, find immense help. A repentant sinner is not one whom He will turn away; he is one who is accepted by Christ. There is great help for sinners who acknowledge their sin.

Then there was the comment about John the Baptist and Jesus' reply

33 Then they said to Him, "John's disciples frequently fast and pray, and the Pharisees' disciples do the same. Yet yours eat and drink."
34 Jesus said to them,
> You can't make wedding guests fast while the Bridegroom is with them, can you?
35 The days will come when the Bridegroom is taken from them; they will fast in those days.
36 Then He told them this parable too:
> Nobody tears material from a new piece of clothing and sews it as a patch on a piece of old clothing. If he did, he would have torn the new clothing and the patch wouldn't match the old clothing.
37 Nobody puts new wine into old wineskins. If he did, the new wine would burst the wineskins and would come pouring out, and the wineskins would be ruined.

(vv. 33-35). It seems that some were comparing the practices of **John's disciples** with those of His disciples. They had found some differences: John's disciples **fast and pray** (like **Pharisees** do); yours **eat and drink**. The idea in making the point is to ask "How come the difference?" Jesus' reply was clothed in language calculated to make them think. A wedding isn't the time for fasting. Everyone rejoices with the Bridegroom while He is present. A time will come in the future when He will be gone; then there will be time and occasion for fasting. Of course, Jesus was speaking of His own presence and of the time when He would leave the disciples. They couldn't as yet understand these words, but they were something to think about when the events took place.

A counselor need not always be entirely direct in his answers. At times he may use language calculated to be memorable, but also calculated to make those who hear ponder the meaning. That is important when he thinks that it is not yet a time when those to whom he speaks are ready to assimilate what he has to say. The parable that follows (vv. 36-39) is another example of the same things.

Jesus speaks of new cloth and new wine. Neither mix well with the old. To **tear** a **patch** of cloth from **new** material to put on an **old** piece of **clothing** would be foolish. First, the new would be ruined and the patch of new material **wouldn't match** the old faded garment. And you don't put **new wine into old wineskins** (the bottles of the day). Fermenting, the new would **burst** the old wineskins which would have lost their elasticity. And, who wants new wine to drink when he can drink aged wine? The old tastes better.

38	Rather, new wine must be put into new wineskins.
39	Nobody, when he has drunk old wine, wants the new. He says, "The old is better!"

Now, there is a batch of thoughts all playing on the idea of the impossibility of mixing the old with the new. What do they mean? Well, they continue the thought about fasting: they show the fitness of things. The old defunct system cannot be simply patched up; something fresh is coming. And one who has tasted how much better it is will not accept anything else. Verse 39 confuses somewhat because it seems to continue the contrast between the old and the new in which previously we are shown that the new is better. Here, however, the facts are reversed: the old is clearly better wine; but the old wine represents the new system, which is better. The old and new differ in import here not simply because, as a matter of fact, old wine tastes better even though that, of course, is the material basis for the use of the figure in this comparison. The **old wine** which is better goes back to that which existed before the old, faded garment. It represents the true, spiritual meaning of the Old Testament ordinances that had become buried under the traditions of the elders. The **new wine**, then, is the substance that true Old Testament saints saw foreshadowed in the Old Testament ordinances. Those holding to the old pharisaical understanding failed to see this because it focused on external factors rather than on their meaning. In the next chapter, we shall see more about this matter.

Traditionalists will try to do anything they can to preserve that which is passe. Plainly, even those things which are wrong, such counselees will try to hold on to at all costs. They fear change. So, in face of clear biblical need for change, you will find them trying to mix their old sinful ways with the new biblical ones. Christ will not settle for any such thing. If He refuses to accept a patched up system which was good in its time but was corrupted, how could He accept that which never was. Merely patching up error with some biblical patches is unacceptable. Nor can the fresh wine of the Spirit be contained in a wineskin grown brittle. How then in one that was wrong from the first?

CHAPTER 6

1 One Sabbath He was going through some grain fields, and His disciples picked and ate some heads of wheat, rubbing them in their hands.
2 But some of the Pharisees said, "Why are you doing what it isn't lawful to do on the Sabbath?"
3 Jesus responded by asking them,
   Haven't you read what David did when he and those who were with him were hungry;
4 how he went into God's house and ate the presentation bread, which it isn't lawful for anybody but the priests to eat, and he even gave it to his companions?

What Jesus was talking about at the end of the fifth chapter is continued into the next, with new ramifications. The coming of Jesus heralded a new era. It was new, of course, in that the true spiritual meaning of the physical accouterments of the Old Testament era would become a reality as the old shadows would give way to the new substance, which is Christ and His spiritual empire. But, beyond that, the deterioration of the old rites into a mere ceremonialistic, legalistic understanding of the ordinances, in which their spiritual meaning was lost, would be condemned as a false, Pharisaical misconstruction. That is a matter about which the very first and second incidents of the sixth chapter is concerned (vv. 1-5; 6-11).

The first incident regards the eating of grain on the Sabbath. Jesus' disciples (who evidently were beginning to recognize the proper meaning and use of the Old Testament laws) rubbed some heads of wheat and ate them while passing through a grain field. The Pharisees, who were looking for a way in which to condemn Jesus, objected, saying, **"Why are you doing what it isn't lawful to do on the Sabbath?"** (v. 2).

Of course, the Old Testament said nothing about forbidding any such activity. While it did forbid the ordinary work one did, thereby making the Sabbath different, this activity was in no sense what the Scriptures meant as work. The Pharisees had extrapolated the fourth commandment to every and all sorts of minute activity that they, legalistically, declared "work." What the disciples had transgressed was not God's law, but the "fence" that the scribes had erected around the law. The disciples had not sinned. But rather than debate casuistic intricacies with them, Jesus countered their charge with a question of His own: "What about **David**, when **hungry** eating the **presentation bread** that was supposed to be eaten only

Luke 6

5   Then He told them, "The Son of Man is Lord of the Sabbath."

6 On another Sabbath He went into the synagog and taught, and there was a man there with a withered right hand.

7   The scribes and the Pharisees watched Him closely to see if He would heal on the Sabbath, because they wanted to find something about which to accuse Him.

8   But He knew how they reasoned, and He said to the man with the withered hand, "Get up and stand here in the midst of us." So he got up and stood there.

---

by the **priests**?" It is plain that if David, out of necessity, could see that the divine command was limited in scope and acted beyond those limits in a legitimate way, Christ's disciples, when hungry, could eat as they did when what they were doing was not even forbidden. Moreover, as He concluded, **The Son of Man is Lord of the Sabbath**. That is to say, since He is God, the One Who established the Sabbath law, He is the One to define its scope and applications. This new wine was refusing to be poured into old bottles!

The counselor will not allow himself to be squeezed into man-made legalistic rules and regulations. When counselees come imposing these upon what he may or may not do for them in counseling, he must make a stand similar to Christ's. "Christ," he should say, "is the One Who must define what is to be said and done, not some church or the tradition of some school or group of persons. We shall see what He says in the Bible and do accordingly." These, or words of the sort, ought to be spoken in reply to such issues as may come up ("We cannot even consider divorce since my church will not permit it under any circumstances," or "We don't practice church discipline in our congregation; so you will have to figure out another way of proceeding").

Not only was this externalism of the Pharisees, who loved to make the law cast as long a shadow as possible, a trivialization of God's great law, but as the following incident shows it could be cruel as well. On **another Sabbath**, while teaching in a synagog, Jesus **healed** a man with **a withered hand** (vv. 6-11). The religious legalists were lying in wait for Jesus to see if they **could find something about which to accuse Him** (v. 7). Jesus purposely made a great demonstration of the healing (v. 8), publicly defying and exposing their hardhearted indifference to human suffering in favor of their false, iron-fisted traditions. Knowing what they were up to, before healing the man, Jesus asked another question [a very important way of driving home a point; a way to be used frequently in

Christian Counselor's Commentary

> 9 Then Jesus said to them, "Let Me ask you, Is it lawful to do good or evil on the Sabbath, to save life or destroy it?"
> 10 Then, looking around at them He said to him, "Stretch out your hand." And he did, and his hand was restored.
> 11 They were mad with rage and spoke to one another about what they might do to Jesus.
> **12** During these days, He went out into the hills to pray; and He spent the whole night in prayer to God.
> 13 When the day came, He called His disciples to Him and chose twelve from among them whom He named apostles:

counseling]: "**Is it lawful to do good or evil on the Sabbath, to save life or to destroy it?**" (v. 9). Then He **looked around at them** and told the man to stretch out his hand. As he did so his hand was healed.

These religionists became **mad with rage** (v. 11). Why? Jesus was showing up their hypocrisy; Jesus was gaining popularity with the people; Jesus was publicly defying them—challenging their interpretations of the law. Consequently, they determined to silence Jesus. Yet they were not sure how to go about it; so they conferred with one another. Some will make trouble for you when you contradict the pet theories that have held counselees in their strangling grip. But you must stand firm so long as you know that you are being true to Christ as He has taught His ways in the Bible. Your biggest problem of this sort will be with man-made laws that, in the long run, strangle counselees by first strangling the Scriptures themselves!

Prior to selecting the full complement of His twelve disciples, Jesus went out into the hills to pray (vv. 12-16). Because of the importance of this matter, He spent the whole night in prayer.

Not only should we pray before important decisions, we must be careful not to pray too long. What does that mean? When you meet counselees who are hallucinating, or those who suffer from other perceptual problems, check out their sleep patterns. In many cases where they are not having some sort of reaction due to drug usage, there may be a problem caused by sleep loss. Significant sleep loss in some persons (2 1/2 days or more) can lead to every effect of LSD! The key thing here is to note that according to the biblical record, Jesus never remained awake longer than one whole night.

The passage indicates that it was Jesus Himself Who named the twelve **apostles**. The word means "sent off ones," and indicates that they were His representatives, sent off on a mission by Him.

Luke 6

14 Simon (whom He also named Peter), Andrew (his brother), James, John, Philip, Bartholomew,
15 Matthew, Thomas, James (Alphaeus' son), Simon (who was called the Zealot),
16 Judas (James's son), and Judas Iscariot (who became His betrayer).
17 Then He went down with them and stood on a level place, and there was a large group of His disciples and a huge crowd of people from all over Judea, from Jerusalem and from the coastal area of Tyre and Sidon,
18 who came to hear Him and to be cured of their diseases. And those who were tormented by unclean spirits were healed.
19 Now everybody tried to touch Him, since power went forth from Him and healed them all.

There are no present-day apostles in the sense of the twelve. The word is sometimes used in a lesser sense of those who were not of the twelve. That is the sense in which, today, we speak of "missionaries." The Latin word "missionary" is the precise equivalent of the Greek, "apostle." Hence, in the proper sense of the word, there are no *women* missionaries. There are wives of missionaries, Bible women who work in harems, etc., but in this office, which is the highest next to the apostle himself, all must be elders, as the apostle Peter styled himself (I Peter 5:1). The eldership is an office forbidden to women in the New Testament (I Timothy 2:11ff.).

In verses 17 through 19 we have the background for the Sermon on the Plain. The group of people to whom the sermon that follows was preached differs from that of which Matthew speaks. The place was also distinct. It would seem that Jesus often said the same or similar things to different groups at different times. Here, we read a condensed version of materials similar to (but not quite the same as) those found in the Sermon on the Mount.

Counselors who do not use the same material in more than one counseling case are foolish. A good illustration, or a somewhat varied adaptation of it, is a valuable piece of material to be used often. It will be varied according to the circumstances. In the case of what Jesus says, that seems to be clearly what He did. Modern scholars, liberal and conservative, tend to enjoy making things more difficult for themselves than necessary. Perhaps that is because they are scholars. Perhaps many of them have never counseled and have preached, if at all, in one place only. As a result they are unaware of the ways of preachers and counselors. Oh, well, be that as it may. Let's go on.

Verses 18 and 19 tell of the healing of many through **power** that

Christian Counselor's Commentary

> 20 Then He lifted up His eyes to His disciples and said to them, Happy are you who are poor, because God's empire is yours.
> 21 Happy are you who are hungry now, because you will be satisfied. Happy are you who weep now, because you will laugh.
> 22 Happy are you when people hate you, when they ostracize you, insult you and despise your name as evil for the Son of Man's sake.
> 23 Rejoice in that day and jump for joy. See, your reward in heaven is great. Their fathers did the same things to the prophets.

went forth from Jesus. Because of this, many others wanted to **touch** Him. Presumably, because of the great crowds, it was impossible for Jesus to heal each person individually. That would account for this method that God, through Him, adopted. Jesus was the Source of healing because, in Him, God had deposited all the fullness of Deity bodily (Colossians 2:9). And we are told that **He healed them all**.

Now for the Sermon on the Plain (vv. 20-49) which was spoken to a group of healthy people (cf. v. 19). The four beatitudes followed by four corresponding woes, are close to some of those in the Sermon on the Mount, but not identical. The **poor** are **happy** precisely because they *are* poor—in spirit. They who recognize that they have nothing to *offer* God are in a condition to *receive* everything. The **kingdom**, with all of its joys, blessings and resources, is *theirs*—now, and for all eternity! Because they recognize that they have no righteousness of their own to offer, they are open, anxious and ready to receive what God gives. On the other hand, Jesus says, "**Woe to the rich, because you have received your comfort**" (v. 24). These are those who *think* they are rich but are, in reality, poor in the **true riches**. (Cf. Revelation 3:17. Incidentally, this letter to the congregation of Laodicea shows that such spiritual poverty is true of members of the church). They are **comfortable** with what they have and see no need for what Christ offers. The same is true of some counselees. Those who recognize fully their great need are the ones who make the greatest changes. Those who do not, if they change at all, usually don't change in lasting ways. It is necessary, therefore, for counselors to help bring some counselees to the place where they acknowledge their spiritual "poverty," in order to receive the good things that God has for those who do.

What Jesus has said in the first beatitude and woe, in general, He now works out in more detail. The second beatitude expresses the **happiness** of the person who **hungers** after righteousness. It is a happiness that occurs because Jesus can satisfy that hunger not only by reckoning His

Luke 6

24 But woe to you who are rich, because you have received your comfort.

Woe to you who are already full, because you will be hungry.

25 Woe to you who laugh now, because you will mourn and weep.

---

righteousness though faith, but also by imparting more and more actual righteousness to the believer who hungers and thirsts after it. Those who consider themselves full already, because they are full of themselves and of this world's goods, in the long run, will find themselves hungry (v. 24). The truth of these verses is often seen in counseling. Those whose tongues are hanging out for God's help in living according to the ways that please Him, having appropriated it, are truly filled with good things. Those who come "knowing" that you have little to offer, go away with exactly what they thought they would!

The third way to **happiness** is by **weeping now** over one's sins and the effects of them on the honor of God and the welfare of others. Those who do, in time, find that they **will laugh**. But that laughter will be with God and His people. It will be joyous, holy mirth. Those who happily enjoy the wrong things now will, at length, **mourn**. All of these beatitudes reveal the fact that things are not as they seem to be. God upsets the ideas of men. By His revelation of truth given here in seemingly paradoxical form, He stops the reader short, makes him rethink his values and sets him on the right track if he will only listen in the right attitude. Counselees should also be brought up short at times by the use of these beatitudes and by statements like them that are calculated to make people think more than once about them.

The last beatitude has to do with persecution (a realism that is worked out in more detail later). Believers are happy about persecution (v. 22) not because they are masochists but because their persecutors make it possible for Christians to receive **great reward** in **heaven**. And it is good to know that you are not alone; when persecuted, remember that this is but a repetition of what happened to the **prophets** of old. People are alike in all ages (v. 23). The persecutor may be one of whom everyone else speaks well (v. 26). But he is in a precarious position too. He will be deceived by the **false prophets** and will end up as his **fathers** who persecuted the true prophets did. It is important to clue in counselees that there are always people in every age who will fight against truth—and those who stand for it. Christians should **jump for joy** when persecuted, Jesus says (v. 23). That is a thought to be pondered!

Christian Counselor's Commentary

26 Woe to you when everybody speaks well of you, because their fathers did the same to the false prophets.
27 Rather, I tell you who hear Me, love your enemies, do good things for those who hate you.
28 Bless those who curse you; pray for those who speak spitefully to you.

Someone says to you, "But you don't know what they are saying about me at work—all because I am a Christian." You reply, "Yes, and I guess that they probably **ostracize** you too?" "Right, you've got it!" "Well, in the light of those facts, let's take a look at Luke 6:22-26."

If everyone speaks well of your counselee, tell him that he probably has been deceived already, as verse 26 intimates. Look for false teaching that he has swallowed hook, line and sinker. It will more than likely be present. Jesus' insight in linking these two things together—speaking well of one and his falling for false teachings—is a valuable one for counselors. Don't forget it. The false teaching may not be overtly religious, but in one form or another it will be present.

Verses 26 and 27 (cf. Romans 12), in general, direct the believer's response to enemies who persecute. They are powerful counseling concepts that he must always have at hand for use. They apply in so many situations. The first is to **love** one's **enemies** and **do good** to those who **hate** you. In other words, overcome evil with good. Love does not mean having a warm, benevolent feeling toward an enemy. If you had to wait until that appeared you might never get around to **doing good** to him. No, one **loves** his **enemy** by feeding him if he is hungry, giving him cold water if he is thirsty. In other words, he looks for a need and, out of the resources he has, meets that need. How often must the counselor teach his counselees this biblical command! Counselees are oriented toward hitting back—either physically or verbally. No, one "strikes back" with love! And this love is concrete; it is not emoting, it is *showing* love by giving.

With reference to verbal responses to verbal abuse, Jesus commands, **"Bless those who curse you; pray for those who speak spitefully to you"** (v. 28). To **bless** is to speak well to, speak pleasantly to, to speak helpfully to another. And, in addition, he is to **pray** for such persons. These truths must be emphasized and reemphasized. Indeed, for some, you must even go to the length of helping them decide what good thing they might do for an enemy. Their minds have for so long dwelled on what harm they could do, it is too large of a paradigm shift for them to

Luke 6

29	To somebody who strikes you on one cheek, turn the other also, and the one who takes your coat, don't keep him from taking your tunic too.
30	Give to everybody who asks you for something, and don't demand that the one who took your things return them.
31	Whatever you want people to do for you is exactly what you should do for them.
32	Now if you love those who love you, what credit is that to you? Even sinners love those who love them!
33	If you do good to those who do good to you, what credit is that to you? Even sinners do that.

---

think of the opposite without help!

The next few verses challenge every counselee about how far he is willing to go to please Jesus Christ. Will you do as little to satisfy Him or as much as you can? That is what the passage is getting at. What about *patience* with another? The smitten **cheek** speaks to this matter. How much are you willing to put up with? The **coat** is a matter of *generosity* (v. 29). How much will you give? The third instance regarding an unpaid loan deals with *charity*. Again, how far are you willing to go—even so far as to allow him to cheat you? This is a very clear indication of the lengths that a believer might have to go in order to win another who hates and/or persecutes him. Pretty powerful stuff, wouldn't you say? Dynamite to use in counseling, I'd say. Try using these verses sometime and watch what happens!

The sum of the matter is found in verse 31 (what is often called the "golden rule"): **Whatever you want people to do for you is exactly what you should do for them**. That does not mean that your desires and interests are the standard for what you do for another. The Bible alone is that Standard. You may possibly want *wrong* things done for you. Rather, it means that you will do good for the other person as you would do good for yourself.

To show love for an enemy is difficult. Don't start telling us about all those others to whom you show **love**—that is, those who show **love** toward you! Even **sinners** do that! You don't keep a list of people who sent you Christmas cards last year and this year send cards only to them. In that simple illustration is the principle that Jesus is inculcating (vv. 32, 33). It is another stick of counseling dynamite!

The same principle is illustrated by another instance of love shown only by reciprocation in verse 34. You must not **lend** only to those who

Christian Counselor's Commentary

34 If you lend to those from whom you expect to receive, what credit is that to you? Even sinners lend when they expect to get an equal amount in return.
35 But you must love your enemies, do good to them, and lend without giving up; your reward will be great and you will be sons of the Most High, since He is kind to the ungrateful and evil.
36 Be merciful as your Father is merciful.
37 Don't judge and you won't be judged; don't condemn and you won't be condemned; forgive and you will be forgiven.

---

can always pay back or lend to you in the future. Rather, you must help out those who might have to default, if they are in genuine need. Again, remember, the main principle is to ask, "How far are you willing to go for Christ?"

Verses 35 and 36 take the matter a bit farther. God wants you to be *like Him*. **He is kind** and gives to those who are **ungrateful** and who violate His commandments by doing **evil**. So you are to be **merciful as your Father is merciful**. There is little **mercy** in the church today; perhaps even less even among those counselees who want vengeance. God is the Standard; your counselee is to be like his **Father** in heaven. "Like Father, like son" isn't a bad saying to repeat in this connection. Just make sure that you emphasize the capital "F." If a counselee has difficulty with this, help him to make a list of all the ways God has been merciful to him this past year. It won't be complete, but if he is conscientious, it will be long. Then, take him to this verse and, in effect, say, "Go thou and do likewise!" **Mercy** is the external result of an internal feeling of pity. It is doing a **kind** act for one who has no claims on you to do so. You might also have the counselee make a list of kindly acts of mercy that he might perform toward an enemy or someone who needs his help.

Verse 37 parallels Matthew 7: **Don't judge and you won't be judged; don't condemn and you won't be condemned; forgive and you will be forgiven.** Granted, the motive here is not so sterling as that in the verse above. But for many people, all that will move them to proper action is fear of reprisals. Here, what is said must be understood in the light of John 7:24, in which passage, Jesus commanded us to **judge a righteous judgment**. This, then, is not an absolute statement about judging. It is a prohibition of the *wrong sort of judging*. That would include such things as jumping to conclusions, failure to get all the facts, hearing only one side of an issue, not bothering to consult all the parties concerned, etc. Though the motive given for not judging and not condemning

Luke 6

38   Give, and it will be given to you—a generous amount, pressed down, shaken together and running over, will be poured into your lap. The measure you use will be used in returning to you.
39 He also told them a parable:
Can a blind man guide a blind man? Won't they both fall into the ditch?

---

is to avoid having this sort of action directed toward yourself, the warning is powerful—and it may be the only one that gets action in a given counseling case. At length, as counseling proceeds, you will want to move the counselee to a higher motivation—pleasing God, becoming like the heavenly Father—but initially, it may be the only thing that brings him to a screeching halt. Jesus' realism about people is apparent throughout the Scriptures. We can be thankful that He was no unrealistic idealist. All that is said about **judging** and **condemning** can here be said about **forgiving** as well. The word used for forgiving in this verse means to "release," and may have in it the idea of "acquitting" another, not holding him to something that he has done. You will meet a lot of the opposite spirit in counselees. Many want to *demand* this and that of another. If this verse teaches anything, it teaches the opposite. There is much here for the counselor who should familiarize himself with the entire passage.

In verse 38 we move on to another similar statement, but with a slightly different emphasis. In each of these commands of the Lord Jesus, there lies behind them the idea of love and grace shown toward others. Each is a facet of that underlying attitude. The motive in this verse is the same as in the previous one, but the application differs: **Give, and it will be given to you—a generous amount, pressed down, shaken together and running over.** That is, rather than being cheated, you will be treated more than fairly—you will be given more than you paid for. I remember as a child buying ice cream at the Arundel ice cream store in Baltimore, Maryland. They would "pack" the ice cream into a cardboard container. When they did so, they not only filled the container, they would press it down hard with the scoop and pile it up on the top so high that the lid never fit precisely. That is what the Lord Jesus is talking about. God's generosity is greater than yours—so why would you hesitate to be generous to another? That is the point.

The parable in verse 39 certainly applies to every counselor. If he is **blind** to the nature of the problem his counselee presents and/or to God's solution to it, he *and* his counselee will end up in the **ditch**. No one should

Christian Counselor's Commentary

> 40 A disciple isn't above his teacher; but everybody who has been thoroughly trained will be like his teacher.
> **41** Why do you see the splinter in your brother's eye but refuse to take notice of the board in your own eye?
> 42 How can you say to your brother, "Brother, let me remove the splinter from your eye," when you don't see the board in your own eye? You hypocrite! First, remove the board from your eye, and then you will be able to see clearly to remove the splinter from your brother's eye.

attempt to counsel unless he has some answers. When he doesn't, he should admit the fact rather than plowing blindly ahead into disaster for all concerned. Then, he should assign the counselee the homework of praying that he will come up with the answer this week. Moreover, he should go find the answer in the Bible (either on his own, or, when necessary by the help of someone else). If he cannot come up with the answer, he ought to admit the fact and refer the counselee (and himself) to a biblical counselor who can. Never bluff your way through a difficult case or you may end up playing blind man's bluff!

Verse 40 contains an important principle. Once a student has been thoroughly trained by another he will not only *think* like him, he will *be* **like him**. That is a serious matter to ponder. Those who spend their time soaking up the teachings of pagan counselors will, in time, begin to think and act like them. One who is thoroughly imbued with Rogerianism, for instance, will find it difficult to give you a precise answer to your questions. He will tend to repeat your own words back to you. Rather than become a *paraclete*, you may find him speaking more like a parakeet! Thank God that every day biblical counselors are privileged to spend time hearing from *God's* Word! To the extent that they appropriate what they study, and are themselves trained by it, they have the joy of becoming more like God Himself.

Jesus demonstrated the truth of His own statement in His disciples. In Mark 3:14 we read that He took the twelve to be *with Him* so that they would become like Him. In Acts 4:13 we read that others saw that they *had become* like Him.

It is dangerous to teach others. One must recognize that he is imparting more than information in teaching. Of almost equal importance with truth is the attitudes, the approaches, etc., that he communicates. These have impact on the truth, which may easily be distorted by them.

Verses 41 and 42 are of significant help to every biblical counselor.

Luke 6

> **43** The fact is that a good tree doesn't produce bad fruit; and it is also true that a bad tree doesn't produce good fruit.
> 44 Each tree is known by its own kind of fruit: people don't gather figs from thorn bushes, nor do they pick grapes from briar bushes.
> 45 A good person from the good treasure that is in his heart brings forth good things, and an evil person from his evil treasure brings forth evil. This is true because a person's mouth speaks from the abundance of his heart.

Neither counselor nor counselee can see properly to remove the **splinter** from another's eye when he has a **board** protruding from his own. The humor in this illustration is apparent. Jesus contrasts a **splinter** (small speck) with a long **board**. The idea, taken literally, is ludicrous, as He intended it to be. But **hypocrites** need to be awakened. Sometimes it is the exaggerated that does the trick. At any rate, both counselors and counselees may profit from an application of the verse. Often people sit in front of the counselor who complain about the nasty language of one another in language that is as nasty as anything the other has spoken. They must be awakened to what they are doing; this verse is calculated to do it. Counselors who themselves harbor some sin in their lives will either come down far too hard on others who likewise have the problem or will avoid it altogether. Their own struggles with sin will distort their dealings with others in one way or another. It is probably true that unless the grace of God intervenes the counselor's effectiveness will rise no higher than his own lifestyle. There must not only be study on the part of every counselor, but according to this verse and the one preceding, counselors must give careful attention to their own lives as well.

In verses 43 through 45, Jesus drives home the principles He has been teaching in another way. He speaks of a **tree**, a **bush** and a **treasure**. **Good trees produce good fruit**. Bad trees don't. One isn't a sinner because he sins; he sins because he is a sinner. Neither **figs** nor **grapes** can be found growing on **thorn bushes** or **briar bushes**. The character of the bush determines what it produces. What is in a **treasure** box will determine what you can take out of it. People are like that. **Good** comes from good persons—those who have been regenerated by the Spirit and are now being sanctified by Him. **Evil** comes from those who have not known regeneration and sanctification. What comes from the **mouth** is first in the **heart**. The **heart** is the inner person. (See my book *A Theology of Counseling* for a detailed discussion of the biblical meaning of **heart**.) Words that are sinful, hurting and cruel, for instance, will be spoken only if one

Christian Counselor's Commentary

> 46 And, why do you call Me "Lord, Lord," and not do what I say?
> 47 Let Me show you what everybody who comes to Me and listens to My words and does them is like.
> 48 He is like a man building a house who dug deep and laid the foundation on the rock, and when a flood came the river dashed against that house, but it couldn't shake it, because it was so well built.
> 49 But the one who hears and doesn't do them is like a man who built a house on the ground without a foundation, against which the river dashed, and it immediately collapsed and it was totally ruined.

first thinks bad thoughts inwardly. When you hear things that are offensive spoken in counseling, you might turn to this passage and show the counselee whose mouth is stained by them the source of his problem. The solution, then, is not merely to stop speaking that way (that, of course is necessary), but also to *repent* of the **evil** thinking that preceded the words. Then, one must begin to fill his **heart** with the proper sort of thoughts.

Then comes a pungent question, one that, when all else has failed in counseling and you are convinced that you are not at fault—that the problem is one of pure disobedience, might be asked of a counselee. But be very sure, first, that there is not some other reason. It is found in verse 46: **Why do you call Me "Lord, Lord," and not do what I say?** The question is sharp, penetrating, one that ought to be used with care. But it is one that you must be sure that you have in your counseling repertoire. There are times to ask it. The best way, perhaps, is to *read* it from this passage. What is so powerful about it is the fact that the Lord Jesus asks it; it is *He* with Whom it brings the counselee into confrontation—not *you*. And that is precisely what is needed in the crunch when one stubbornly resists doing what the Scriptures clearly require and admits it.

Finally, the chapter (and the Sermon on the Plain) ends with the story of the two **houses**. The point that Jesus is making (contrary to the child's ditty that is based on this story) is that one's life will either stand or come crashing down in times of trouble according to whether it has been built on the teachings of Christ (v. 47). But it is not enough to **listen to** and be able to repeat what Christ has commanded—one must *do* **them**. Here is the conclusion that hearkens back to all that He had been teaching. The counselee who knows all he should but does not do it is one who needs to hear this story all over again. Christian living is built by observing all that He has commanded—especially in this sermon and the sermon on the mountain. Use Luke 6 frequently, freely!

CHAPTER 7

1 When He had finished delivering all of His sayings in the hearing of the people, He went into Capernaum.
2 Now there was a slave of a centurion, who was dear to him, who was sick and about to die.
3 So when he heard about Jesus, he sent some Jewish elders to Him to ask Him to come and heal his slave.
4 When they came to Jesus, they urged Him earnestly, saying, "He deserves to have you grant this request,
5 because he loves our nation and he built our synagog for us."
6 So Jesus went with them. When He was not far from the house, the centurion sent friends who said to Him,
> Don't put Yourself to such trouble Lord; I don't deserve to have You come under my roof.
7 > That's why I didn't count myself worthy to come to You. Instead, just speak the word and let my servant be healed.

The healing of the **centurion's slave** is the subject of the next item (vv. 1-10). We are told that he was **about to die** (v. 2). There are some who think that because the providence of God is unknown and because of the little we know of the human body it is always wrong to say that one is dying. Luke, a physician, must have known the signs of death and heard that this slave exhibited them. He does not hesitate to say so. As a matter of fact, it is the near death condition of the slave that sets the stage for the miracle of Christ. Don't let counselees be overly precise in this matter.

The **centurion** seems to have been a remarkable man. He had a warm relationship to his slave (v. 2), he was a proselyte of the gate, he had built a **synagog** for the **Jews** of **Capernaum** and the **Jewish elders** spoke very highly of him. Moreover, as we see how he relates to Christ and what Jesus' expressed opinion of him was, we can only marvel at this man of **faith**.

Luke's concern in these verses (as elsewhere) is to show that Jesus is the Master over all of life and death. This incident and the next speak of His power over sickness and death. It is important always to remember that death comes by the will of God, in His way and according to His timetable. Sometimes counselees who cry out "Why? Why him? Why now?" must be told simply but plainly, "Because God, Who does all things well, thought it best."

In this episode, it is not healing only that is mentioned, but healing at

Christian Counselor's Commentary

> 8   I am also a man under authority who has soldiers under me. So I tell this one, "Go," and he goes, and that one, "Come," and he comes, and to my slave, "Do this," and he does it.
> 9 When Jesus heard these words He was amazed at him, and He turned and said to the crowd that was following Him, "I tell you I haven't found such faith in all of Israel."
> 10 Now when those who had been sent returned to the house, they found the slave well.

---

a distance. That is the remarkable thing about it, so far as the act is concerned. The other remarkable thing is the **faith** of the **centurion**. Here is a man who, according to Christ, had **faith** that exceeded that which Jesus had **found in all of Israel** (v. 9). That is quite a statement! We have seen faith that existed among those pious Jews who were awaiting the Messiah, the faith of John the Baptist (about whom Jesus will say some very commendable things) and the faith of the four men who brought the paralytic. Yet as great as their faith was, this gentile's faith exceeded them all. From time to time, it might be well to ask a counselee how solid his faith is. For instance, does he believe that Jesus can solve his problem? If he has weak faith, it may be necessary to help him to attain a greater faith. Remember faith comes by hearing, and hearing by the Word of God. Set him to work reading the Bible. Read this story of the healing of the centurion's slave, etc.

    The humility of the centurion also stands out (cf. vv. 6, 7). Moreover, he understood **authority** when he saw it. He was a man **under** the **authority** of others, and he exerted authority toward those under him. He knew that Jesus' Word was authoritative. If He commanded healing it would take place as surely and as quickly as when he gave an order to those under him (v. 8). The authority of Christ, mentioned here as well as elsewhere, is important. Every counselor, so long as he asserts biblical authority, counsels with the authority of Christ. No other sort of counseling is authoritative. But if Jesus commands a Christian counselee to love an enemy (as we saw in the last chapter He did), the counselee has no right to object, and ought to respond instantly. After all, he also is a man **under orders**! Why should a man like this be so responsive and counselees today so unresponsive? Is it in part, at least, because the authority of Christ has not been rightly emphasized? Are churches, counselors and others all too relaxed, willing to cajole, beg and coax, rather than order? Have we cultivated a mentality that runs adversely to that which we should have (cf. Matthew 28:18-20)?

11 Shortly afterward, He went to a city called Nain, and His disciples and a large crowd accompanied Him.

12 As He came close to the city gate, He saw a dead man being carried out for burial. He was the only child of his mother, who was a widow, and a large crowd from the city was with her.

13 When He saw her, the Lord was moved with compassion for her and said to her, "Don't cry."

14 He approached the coffin and touched it, and the pallbearers stood still. Then He said, "Young man, I tell you, get up!"

15 The dead man sat up and began to speak. Then He gave him to his mother.

16 They were all seized with fear and praised God, saying, "A prophet has been raised up among us! God has shown concern for His people!"

Verses 11 through 17 carry the power of Christ one step beyond. He may heal those who are dying, but what of those who have already died? Outside of the city of **Nain** we receive the answer. The **widow's only son has died**. As Jesus and those with Him approach the city, they meet the funeral procession. Out of **compassion** Jesus told her not to **cry** and raised her son from the dead (vv. 13-15). That same Savior, Who has no less **compassion**, sees your counselee's situation today. He is still the compassionate One, Who acts in compassion. But what the compassionate thing is may differ from situation to situation. Yet, you may always assure counselees that Jesus does the compassionate thing—even when they cannot understand how that can be.

There is another factor here. The centurion had great faith. Nothing is said of the widow's faith. It was merely Jesus' compassion that moved Him to action. Surely, that led to her faith. But it is not necessary to have great faith to receive a response from Jesus. Faith healers may say so, but this incident proves otherwise, and may be one reason why it is placed in contrasting juxtaposition to the previous one.

Verses 16 and 17 tell us about the way in which the news of what Jesus was doing and teaching **spread**. The two **large crowds** (vv. 11, 12) that had converged into one around this miracle went out and spread this word. They could not easily forget what had happened, indeed, they had all been **seized with fear** (v. 16). They **praised God** and realized that Jesus was a **prophet**. The last phrase, **God has shown concern for His people**, hints at the idea that they were aware of a new visitation of God. Whether they realized Jesus was more than a prophet—the Messiah—or whether they thought that He was merely the herald of the Messiah, we do

Christian Counselor's Commentary

17 And this word about Him spread all over Judea and the surrounding countryside.

18 Now John's disciples reported to him about all these things. So John called two of his disciples

19 and sent them to the Lord, saying, "Are you the Coming One, or should we expect another?"

20 When these men came to Him, they said, "John the Baptist sent us to you to ask, 'Are you the Coming One, or should we expect another?'"

21 At that very time He healed many of diseases, plagues and evil spirits, and He helped many blind people to see.

22 So in answer He said to them,
> Go tell John what you saw and heard: **blind people see again,** lame people walk, lepers are being cleansed, deaf persons hear, dead persons are raised, **poor people have the good news announced to them.**

23 So, happy is the person who doesn't turn away from Me.

---

not know. But they were aware that something new was in the wind, and that God was behind it, somehow blessing His people.

We turn to a longer narrative that is in three parts. But it all pertains to Jesus and John the Baptist (vv. 18-35). The first has to do with John's doubts. Some think that John doubted everything about his mission, but that is not so. We hear nothing of his saying, "Was it all for nothing?" or words to that effect. Jesus had not yet swung the axe and taken down the tree; His shovel had not yet separated between the wheat and the chaff. John was wondering whether, therefore, he had been right about Jesus. Perhaps He was only a precursor of the One Who would come. Listen to his words: **"Are you the Coming One, or should we expect another?"** There were many traditions about the Messiah. Some even said that two Messiahs would appear. In prison, John wondered if he had things altogether straight. At that very time when John's disciples arrived with John's question Jesus was doing many miracles (vv. 20, 21). He pointed to these, which they had the opportunity to observe, and (quoting Messianic passages from Isaiah) simply referred John to the Bible. He was the fulfillment of these predictions (v. 22).

For the sake of those who were listening to the disciples of John and Jesus' answer, He said, **"Happy is the person who doesn't turn away from Me."** It was a warning that they and John's disciples needed to hear. There were all sorts of ideas floating around about who He was. Jesus would have them understand that there would be no other person to whom

Luke 7

24 And as John's messengers went away, He began to speak to the crowds about John:
> What did you go out into the desert to see—a reed that was shaking in the wind?
>
> 25 No? What then did you go out to see—a man dressed in soft clothing? Listen, those who have beautifully styled clothes and live in luxury are in royal palaces.

---

they should turn. He was not a forerunner of another; *He* was the **coming One**.

When a counselee is confused, mixed up about things, there is One Person to Whom and one place to which to turn: he should turn to Jesus Christ as He speaks in the Bible. Prayer and Bible study, help in understanding and applying Scripture from a counselor: these and any other ways one may come to understand from the Bible what is uncertain is the way to go. One should not go bouncing around from person to person asking his opinion. There is one source alone to which to turn, from which he should never **turn away**.

After the **messengers** from John had departed, Jesus spoke to the **crowds** about John. He didn't want a wrong impression about him to be left with them. After all, John and his baptism had served a very important purpose. In no way would He disassociate Himself from John. Rather, in all that He says, He does the opposite. And He strongly upholds the person and the ministry of John.

How important it is when a truly biblical counselor's ministry might be brought into disrepute through misunderstanding not to abandon him but to stand with him. This is important both in order to uphold his ministry (which is biblical) and to vindicate the person who exercised it. Too often in biblical circles there is an independence among us that is unhealthy. We need to fight and work for one another as we jointly seek to honor Christ. Moreover, we must always avoid the tendency to build one's self up at the expense of another—even a fellow biblical counselor! It is to be regretted that there have been instances of this. It must stop!

What did Jesus say about John? We read His words in verses 24 through 28. John was no **reed shaking in the wind** (v. 24). How important it is to emphasize that it is Jesus speaking. He commends John for his steadfastness, for his ability to withstand every pressure to bend. He is sturdy, consistent, a man one can depend on to stand for truth and to keep his word. Every counselor must have that sort of character, and must inculcate it in his counselees.

26   Well then, what did you go out to see—a prophet? Right! But, I tell you, he was more than a prophet!
27   He is the one about whom it is written, **See, I send My messenger before Your face who will get Your road ready for You**.
28   I tell you among those born of women, nobody is greater than John; yet he who is least in God's empire is greater than he.
29 All the people, when they heard Him—even the tax collectors—acknowledged that God is right by being baptized by John,
30 but the Pharisees and the lawyers rejected God's counsel about themselves by not being baptized by him.

In addition, Jesus says John was rugged, tough and unmoved by every pretension of **luxury** (v. 25). He fascinated and convicted Herod by his preaching. Doubtless, if he had toned down his words (as many friends, in one way or another, keep telling me to do) he could have enjoyed all the finery and luxury of Herod's court. He might even have been appointed court chaplain! John was untouched by any such thing; he had truth to preach, and preach it he will, at any cost. Too many counselors tone down what they have to say. Thereby they weaken their ministries and fail to help counselees as they might.

If not a **reed**, if not someone **dressed in fine clothes** enjoying all the **luxuries** of a **royal court**, what was John? That is what Jesus asked (v. 26). He was a **prophet**. Yes, he was that, but he was also **more than a prophet**. He was the forerunner of the Messiah. To substantiate this, Jesus quoted Malachi 3:1 (v. 27). And in Jesus' words, no one is greater than John. Yet, those who would become members of the new era, **God's empire** that was now coming on the scene, would be **greater than he** (that is, greater in their opportunities and knowledge). These were high words of commendation for John. His question to Jesus had not shaken Jesus' opinion of him. Not for a moment! And He wanted the crowds who had been baptized by John to know so. They had made no mistake in heeding his message of repentance. After all, they had agreed with God's estimate of their sin in that baptism (v. 29).

But the Pharisees and the lawyers rejected God's counsel about themselves by not being baptized by him (v. 30). That is to say, they thought they needed no repentance, so why be baptized with a baptism that indicated that they did?

Jesus, exasperated by their response both to John and to Himself, then told them a parable. The present **generation** of religious leaders (and those who followed them) is **like children playing games in the** market-

Luke 7

31 To what then shall I compare the people of this generation? What are they like?

32 They are like children sitting in a marketplace and calling to one another, who say, "We piped for you, but you didn't dance; we sang funeral dirges, but you didn't cry."

33 I say this because John the Baptist came without eating bread or drinking wine, and you say, "He has a demon."

34 The Son of Man has come both eating and drinking, and you say, "See, the man is a glutton and a drunkard, a friend of tax collectors and sinners."

35 But wisdom is shown to be right by all her children.

36 One of the Pharisees asked him to eat with him, so He went into the Pharisee's house and reclined at the table.

37 And a woman, whose sinful life was known to the city, learned that He was dining in the Pharisee's house, and she brought an alabaster box of perfume.

---

place. They **piped** but the leaders didn't **dance**; they **sang dirges**, but they didn't **cry**. John came solemnly, fasting, acting like a Nazarite, calling for repentance, but the leaders failed to respond appropriately. Jesus came joyously, **eating and drinking,** but they wouldn't respond to that either. Instead, they claimed that John was **demon-possessed**, and they accused Jesus of being **a glutton and a friend of society's outcasts**.

The way in which many respond to biblical teaching is clearly exposed. No matter what approach you take, no matter which biblical truths you emphasize—those which are hard and austere or those which are kind and loving, it really doesn't matter. When one's mind is set on doing as he pleases, when he is satisfied with his own self-righteousness, he will always invent excuses for not heeding God's Word. Usually, too, he will attack the messenger. You haven't been counseling very long if you haven't discovered these things to be true.

Yet, even in a day like that, **wisdom's children** vindicate the truth, showing what is **right**. No matter how bad the times, God has always had His own who support the truth, who understand it and who respond appropriately to God's Word. There are those who in wisdom agree to what both John and Jesus taught and did.

Having ended His discourse on John the Baptist, he was asked **to eat at the home of a Pharisee** (v. 36). Jesus went. The Pharisee didn't invite Jesus because he believed in Him; it seems that he was interested in learning more about Him, possibly in order to condemn Him. When reclining

Christian Counselor's Commentary

38 She stood behind His feet, crying, and began to wet His feet with her tears. So she wiped them with her hair and tenderly kissed His feet and anointed them with the perfume.

39 Now when the Pharisee who had invited Him saw it, he said to himself, "If this man were a prophet he would have known who and what this woman who is touching him is—he would have known that she's a sinner."

40 But Jesus said to him in response, "Simon, I have something to say to you." He said, "Say it, teacher."

41 A certain creditor has two debtors. One owed five hundred denarii and the other fifty.

42 Since neither of them had anything with which to repay him, he freely forgave both. Now, which one of them will love him more?

43 Simon replied, "I suppose the one to whom he forgave the most." And He said to him, "You chose the right one."

44 Then He turned toward the woman and said to Simon, Do you see this woman? I came into your house, but you didn't offer Me water for My feet. But this woman has wet My feet with her tears and wiped them with her hair.

45 You didn't greet Me with a kiss, but this woman from the time I came in hasn't stopped kissing My feet.

46 You didn't anoint My head with oil, but this woman anointed My feet with perfume.

---

at the table, a woman appeared who brought **an alabaster box** [or vial] **of perfume**. She was a notorious **sinner**, known as such in the **city** (v. 37). She first **stood** at Jesus' **feet** then, crying, **wiped** His tear-wet feet with her hair. And **she tenderly kissed His feet and anointed them with the perfume** (v. 38).

The **Pharisee**, however, said to himself that Jesus couldn't be a prophet or he would have known who and what this woman is. He implied by this that Jesus would then have had nothing to do with her. The fact of the matter is that Jesus *did* know all about her and that was precisely why He allowed her to do as she did. His standard differed radically from that of the Pharisee.

At this point Jesus spoke to **Simon** the **Pharisee**. He told him a parable about two **debtors**, each of whom could not **repay** his debts, which differed radically. Yet, their **creditor freely forgave** both. Then He asked, **"Which one of them will love him more?"** Simon, cornered, answers hesitantly, **"I suppose the one to whom he forgave the most."** Jesus assured him that he had chosen the correct one (v. 43).

Now that He has Simon safely caught in His net, He pulls the string

Luke 7

47 I tell you, then, (it is clear that) her sins—which are many—have been forgiven her because she loved much. But the one to whom little has been forgiven loves little.
48 Then He said to her, "Your sins have been forgiven you."
49 Now those who were reclining at the table with Him began to say among themselves, "Who is this who even forgives sins?"
50 Then He said to the woman, "Your faith has saved you; go in peace."

---

and there he is dangling. This is a useful tactic to use in counseling (cf. Nathan and David: "You are the man"). Unlike you, **Simon** (who failed to show Me the amenities one always shows a guest), Jesus says, this woman, in her ways, has done all the things you should have done. In other words, she stands head and shoulders above you, even though you look down on her! (vv. 44-46). **It is clear** that she loves more **because** her actions give proof of the fact (v. 47). Then Jesus tells her that her **sins** have been **forgiven** (v. 48) assuring her of what she had assumed already. The guests wondered at this since it meant that Jesus was taking upon Himself the prerogatives of Deity—forgiving sins (see the story of the man on the stretcher who was let down through the roof for an understanding of the teaching of the time about this). To the woman He explained that her **faith** in Him had led to her **salvation**, and that she could leave there in **peace**.

What does this incident and Christ's exposition of it tell counselors? Many things, but we will mention only a few. It shows what true repentance is like. The woman's actions might have been unusual, embarrassing to many; to her they were absolutely natural. The account reveals the attitude of self-righteousness, where one is concerned with himself (touch a filthy woman like this?) and not with the need of another. Counselors must be careful not to become Pharisees in their selection and treatment of counselees. Again, the story explains how to discover true love for Christ; it comes to the fore—even when it must take (in the eyes of others) seemingly foolish form. Those who have been forgiven much do not mind becoming "fools for Christ's sake." **Peace** is what everyone who believes may (should) have. Assurance is a clear right of every saved sinner—not on the basis of his works or holiness, but on the basis of God's promises. Counselors must be clear about this (for help, see Horatius Bonar, *The Everlasting Righteousness*).

Chapter 8

1 Afterwards, He traveled through cities and villages, preaching and announcing the good news about God's empire. And the Twelve went with Him,
2 as well as some women who had been healed of evil spirits and diseases: Mary called Magdalene, from whom seven demons had gone out,
3 Joanna, the wife of Chuza, Herod's steward, Susanna and many others, who helped support them from their own resources.
4 As a large crowd was gathering and people from city after city were coming to Him, He told a parable:
>5 A sower went out to sow his seed. Now as he sowed it some fell along the road and was stepped on and the birds of the sky ate it.
>6 Some fell on rock and sprouted and dried up because it didn't have any moisture.
>7 Some fell among thorns that grew up with it and choked it.
>8 And some fell on good soil and grew up and produced fruit a hundred times over.

After saying this He called out, "Whoever has ears to hear, let him listen."

Chapter eight begins with another summary statement about Jesus' **preaching** itinerary in Palestine. He took the **Twelve** with Him. But mention is also made of some women who traveled along, presumably to minister to and help Jesus and the disciples. These were people who had been healed or exorcised by Jesus. Their gratitude was translated into action. Counselees, helped by biblical counselors might wish to do something to further the ministry. That, it seems, from the example of Jesus, is perfectly acceptable. Some, who may be overly scrupulous, might otherwise object. Mary Magdalene, from whom Jesus cast seven demons, was prominent enough to be mentioned by name (incidentally, there is no reason to think that the woman in the previous chapter was Mary).

There were others, some of whom had close ties to royalty, mentioned. It is specifically stated that they supported the ministry of Jesus and the Twelve financially (v. 3). That there is need for such support is absolutely true. People must eat, etc. The laborer is worthy of his hire. On the other hand, there is no record of Jesus having solicited these funds. It seems that they were voluntarily given. Some counselors, it seems, go overboard on seeking funds. If their counseling is done effectively, the Lord will raise up people to support their work.

On one occasion, as **a large crowd was gathering**, Jesus stopped to

9 Then His disciples asked Him what this parable meant.
10 So He said,
> To you has been granted knowledge of the secrets of God's empire, but to the rest I speak in parables, so that **though they see, they won't see, and though they hear, they won't understand**.

---

tell them a **parable** (vv. 5-18). It is the parable of the **Sower and the Seed**. The point of this parable is to urge listeners to **be careful how** they **hear** (v. 18). There are ways and ways of listening to Jesus. We saw something of this in Luke four, which you may wish to reread in the light of this parable.

The parable is sketched in verses 5 through 8. The Sower sows. Some seed fell on the hard **road** only to be **stepped on** and **eaten** by birds. Some fell on **rock** beneath thin soil; it sprouted but died because there was no depth or **moisture**. Some fell among **thorns** which **choked** it as soon as it began to grow. Some fell on **good soil** and produced a crop one **hundred times** over. Having given the parable, Jesus called on the crowd to **listen** (v. 8). By that He doubtless meant how you **listen** is the factor that determines whether you are good or bad soil. The Word He, the **Sower**, preached would fall on all kinds of ground. But only in those who listened properly would it bear fruit (cf. John's comments on works appropriate to repentance and Jesus' words about **listening and doing** at the conclusion of His Sermon on the Plain: Luke 6:47).

The **disciples** asked for an explanation of the **parable** (v. 9). The word *parabole* has in it the idea of a comparison of two things. One thing is "thrown alongside another" as a way of getting across the truth one wishes to teach. Jesus' parables were memorable, often had a twist to them that made all the difference (as we shall see vividly in chapter fifteen) and were left hanging for those who heard to figure out. They often involved two sorts of responses (as here and in the parable of the two houses) that those who heard might make.

Jesus willingly explains the meaning of the parable to His disciples, telling them that to them God has **granted knowledge of the secrets of** His **empire**. To others, there were to be no explanations of the parables that He left with them. They would have to figure them out. But many would not (v. 10). Because, as Isaiah, to whom He referred, said, "though they have eyes and ears, nevertheless **they won't see and hear**." That is to say, they will hear the story, but they won't **understand** (v. 10). That is

Christian Counselor's Commentary

> 11 This is what the parable means: The seed is God's word.
> 12 Those beside the road are those who hear, but then the devil comes and takes the word from their hearts, so that they won't believe and be saved.
> 13 Those that are on rock are those who hear and receive the word with joy, but they don't take root. They believe for a while, but during time of trial they fall away.
> 14 Those that fell among thorns are those who hear, but as they go on are choked by the worries and riches and pleasures of life and their fruit doesn't mature.
> 15 And those on good soil are those who, when they hear the word, hold on to it with a fine and good heart, and persevere until they produce fruit.

because they fail to heed the admonishment **Whoever has ears to hear, let him listen!** Parables are enlightening to those who hear well; they are confusing to those who do not.

Jesus now explains. There are those who hear, but the devil (through his enticements) makes them forget by making other things more important, so that the seed doesn't even take root in their hearts (v. 12). There is no saving faith.

Others hear and receive the message with joy (that is, they make an emotional response to the Gospel, but their "faith" is not saving faith because it does not last). At first, they think they are Christians, but it becomes apparent later when trials come and they fall away that they never were saved (v. 13).

A third group—who are not good soil either—hear, but worries, on the one hand, or riches and pleasures of life, on the other, are of greater importance to them. When they discover that the Gospel doesn't alleviate all of their suffering and doesn't add to life's luxuries, they lose interest. They are those who want to "add Jesus on" to their lives in order to make them more pleasant, and find that He is not in the business of being added on. He shakes everything up and changes one's life radically. They don't want that (v. 14)!

Then there is the seed that falls on the good soil (notice the seed is the same; the soil is what differs). These are those who **hear the word, hold on to it with a fine and good heart and persevere until they produce good fruit** (v. 15). These are those whose faith is genuine, who have truly been saved. The others may for a time associate with God's people, may seem to be saved, but like those mentioned in Hebrews 6 and 10,

Luke 8

> 16 Nobody, when he lights a lamp, covers it with a container or puts it under a bed. Rather, he puts it on a lampstand, so that those who come in can see the light.
> 17 I say this because there is nothing hidden that won't be uncovered, and nothing secret that won't be known or made apparent.
> 18 So then, be careful how you listen. Whoever has will be given more; whoever doesn't have will have even what he seems to have taken away from him.
> 19 Then His mother and His brothers came to Him, but they couldn't get to Him through the crowd.

---

eventually fall away (see the commentary in this series on those two passages for details).

Counselors will do well to use this parable on appropriate occasions. There will be times when those who, having problems, come, and it seems like they may be falling away. Check out the various possibilities mentioned in the parable. You may try to counsel supposed believers who have made a false profession of faith. On the other hand, believers are not immune to the foibles mentioned in the parable. They too can be taught from its contents by relating to them what Jesus has to say about these wrong ways of **hearing**. Many counselees do not listen carefully to what you say, and, as a result, get themselves into additional trouble. Urge people, as Jesus did, to **be careful how** they **hear**. Much failure in counseling can be attributed to failure to observe this command diligently. In 8:18, 8:21 and 11:28 the importance of good hearing is stressed as the climax of a paragraph.

The lamp on the **lampstand** that is mentioned here (a frequent image Christ used) speaks of the disciples. They must **hear**, because the time will come when, like that **lamp** spreading light to all corners of the room, throughout the world they will herald the truths that Christ is explaining to them. There is nothing esoteric about His teaching (vv. 16-18). Yet there is a condition for learning: listen **carefully**, because the more you have the desire to learn, the more that will be given to you. But on the other hand, failure to learn means less will be given; indeed, even the little you have will be removed. And learning means learning for doing. That is the bottom line. It is a principle of learning that also holds true for counselees.

Still emphasizing the importance of hearing God's Word (v. 21), there is a brief interlude telling of a visit of Jesus' family members (vv. 19-21). Because of the crowds, Jesus' **mother** and **brothers couldn't get**

Christian Counselor's Commentary

20 So they told Him, "Your mother and your brothers are standing outside and want to see you."
21 But in reply He said, "My mother and My brothers are those who hear God's word and do it."
22 One day He got into a boat with His disciples and He said to them, "Let's go over to the other side of the lake." So they put out into the lake.
23 As they sailed He fell asleep. Now a storm blew up on the lake, and the boat began taking water and they were in danger.
24 So they went to Him, awakened Him and said, "Master, we're going to die!" But He awakened, rebuked the wind and the rough water, and they stopped raging and there was a calm.

---

to Him. But word was passed through that they were **standing outside**. His reply was, **My mother and My brothers are those who hear God's word and do it**. In other words, there is a family to which we all may belong by the saving faith that leads to works. Faith is thicker than blood! Note especially, Jesus virtually defines a member of the family of God in terms of **hearing**. Few emphases are made so strongly throughout the book of Luke. Counselors find that the problem among counselees is rife. Many are in trouble because they have refused to "hear" God's word. Others fail to get out of trouble (and usually get into worse trouble as a result) because they will not hear. Now, it is important, then, for you to stress (as Jesus does) the need to **hear** in the sense of His words. Remember, it is *how* one hears that is critical. A person may hear words, be able to repeat them, etc., but **hearing**, he does **not understand** (v. 10). Then there are those who **hear and** *do*. And, by the way, be sure that you make this hearing a matter not of how they hear *you* but how they hear God—as Jesus does (v. 21). You have no issue with your counselees; the issue is between God and them.

In verses 22 through 25 we read of the story of the storm. The disciples and Jesus were sailing toward the East across the sea of Galilee when one of those sudden violent **storms**, that sometimes do, arose on the lake. The wind and the waves were treacherous; they began to take in water, and the boat was (it seemed) in danger of sinking. During this Jesus was **asleep** (v. 23). They awakened Him, crying out **Master, we're going to die!** But, calmly, Jesus **rebuked the wind and the rough water** and the storm ceased. All became as calm as Jesus. It must have been very severe when seasoned fishermen despaired of life and turned to a non-sailor for help! Then Jesus asked, **"Where's your faith?"** These men had been appointed by Jesus for a task of carrying the gospel throughout the world.

Luke 8

25 Then He said to them, "Where is your faith?" But they were afraid and amazed and said to one another, "Who, then, is this man that commands even the winds and the water, and they obey him?"

26 Then they sailed down to the country of the Gerasenes, that is opposite Galilee.

27 As He stepped out on the shore He was met by a demoniac from the city, who for a long while hadn't worn clothes, and lived among the tombs rather than in a house.

They were immortal until they had completed the task. To say, "**we're going to die**" was a denial of Christ's Word. Note, He didn't deny that they had faith; simply that they did not exercise it (a frequently-occurring counselee problem in times of fear). And, He didn't ask the question for information; He asked to put the pressure on them to make them think—then left it there.

The disciples were impressed by His ability to control the forces of nature and said, "**Who is this man?**" Jesus still controls all of life. He still can quiet the storms of life for those who cry out to Him for help. But, it would seem, He also expects counselees to exercise their faith during the stormy hours and not always ask Him to do more for them. He has given faith for those times (Ephesians 2:8, 9). It is to be used. It isn't wrong for counselors from time to time to repeat Jesus' question to counselees who are terrified about life's hard times.

Notice also that Jesus dealt with the disciples' problem, then asked the one question. That is often the technique to use in counseling. Help the counselee to solve his problem. Then, after he stands amazed that all the while God had the answer in His Word, ask the question. In that context it means, "Have you been a Christian, and a Bible student, so long and yet you haven't learned that there are answers in the Book for all of life? Why are you so surprised? Where is your faith?" No matter what you do, bring the counselee to see that it is his right and obligation to find all things necessary for life and godliness in the Bible.

We come now to the long account of the healing of the demoniac (vv. 26-39). We will not take the time to refute Huxley's tragic attempt to destroy one's faith through debunking it. Let it suffice to say that if that is the best a notable skeptic can do, it is precious little. Here was a person who lived among the rock-hewn tombs outside the little cities on the Eastern cliffs of the lake. He stripped himself of clothing. People tried to restrain him by putting him in shackles, but when seized by the demon, he was able to tear the chains apart. As we saw before, the demons in him

Christian Counselor's Commentary

28 When he saw Jesus, he shouted out, fell down before Him and said in a loud voice, "What do you want with me, Jesus, Son of the Most High God? I beg you, don't torture me!"
29 (He said this because He had ordered the unclean spirit to come out of the man. Often he had seized him, and though he was bound with chains and shackles and put under guard, he tore the chains apart and was driven into lonely places by the demon.)
30 Jesus then asked him, "What is your name?" And he said, "Legion" (Because many demons had entered into him).
31 Then they begged Him that He wouldn't order them to go away into the abyss.
32 There was a large herd of pigs feeding on the mountain, so they begged Him that He would let them enter into them, and He agreed.
33 The demons left the man and entered into the pigs, and the herd rushed down over the cliff into the lake and was drowned.
34 And when the herdsmen saw what had happened, they fled and reported it in the city and in the farms.
35 So people came out to see what had happened, and they came to Jesus and found the man from whom the demons had departed sitting at Jesus' feet, clothed and in full possession of his senses. And they were afraid.

---

were aware of Who Jesus was, begging through him, "**Don't torture** us" (v. 28). Jesus asked the man, "**What is your name?**" To which the demons replied, "**Legion**." This reply was given because there were so many **demons** in him. A full Roman legion contained 6,826 soldiers. Doubtless, it did not mean that there were exactly this number in him. But it did mean that there were so many that it was like a legion of them! Indeed, there were enough to enter into every one of the large herd of swine in the area.

The demons did not want to be sent away into the abyss (either hell or the lake in front of them; commentators differ. Probably, in this context, the depths of the lake). Jesus cast them out and sent them into the herd which immediately **rushed down over the cliff** and **drowned** in the sea (v. 33). Then comes the point of the story. The people saw that the demoniac had been cured of his problem and was **clothed and in possession of his senses**. Knowing that something far beyond them had been happening, the passage says that they were **afraid** (v. 35). Before them there was a choice: the human being or the herd of pigs; a soul or swine? Which would they choose? Would they rejoice at seeing the healing or would they regret it because of the loss of the herd (one that had no place in Jewish circles anyway. See Lenski for an argument that the herd was in

Luke 8

36 Then those who had seen it reported how the demoniac was healed.

37 So the entire group of people from the country of the Gerasenes asked Him to leave them, because they were in the grip of great fear. So He got back into the boat and returned.

38 And the man from whom the demons had departed begged Him to let him stay with Him, but He sent him away, saying,

39 "Return to your house and tell what God has done for you." So he went throughout the whole city, preaching what Jesus had done for him.

40 Now when Jesus returned, the crowd welcomed Him, since they were all expecting Him.

41 Then a man named Jairus, who was a synagog ruler, came and fell at Jesus' feet and begged Him to come into his house,

42 because he had an only daughter about twelve years old who was dying.

Jewish, not Gentile, hands). Sadly, the whole crowd that had gathered, out of **fear**, asked Jesus to leave (v. 37). He did.

That is a sad conclusion to the story, but not one that is unusual. Yet, Jesus ordered the man to go back to his home and tell everyone what had happened. Which he did—and more. Jesus was not returning; He left the man as His missionary to any who would hear.

The operative term here, it seems, is **fear**. Many fear the supernatural, as did these people. But that was not all. If Jesus remained, He would probably have done much more to upset their ways, and their economy. No, He must go before anything else happened. Today, **fear** is still a great problem among counselees. People are afraid of what Jesus will ask them to do—or what He might do in their lives. They, too, invite Him to leave. They can handle their own lives themselves, thank you! What a mistake; what a tragedy! How important for counselors, in those situations in which people are afraid of what Jesus will require of them, to stress the fact that He only wants to do good. Fear is a powerful emotion that leads people to unreasoned action. It is gracious of Jesus to leave behind one who would proclaim the truth, even when rejected by the crowd. It is possible that when their fear subsided, some eventually believed through this man's testimony. You may be the last one that your counselee hears. Make the most of it.

As for the casting out of demons today, let it be noted that there is no command to anyone to engage in this practice. We are to preach the Gospel. For more on this matter, see my book *The Christian Counselor's Manual*.

Christian Counselor's Commentary

As He went, the crowds were pressing against Him.
43 A woman who had suffered from bleeding for twelve years and couldn't be healed by anybody
44 came up behind and touched the fringe of His clothing, and instantly the bleeding stopped.
45 And Jesus said, "Who is that touching Me?" When everybody denied that he did it, Peter said, "Master, the crowds are pressing you all around and shoving you."
46 But Jesus said, "Somebody touched Me; I sensed the power leaving Me."
47 When the woman saw that she couldn't hide, she came trembling and fell down before Him and declared in front of everybody the reason why she touched Him and how she was cured instantly.
48 Then He said to her, "Daughter, your faith has healed you. Go in peace."
49 While He was still speaking, someone came from the synagog ruler's house and said, "Your daughter has died; don't trouble the teacher any longer."
50 But when Jesus heard this, He answered him, "Don't be afraid; only believe, and she will be healed."

We close this chapter with the double story of **Jairus' daughter** and the **woman** in the **crowd** (vv. 40-56). At this point, crowds followed Jesus wherever He went. The crowd **welcomed** Him, **expected** Him to return from the other side of the lake (v. 40). **Jairus**, the **synagog ruler**, came and **fell** at Jesus' feet **begging** Him to heal his **twelve** year old only child, a **daughter**, who was **dying**. Jesus went. But as He did, the **crowds were pressing** Him on all sides (v. 42). A woman, who had suffered from bleeding for twelve years (the same amount of time Jairus' daughter had been alive) touched the fringe of Jesus' robe and was healed. He asked, **"Who is that touching Me?"** How could He or others know with the crowds pressing in on Him that way? But He had sensed power going out from Him (cf. the story of the cripple in chapter 5; cf. also 6:19). The woman admitted that it was she who had touched Jesus (v. 47). And He made it clear to her, before the crowd, that her faith had healed her (v. 48). Those who confess their dependence on Christ by faith usually have the opportunity to become a witness for Him before others.

Finally, he reaches Jairus' home. By now, death has occurred. But Jesus rebuts the suggestion that it is too late, and it would be unnecessary for Him to come. He says, **"Don't be afraid; only believe, and she will be healed"** (v. 50). Only three disciples and the parents went into the

51 So when He went into the house, He wouldn't let anybody go in with Him except Peter, John, James and the girl's father and mother.
52 They were all weeping and wailing over her. But He said, "Don't cry. She isn't dead; she's asleep."
53 So they ridiculed Him, knowing that she had died.
54 But He took her by the hand and called her, saying, "Little girl, get up."
55 Her spirit returned and she got up right away, and He ordered that she be given something to eat.
56 Her parents were amazed, but He instructed them to tell nobody what had happened.

---

house with Him. He forbade entrance to the rest, many of whom **ridiculed** Him for what He said. But He raised her from the dead, as if He were awakening one from **sleep**. She arose and **ate** something (not because she was hungry, but as evidence that this was a true, bodily resurrection; cf. 24:14-43). He left the entire matter as quiet as possible, instructing the parents not to tell what He had done (v. 56).

People still **ridicule** Jesus when they are told that He has the solution to problems in His Word. They prefer to disbelieve. Counselees may rest assured that when they seek biblical counsel they will have their share of detractors. They must persevere, however, regardless of the ridicule, if they would receive help. His word to them is still the same: **Only believe**.

CHAPTER 9

1 And He called the Twelve together and gave them power and authority over all the demons and to heal sickness.
2 Then He sent them to preach God's empire and to heal.
3 He said to them,
> Don't take anything for the road, not a staff, a wallet, bread, or money, and don't take a second change of clothing.
4 When you enter a house stay there until you leave the city.
5 Wherever they don't receive you, when you leave the city shake the dust off your feet as a testimony against them.

Jesus sends His future apostles out to preach. He gave them the **power and authority over all demons and to heal sickness**. This is of importance to understand. Jesus can, when He wishes to do so, delegate His authority. While the same sort of authority is not present with us today, nevertheless, the authority of church government and discipline is. Elders, who counsel, do not counsel as those who have no authority to do so. While all Christians should counsel *informally*, only those to whom authority to rule has been delegated must be obeyed when they exercise that authority properly (Hebrews 13:17). There is still authority in Christ's church. The presence of so many independent parachurch agencies has weakened the authority of the church in the eyes of the average church member; it is time to restore it to its rightful place. All authority given by Christ to those He sends is for the benefit of those over whom it is exercised.

So, they were **sent** to **preach** and to **heal** (v. 2). How He sent them on this first preaching mission is indicative of the urgency and the temporary nature of it. They were to take nothing **for the road**. What this means is spelled out in the rest of verse 3. And when they entered a house (for lodging) they were to stay there until they left the city. They were to accept the first invitation and not change their minds if they happened to get a more attractive offer later on. They were there for the benefit of others: not their own benefit. And if no one would **receive** them in a given city, they were to **shake the dust off their feet as a testimony against them** (v. 5).

Jesus was doing several things at once. He was training the disciples for the future. He was spreading the word throughout Palestine in a way one Person alone could not; He was showing them something of the aus-

Luke 9

6   So they departed and went throughout the villages, announcing the good news and healing everywhere.

7   Now Herod the tetrarch heard about everything that was happening and was confused, because some said that John was raised from the dead;

8   some said that Elijah had appeared, and others that one of the ancient prophets had risen.

9   But Herod said, "I beheaded John; who is this about whom I am hearing such things?" And he tried to see Him.

---

terities with which they would be faced in the future, and He was impressing on them the urgency with which their training must be completed. The days were growing fewer, and there was much yet to be accomplished. Though we sometimes think that the disciples hadn't learned much, certainly they had learned enough to preach the basic message with which He entrusted them.

Sometimes we are reluctant to allow counselees to move forward rapidly enough. The record shows that the Twelve had much more to learn. They would not receive most until after the resurrection and the Pentecostal descent of the Holy Spirit, but they knew enough to be sent out at this time. We, too, must learn to trust people a lot sooner than we sometimes think we should. Often, entrusting responsibilities to them is what stretches them. Verse 6 shows that Jesus' trust was well-founded; they accomplished their mission.

The word about Jesus got around (perhaps largely because of this mission of the Twelve), even into Herod's headquarters. (v. 7). He was confused, thinking that John the Baptist had risen from the grave. Others said that Jesus was the Elijah of Old Testament predictions, and still others, that one of the ancient prophets had been raised from the dead. In other words, rumors and reports were spreading everywhere. You won't be able to keep down false rumors about you and your counseling when it becomes well-known enough for people to talk. You will be amazed at the things people suppose.

Herod is concerned and tries to see if this Jesus was, indeed, John the Baptist (v. 9). Obviously, his conscience is bothering him. Conscience is the friend of every counselor, who should learn how to appeal to it, how to speak to it, how to quiet it through repentance and obedience. Jesus, however, seems not to have had any interest in accommodating him in order to satisfy his curiosity and quell his fears. There are times not to accede to such requests.

The disciples (now officially called apostles) returned (v. 10). Jesus

Christian Counselor's Commentary

10 When they returned, the apostles related to Him what they did. And He took them and departed privately to a city called Bethsaida.
11 But the crowds knew it and followed Him. He welcomed them and spoke to them about God's empire, and He cured those who needed to be healed.
12 As the daylight began to disappear the Twelve went to Him and said, "Dismiss the crowd, so that they can go to the villages and farms around to find places to stay and eat; the spot where we are is a desert."
13 He said to them, "You give them something to eat." But they said, "We don't have anything but five pieces of bread and two fish, unless you want us to go and buy food for all these people."
14 (The men numbered about five thousand.) Then He said to His disciples, "Have them sit down in groups of about fifty each."
15 They did so and had everybody sit down.
16 Then He took the five pieces of bread and two fish, looked up into the sky, blessed them, broke them and kept giving them to the disciples to set before the crowd.
17 So they ate and all were satisfied. And they took up twelve baskets of leftovers.

---

took them apart privately for a briefing. But the crowds found out where He was and came anyway. Jesus welcomed them, and preached and healed. The disciples then asked Him to dismiss the crowds to go get something to eat. Jesus said, **"You give them something to eat."** They protested that they had nothing except five loaves and two fish (vv. 12, 13). Then Jesus had them organize the crowd of 5,000 men (how many women and children there were, we don't know) in groups of about fifty each. And they did so, sitting down. Then He kept giving bread and fish for them to distribute to the crowd until **all were satisfied**. At the end, they took up twelve baskets of leftovers (vv. 16, 17).

The resources upon which you and your counselees may draw are unlimited. Christ is the One Who always has enough. That means so far as your counseling is concerned, you have all that is necessary. And He will never run out. If *you* run out that is your fault; God's Word contains so much wisdom for counseling that none of us will ever begin to fathom it. When we are through counseling as we ought to, we will still have baskets of leftover material that we never thought of or got the opportunity to use. The wonderful fact is that, while you ought to learn all that you can of the Bible, you don't need to wait until you learn it all. Since there is more than enough, if you have enough to deal with a case, that is all you need

Luke 9

18 As He was praying alone the disciples were with Him and He asked them, saying, "Who do the crowds say I am?"
19 They replied, "John the Baptist; but others, Elijah; and others that one of the ancient prophets has risen."
20 Then He said to them, "Who do you say I am?" Peter, answering, said, "God's Christ."
21 But He warned them and ordered them to tell this to nobody.
22 And He added,
> The Son of Man must suffer much and be rejected by the elders and chief priests and scribes and be killed, and be raised the third day.
23 Then He said to all of them,
> If anybody wants to come after Me, he must deny himself and take up his cross daily and follow Me.

---

for that one.

In verses 18 through 22, Jesus addressed the disciples to cause them to think. Again, He asks a question: **"Who do the crowds say I am?"** They answer precisely as we have seen (vv. 7, 8). Then He asked them what *they* thought. They come through with the correct answer: **"God's Christ"** (Messiah). But He warned them, giving orders not to tell this to anyone at the present time (v. 21). Doubtless, this restriction was laid down for reasons we have already discussed. Then, since they had come that far, Jesus lets them in on the vital part of what He had come to do—He tells them of His **rejection**, His **death** and His **resurrection** (v. 22). In other words, He presents the Gospel to them in clear, succinct form. That is something every counselor must be able to do.

Then He spoke to all of those who had gathered. He told them what the conditions for **discipleship** would be: to **deny** (lit., "say no to") **self**, to **take up his cross** and to **follow Him**. What does that mean? To **take up the cross daily** means, like Jesus, to carry out the cross to crucify yourself (your sinful desires) on it every day, saying "no" to self. Positively, it meant to say "yes" to Jesus as one follows after Him, doing His will. The two-factored, put off/put on methodology of sanctification was invented neither by Paul nor by Peter, but by Jesus Himself.

Spell out to counselees that to **take up the cross** doesn't mean something like "my wife is my cross," or anything of the sort. To **deny self** doesn't mean to deny something to yourself. Explain clearly that it means death to self and its desires every day. There is a common misunderstanding of this passage. And make it equally plain that this is not a once-for-all

Christian Counselor's Commentary

24   This is true because whoever wants to save his life will lose it, and whoever loses his life for My sake will save it.
25   What does it profit a person if he gains the whole world and loses or forfeits himself?
26   Whoever is ashamed of Me and My words, of him the Son of Man will be ashamed when He comes with His glory and with the glory of the Father and of the holy angels.
27   I tell you the truth when I say that there are some standing here who won't taste death until they see God's empire.

28   Now about eight days after these teachings, He took with Him Peter, John and James and went up on a mountain to pray.

29   As He prayed, the appearance of His face changed and His clothing became gleaming white.

---

thing; it must be done **daily**. There are counselees who want a three-step formula that will land them on cloud nine from which they will never fall. It doesn't work that way. So long as we live in this life, we will have to struggle with putting to death sinful desires.

Jesus goes on, saying that if you are interested in holding on to your **life**, you will lose it, but if you lose it for His sake, you will actually save it. To gain everything now in this life, but to lose one's own soul for the future is total loss. Christians must not be ashamed of Christ now, lest He be ashamed of them at His coming (vv. 24-26). That is a very strong warning. Many counselees are ashamed to confess Christ at work, before relatives, etc. Are they genuine? Here is the passage to quote to them.

Some in the crowd who were standing there would live until the time when Christ's empire would supersede the Old Jewish order. Less than forty years later, the old was finally torn down and replaced entirely by the new. The grace period for Israel in between was a time of transition. The church would formally begin with the resurrection and ascension (cf. John 20:21-23 and comments on that passage in the commentary in this series). The disciples would be sent out into the world on Pentecost. But until the destruction of the city and the temple in 70 AD, the old order, hollow though it was, remained and the new overlapped it.

In verses 28 through 36, we read Luke's account of the transfiguration. It was a tremendous time. Jesus and His three favorites (three witnesses were necessary, as at the raising of Jairus' daughter) went up into a mountain to **pray**. As Jesus prayed, He was **transformed** before their eyes. His **face** and His **clothing** became **gleaming white**. The Deity within was being partially manifested. **Moses** and **Elijah** (two about

Luke 9

30 Two men—Moses and Elijah—appeared in glory and talked with Him,
31 speaking about the exodus that He was going to bring about in Jerusalem.
32 Peter and those with him had become very drowsy, but they became wide awake when they saw His glory and the two men who stood with Him.
33 Now, as they were leaving Him, Peter said, "Master, it is wonderful for us to be here. Let's make three tents, one for You, one for Moses and one for Elijah." (He didn't really know what to say.)
34 As he spoke these words a cloud came and overshadowed them, and they were afraid as they entered the cloud.
35 Then a voice spoke from the cloud, saying, "This is My Son Whom I have chosen; listen to Him."
36 When the voice had spoken, they found that Jesus was alone. But they kept quiet and didn't report anything that they saw.

---

whose deaths there was something unusual) **appeared** in a blaze of **glory**. And these brothers, who represented the law and the prophets, spoke with Jesus about the **exodus He was going to bring about in Jerusalem**. This exodus from the Egypt of Satan's kingdom into the holy land of Empire through the cross was the subject matter. Peter, ever the first to say something, no matter how foolish, said let's make three tents for You, Elijah and Moses. A cloud overshadowed them at this moment, and God spoke from the cloud, **saying, "This is My Son Whom I have chosen; listen to Him."** Once more, the emphasis on listening is made. It was neither the law nor the prophets (represented by Moses and Elijah) to which they were directed, but to Jesus Christ Who fulfilled them. They were to listen to *Him*. The cloud left with the two men, and they were alone with Jesus. Until much later, they kept quiet about what they had seen. Later on, they might be free to allude to the experience.

There are times to keep quiet, lest one show how much of a fool he is. There are times to keep quiet when it is not yet appropriate to speak. Counselors must not only deal with times and places when counselees ought to speak, but those times and places in which they ought to say nothing. To know which is which is a large part of wisdom. And counselors must seek to be wise.

Verses 37 through 43 relates another story of exorcism—with a slightly different twist. Again, we are introduced to an **only child** who, this time, was possessed with a demon. The father cried out for Jesus to

Christian Counselor's Commentary

37 The next day, when they came down from the mountain, a large crowd met Him.
38 A man from the crowd shouted, saying,
    Teacher, I beg you to look at my son; he is my only child.
39   A spirit seizes him, and suddenly he yells, and it throws him down, foaming at the mouth. It hardly ever leaves him, and is bruising his body.
40   I asked your disciples to cast it out, but they couldn't.
41 Then Jesus answered and said, "You unbelieving and twisted generation! How long must I be with you and put up with you?"
42 As the boy was coming the demon threw him down and convulsed him. But Jesus rebuked the unclean spirit, healed the boy, and restored him to his father.
43 And everybody was astonished at God's majesty.
    Now while they were all marveling at everything He did, He said to His disciples,

---

heal him (vv. 38, 39). The demon was doing physical harm to the boy. But the different twist is found in verse 40. The father explained that the disciples had tried, but failed, to cast out the demon. Whether these disciples were members of the Twelve or not we do not know from the narrative. But Jesus first rebukes them for their failure (v. 41). He calls them an **unbelieving and twisted generation**. The generation was **twisted** because it did not **believe**. It did not **believe** because it was **twisted** in its thinking and living. The one fed the other in a vicious circle. The reason that these disciples were ineffective was precisely because they were **unbelieving**. There is no more frequent cause of failure among Christian counselors than that which stems from unbelief. If one thinks that a particular case is beyond help, what he is saying is that Jesus Christ can't help. That is unbelief. And so long as he thinks that way (whether he recognizes the implications or not) he is likely to be ineffective. It is important for counselors to tell counselees when they say, "I don't think that my husband can make that change" (or whatever), "What you really mean is that Jesus Christ can't help him do so." Ask, "Do you really believe that your husband is stronger then the Lord Jesus?" The answer might be, "Well, no, but we are discussing my husband's stubbornness; not Christ's power." Then you should reply in words to this effect: "No, we are discussing both. Jesus can overcome even *your* husband's stubbornness!" That's the basis for counseling—belief! And the point here is that the unbelief was on the part of the disciples, not the father. Verses 42 and 43

Luke 9

44 "Let these teachings sink into your ears. The Son of Man is about to be betrayed into the hands of men."
45 But they didn't understand this statement; it was hidden from them so that they couldn't perceive what He meant. But they were afraid to ask Him about the statement.
46 Then an argument arose among them about who was the greatest.
47 So when Jesus knew what they were debating in their hearts, He took a child, stood him beside Himself
48 and said to them,
> Whoever receives this child in My name receives Me, and whoever receives Me receives the One Who sent Me. The one who is least among you is great.

---

record the eventual healing by Jesus Himself.

Once more Jesus addresses His disciples about the cross. And, interestingly, He has to emphasize their hearing once more (v. 44). They had not understood when He told them previously. From the conversation that follows hard on this announcement it is clear that they failed to **understand** now either (cf. also v. 45). It may be that they *didn't want to hear* that Jesus would be **betrayed**. At any rate, because they were not **careful how they listened** in the past, it is clear that they were not able to receive more when it was given (v. 45). Presumably, because Jesus had rebuked them, they were afraid to ask what He meant.

Often counselees don't understand what you are telling them. It is necessary at times, therefore, to ask them to repeat in their own words what you have told them. Frequently, you will find that they haven't got a clue—or they have it twisted up. They will not tell you they didn't understand for fear of embarrassment. Take the initiative. However, even then, you will run into cases where, because people previously wouldn't hear, it has now become impossible for them to do so.

Verses 46 through 48 follow upon the statements about Jesus' death. Having heard this, they are so oblivious that the disciples are next found arguing about who would hold the supreme position among them (v. 46). What utter self-centeredness!

Jesus disposes of this spirit on their part by humbling them. Taking a child as an object lesson, Jesus said that whoever receives a child in His Name receives Him, and also the Father. And He continued, "**the one who is least among you is great**" (v. 48). The child was the symbol of weakness and was anything but important in the scheme of things. What Jesus was saying is that those who are childlike in these respects are those

Christian Counselor's Commentary

> 49 Then John said, "Master, we saw somebody casting out demons in Your name and we stopped him because he doesn't follow along with us."
> 50 Jesus said to him, "Don't stop him. Whoever is not against you is for you."
> 51 As it grew near to the time of His ascension, He set His face to go to Jerusalem.
> 52 So He sent messengers before Him. And they went into a Samaritan village to get things ready for Him,
> 53 but the villagers wouldn't receive Him because He was heading for Jerusalem.
> 54 When His disciples James and John saw this, they said, "Lord, do you want us to command fire to fall from heaven and destroy them?"

who are **great**. Proud counselees may be helped by these verses. There is no place for pride among Christ's people.

Verses 49 and 50 reveal another problem that must be rooted out from among God's workers: a spirit of rivalry. Here was someone doing the work of Christ that the disciples tried to stop because he was not formally a part of their group (v. 49). Jesus says, **"Whoever is not against you is for you"** (v. 50). So he shouldn't be stopped. This is not contradiction of the word in Matthew 12:30, **Whoever isn't with Me is against Me**. The two complement each other. If one is with Christ, it isn't necessary for him to be of a certain group of those who are working for Him. Denominational differences today immediately come to mind. Just because someone **doesn't follow along with** *us* doesn't mean that he is not a faithful follower of *Christ*.

You will find yourself needing to reconcile these two verses from time to time for counselees. Be sure that you understand how they fit together. Bigots, those who engage in rivalry, intolerant Christians, will all truck out the Matthew passage. But they will neglect this one!

Now, coming to verses 51 through 55, we learn something of Jesus' determination. He **set His face toward Jerusalem**—that is the place where the cross would occur. This determination to face a difficult situation is something every Christian must also learn. Call on counselees to **set their faces** toward it. Without this sort of determination, there would have been no redemption. Yet it took a deliberate effort on Christ's part to go the Jerusalem.

In **Samaria** He was turned down by one **village** because He was headed toward the hated **Jerusalem**. Though He sent messengers to prepare lodgings there, they refused to take Him and His entourage in

Luke 9

55 But He turned and rebuked them.[1]

56 Then they went to another village.

57 And as they were going along the road, somebody said to Him, "I will follow you wherever you go."

58 So Jesus said to him, "Foxes have holes and birds of the sky have nests, but the Son of Man doesn't have a place to lay His head."

59 Then He said to another, "Follow Me." But he said, "Let me first go bury my father."

60 But He replied, "Let the dead bury their own dead. You go and announce God's empire."

61 Then another said, "I will follow you, Lord, but first let me go say good-bye to my family."

62 Jesus said to him, "Anybody who puts his hand on the plow and looks back isn't fit for God's empire."

---

[1] Some MSS add, *And He said, "You don't know the kind of Spirit you have; the Son of Man didn't come to destroy men's lives, but to save them."*

(thereby missing the blessings that His presence always brings). Instead of adopting James and John's proposal (v. 54) Jesus rebuked them. The answer was simple: **Then they went to another village** (v. 56).

Verses 57 through 62 conclude the chapter with the various ways in which people seek to follow Jesus. The first said, **"I'll follow you wherever you go."** To him, Jesus responded I have no place to lay my head. Are you willing to take up such a life? Disciples must count the cost.

A second said, **"Let me first go bury my father."** He meant, "When I am free and on my own, I'll do so." He was not ready *yet*—even though the Lord called him. Such people, who put things off, are rarely ever ready. If one thing doesn't stand in the way any longer, then another does. Jesus told him to let those who are spiritually dead take care of such matters; you have been called to a work; go do it! Counselors may have to say the same at times. Good intentions are not enough.

A third said, **"First let me go say good-bye to my family."** This sounded like a reasonable request, but Jesus knew the ties at home that might change his resolve. He said, If you put your **hand to the plow and look back** you **aren't fit for God's empire**. Remember Lot's wife!

Excuses, excuses! That was what Jesus was dealing with. So will you, counselor. Put it off, put it off, as long as possible. That is what you will hear again and again. And those who are allowed to do so will discover that they rarely, if ever, get around to doing what they should.

CHAPTER 10

1 After this the Lord appointed seventy[1] others and sent them out ahead of Him by twos into every city and place where He was about to go.
2 He said to them,
> Indeed, the harvest is great but the workers are few. So ask the Lord of the harvest to send out workers into His harvest.
3 Go. Take note of this: I send you as lambs into the midst of wolves.
4 Don't take a wallet or bag or sandals and don't get into conversations along the road.

---

[1] Some MSS read, *seventy-two*.

There is no doubt about the purpose of the sending of the seventy. Their mission was similar to that of John the Baptist. They were to prepare the way for the Lord. But this time, the end of His ministry was drawing near and it was important to reach all the territories in Palestine that He had not sufficiently covered previously. Looking at the urgency of Jesus' words in the last verses of chapter nine (vv. 57-62) it is apparent that He is concluding matters before taking His disciples aside for their final pre-resurrection instructions, and then going to the cross. Time was growing short.

That is why the strong verb in verse 2 (**send,** literally, *"thrust out"* **workers into His harvest**) is used. The **seventy** went **by twos**. That is, of course, a wise way for these disciples to go. In Ecclesiastes 4:12 we read that two are better than one. The one may help the other in time of difficulty. And the verse further indicates that three is an even stronger force ("a threefold cord is not easily broken"). In counseling, it is not unwise, when possible, to do team counseling (for more on this see *Competent to Counsel*). The Freudian idea that no one else but the counselor and one counselee may be in the room at a time (in order to bring about transference) has long since been exploded. If for no other reason, when counseling a woman it is wise for a pastor to have an elder present so that no hanky panky on the part of the counselee can take place, and none can be charged to the counselor.

The urgency of this task also appears in verse 4 where those fine, luxurious or extra accouterments which one may want to take on a trip are forbidden. Even chatting along the way (sometimes an elaborate process

5	Whatever house you enter, first say, "Peace on this house."
6	If a son of peace lives there, your peace will rest on it. Otherwise it will return to you.
7	Also, stay in the same house, eating and drinking whatever they provide; the worker is worthy of his pay. Don't move around from house to house.

---

in oriental countries) was to be avoided. There are occasions in counseling when it is not possible to take the time and the patience to deal with all the aspects of a problem that one normally would. Something must be done in a hurry—otherwise, with bags packed, for instance, a spouse may leave. Data gathering would be preferable, if there were time. But on this occasion, to extract the promise that he not leave before serious counseling takes place, and willingness to set the date for the same, is all you may be able to opt for. It will be sufficient. The longer counseling can take place later. Now, obtaining those two promises is adequate.

Verse three indicates that the trip would not be without its hazards. **Lambs** sent **into the midst of wolves** is an apt description of what counseling involves at times. People, who want their way, sometimes get very angry when you point out that the Bible does not allow it. Others become angry when you help counselees in ways that don't square with their agendas. You may get a phone call that will fill your ear—or even a visit from an irate family member or friend. The counselor should be aware of these possibilities. Ministry is not the "safe" calling it often has been represented to be. Of course, if one does little or no counseling, he may not run many risks.

Note, also, the precision and specificity of the instructions that Jesus gives the seventy. God did not leave everything to us to work out when He called us to ministry. Indeed, He laid out many elements of the task, and He expects us to abide by those. Matters of church discipline, for instance, are not optional. They are laid out *as God's way for His servants to follow.* They may not choose to ignore them.

In verses 5 through 7 more specifics are given. One is to remain in any house into which he is invited to stay; he is not to shop around or relocate when he finds "better" accommodations. This would indicate several things: first, that he is not there to "get" something but rather to *give*; second, that he is to express his appreciation to the one who first showed concern for his welfare. Third, it would indicate something of the urgency that is apparent elsewhere in the passage: he is not there to stay long so as

8	Whenever you are welcomed by a city that you enter, eat what is set before you.
9	Heal the sick in it and tell them, "God's empire has drawn near to you."
10	Whenever you are not welcomed by a city that you enter, go out into its streets and say,
11	"Even the dust of your city that sticks to our feet we wipe off before you. Nevertheless, know this—God's empire has drawn near."

to take the time to settle in.

There are instructions, also, concerning **peace**. *Shalom* ("**peace**") was the usual Jewish greeting. Jesus makes it meaningful. They were to speak a word of peace in Christ's name to those who invited them into their **house**. If those who lived there were truly seeking **peace** with God and neighbor (and the members of the preaching team), their greeting would be more than a perfunctory word—God would bless those who live there with peace. If, however, they turn out to be other than those who seek and promote peace, the import of their greeting would fail to bear fruit: the **peace** they might have received from God will not fall upon them.

In all ministry, including the ministry of counseling, there will be one of two results. You will counsel "sons of peace" (those who want to hear and do God's will, and thus bring about peace) and those who are not. You must never be surprised at the latter outcome, however, since Jesus, Himself, predicted it.

More instructions were given regarding a **city** (vv. 8-15). Again, they are to be easygoing missionaries (**eat what is set before you**). And, at the outset, they are to exercise their newly-given power to **heal** (v. 9). Their credentials thus established, they were to preach the message that John and Jesus preached: **God's empire has drawn near to you**. Obviously, this terminology, for those who had believed the prophets and were looking for the fifth world empire of Daniel, would herald the fact that the Messiah had come. If those in the city were responsive, doubtless they would be told the story of Jesus as the Messiah in detail. If they were not, but rejected the preachers, they were to **go out into the streets** (i.e., publicly) and say, **Even the dust of your city that sticks to our feet we wipe off before you**. This was a sign of *total* rejection. The city was rejected so as to be remembered no more—not even by a speck of dust incidentally carried away from it (v. 11). Then Jesus tells them that it will be more tol-

12	I tell you that on that day it will be more tolerable for Sodom than for that city!
13	Woe to you, Chorazin! Woe to you, Bethsaida! If the powerful works that took place in you had taken place in Tyre and Sidon long ago, they would have repented sitting in sackcloth and ashes.
14	Still it will be more tolerable for Tyre and Sidon in the judgment than for you.
15	And you, Capernaum; will you be lifted up to the sky? No, you will go down to Hades!
16	Whoever hears you hears Me, and whoever rejects you rejects Me. And whoever rejects Me rejects the One Who sent Me.

erable for pagan cities than for the Hebrew city that rejected His missionaries.

Yet, in grace, there is to be a parting shot: they were instructed to say, **Nevertheless, know this—God's empire has drawn near** (v. 11). A merciful, last chance is given. It was a word that might linger in the minds of some who would take advantage of it and seek them out in the next town, etc. That is what I have always made a policy in counseling whenever possible. If a person rejects the Word of God offered, I warn of the danger into which he is coming (**more tolerable . . .**) and also try repeatedly to weave a Scripture verse into the conversation so that he will have something to remain with him after we have said good-bye. I want to put a Scriptural burr under his saddle as he rides off into the sunset. I would advise you to do the same. People (not all of them) have returned. And, sometimes, their explanation is that the passage of Scripture continued to work on them. God uses His Word. The verse that I usually use is Proverbs 13:15^b.

People will think that they are merely turning you down when they refuse to do as God says. They are not (cf. v. 16). To turn down the word of Christ's servant, when he is truly telling him what God says, is serious business—it is to turn down Christ Himself. And rejecting Christ, is also rejecting God. This is a very important point that you must frequently make with counselees when it is clear that they are (wrongly) of this opinion. You may have to say to them something like this: "Now, you may think that you are **rejecting** *me*. That isn't so. As you know, I have presented nothing to you but what the Bible says to do. (Here, you may want to quote a crucial verse to solidify the point.) If you turn down that word from Jesus, you are **rejecting** *Him* and, with Him, God the *Father*." You may then want to quote this verse from Luke 10. This is powerful backing

17 The seventy returned with joy, saying, "Lord, even the demons submit to us in Your name."
18   He said to them,
    I saw Satan fall like lightning from the sky.
19   See, I have given you authority to step on snakes and scorpions, and over all the enemy's power; nothing at all shall hurt you.
20   However, don't rejoice that the spirits submit to you; rather, rejoice that your names have been enrolled in the heavens.

---

for the counselor who uses the Word of God.

The **seventy** return after some time. They are thrilled that **even demons are subject** to them. It is of interest how they focus on their new capacities rather than on the effects in the lives of those to whom they preached. This is ever a temptation for the Christian minister. Especially, if his counseling is successful. He can become so happy over his success, his newfound abilities, that he loses interest in the purpose for which they were given and developed. Don't let this happen to you.

Jesus responds to this misdirection of their interests. Yes, it is true that I have given you such powers (v. 19), and they have been successfully used (v. 18). You did bring Satan down from His perch as the god of this world. But that isn't the thing that is important concerning you. If you must focus on yourself, be grateful that you are saved (v. 20).

It is always of the greatest importance to keep first things first. That is what Jesus is pointing out to the seventy in verse 20. That is what you must do in your own ministry and in the advice that you give to the counselee.

There is one other fact of importance here. We ought to give people opportunity to serve sooner than some are in the practice of doing. Jesus entrusts this work to seventy who are rather immature. If we wait until people have everything in line before setting them out to help others, hardly any will be encouraged to go. The same is true of training people to counsel. Often, trainees must be given work to do and then, having accomplished it, the work and the worker must be critiqued.

In verses 21 through 22 we read of Jesus' response to the ministry. Fundamentally, it is summed up in the words **He exulted**. Don't say that Jesus never showed joy and let others recognize it! Here, in the great joy of victorious exultation, motivated by the **Holy Spirit**, Jesus praises God. The difference between the way we cry out for joy and the way that Jesus did is that we so seldom praise God as the Source of our victory. We fail to acknowledge Him as the One who deserved praise. Rather, in the spirit

Luke 10

> **21** In that same hour He exulted by the Holy Spirit and said, Father, Lord of heaven and earth, I praise You because You hid these things from the wise and intelligent and revealed them to babies. Yes, Father, that is what You were pleased to do.
>
> **22** Everything has been handed over to Me by My Father, but nobody knows Who the Son is except the Father or Who the Father is except the Son and any to whom the Son wants to reveal Him.

of the football player having made a touchdown, we virtually say "We're no. 1!" meaning, *we* did it and *we* should be praised. Counselees, joyously responding to God's great mercies to them, must have their praise directed to God.

For what did Jesus praise God? That the message went forth and that many of those who were childlike in heart and spirit had received it in faith. The sad note is that those who thought they were too intelligent to believe were hardened in their unbelief (the message was **hidden** from them). You will see the same in counseling from time to time. Those **wise and intelligent** in this world's eyes (and their own) often allow their "wisdom" to get in the way of faith. On the other hand, **babies** in worldly wisdom readily conform to God's will as soon as it is made known from the Bible. Counselors, also, have problems with understanding. They are so often blinded by the "brilliance" of men's theories, enticed by the prestige and money that practicing eclectically brings, and the like, that they refuse to trust in the sufficiency and the simplicity of biblical counseling. Simple is not simplistic—a charge often made by such persons. While Jesus made things simple so that **babies** intellectually could benefit, what He said is anything but simplistic. And because some of us have worked hard at making the truth of the Bible as it applies to counseling as clear as we can, so that all might understand, the results of that effort are used against us as they claim what we have taught is simplistic. It is not.

Jesus went on to talk about His authority. It had been **handed over** to Him by the **Father**, Who gave Jesus all authority in heaven and in earth (Matthew 28). The wicked one no longer could be called the prince of the power (authority) of the air. He was **falling** swiftly like **lightning** from heaven. Yet, it was not the time when large numbers would understand. Indeed, until the cross and resurrection, most of His followers had only an implicit faith which excluded their full knowledge of the Trinity and the interrelationships of its Members (v. 22). In time, all of this would be made clear.

Counselees do not have to understand everything at once. But they

Christian Counselor's Commentary

> **23** Then He turned to his disciples and said privately,
> Happy are the eyes that see what you see!
> 24 I tell you, many prophets and kings wanted to see what you see, but didn't, and wanted to hear what you hear, but didn't.
> **25** It happened that a certain lawyer stood up and tested Him, saying, "Teacher, what must I do to inherit eternal life?"
> 26 He replied, "What is written in the law? How do you read it?"
> 27 And he responded, "You must love the Lord your God with your whole heart, with your whole soul, with your whole ability and with your whole mind, and your neighbor as yourself."
> 28 Then He said to him, "You have answered correctly. Do this, and you will live."

---

should grow in their comprehension of the truth. Counselors may be patient, as Jesus was, but must always hold out the fact that there is more to learn. No one who leaves counseling should do so with the misapprehension that he now knows it all—or even much!

The sovereignty of God in all of these matters is also apparent. God **hid** and God **revealed** (v. 21). The **Son** understands about the Trinity and all **to whom the Son wants to reveal** the **Father** (v. 22). That God works sovereignly is the message of the whole Bible. But, He never does so apart from human responsibility. He so plans and executes His will that the individuals involved in fulfilling it do so because they want to in a thoroughly responsible manner. He does not violate their will but on the contrary works by it to achieve His ends.

In verses 23 and 24, Jesus makes a brief, but important, statement to His disciples. He tells them that they have been deeply privileged to see the things that they have been **seeing**. He says that many of the believing Old Testament prophets and Kings (like David) **wanted to see** what they see, but didn't (cf. Hebrews 11:13; I Peter 1:10-12). When counselees complain (as they sometimes do) that they are living in difficult times when it is hard to comply with God's biblical requirements, show them how much more that they have than many did in biblical days—how very privileged they are in *this* day. Such excuses must be stifled.

In verses 25 through 37 we have the lawyer's question and Jesus' response. It is a powerful passage of Scripture that may be used for many purposes. Learn to use it effectively in counseling. The professional student of the Bible (that is what **lawyer** means in the New Testament) asked a question of Jesus: "**what must I do to inherit eternal life?**" It was a good question that we would like to hear asked more often than we do

Luke 10

29 But because he wanted to justify himself, he said to Jesus, "And who is my neighbor?"
30 Jesus took up this question and answered:
> A certain man was going down from Jerusalem to Jericho and ran into robbers who stripped and beat him and left him half dead.
31 A priest who happened to be going down that road saw him and passed by on the other side.
32 So too a Levite, when he came upon the place, saw him and passed by on the other side.
33 But a certain Samaritan, as he traveled, came upon him, and was filled with pity when he saw him.
34 So he went over to him, bound up his wounds and poured oil and wine on them. Then he put him on his own donkey, took him to the inn and cared for him.
35 The next day, he took out two denarii and gave them to the innkeeper and said, "Take care of him. And whatever more you spend, I'll repay you when I return."

---

from unbelievers. Jesus gave the right answer: You claim to know the Law of God; well, then, *you* tell *Me* what it says about the matter. He turned him to the Bible. More counselors should use the same method of responding to counselee questions by asking them, "What is the Bible's answer to that question?" That is, it is a good method to make the person think—if he knows the answer. Obviously, since he came up with the proper answer (vv. 27, 28), he did. There was no reason to ask Jesus except to try to catch Him up in some way.

In verse 28, Jesus makes it clear that fulfilling the law would truly merit **eternal life**. But of course, as the entire New Testament (and Jesus' death for sinners) attests, no one is able to fulfill the law of God. Only Jesus, made under the law and sinless, could do so. Indeed, eternal life eluded this **lawyer** because, like other Jews of his time, he knew that he was a sinner who had not **do**ne it (v. 28).

Notice that this man was insincere; verse 29 makes it plain that he **wanted to justify himself** since Jesus had put him on the spot. So, like all good theologians, he had another question in reserve to which there were a variety of answers in that day. He asks, "but **who is my neighbor?**" This lawyer wanted to go on as he had in the past; he didn't want to change, so he posed the question in a frame of mind that, in effect, said, "How can one fulfill the commandment if he isn't sure who his neighbor is?"

Many counselees will make similar objections. They will have

Christian Counselor's Commentary

36   Which one of these three do you think became the neighbor to the man who ran into the robbers?
37   He said, "The one who showed mercy to him."
         Then Jesus told him, "You go do the same thing yourself."
38 As they went along, they entered a village, and a woman named Martha welcomed Him into her house.
39 She had a sister named Mary, who sat at the Lord's feet and listened to His word.
40 But Martha was distracted by all the work she was involved in doing, so she went to Him and said, "Lord, don't you care that my sister has left me to do all the work by myself? Tell her to help me."
41 But the Lord replied,
        Martha, Martha, you're worried and upset about many things,
42   but there is only one real need—Mary has selected the best portion, one that won't be taken away from her."

"problems" knowing how to apply the Bible when they know that they haven't done so. To get you off their back (to **justify** themselves for failure to obey the Bible) they raise these questions. How does Jesus deal with his question? By telling him a story—a story that neither he nor anyone who has ever read it can forget. The story of the Good Samaritan. There is no need to detail the story for you simply because having once heard it, you cannot forget. But look carefully at the conclusion: in it, Jesus forces the right answer from his lips (vv. 36, 37^a). He has answered his own question; his excuse is gone. Then comes the punch line (v. 37^b). Obviously, to show love to a person—any person—is to make him a neighbor. And one ought to show love to everyone, even if you are a Samaritan and he is a Jew!. Using the Samaritan as the one showing love was a brilliant stroke—Jews didn't consider them neighbors.

Finally, we come to the story of Mary and Martha (vv. 38-42). **Mary** chose **the best portion** (a play on words—since **Martha** was all concerned about what to do, which portion of food to serve to Jesus, etc.). That is to listen to and learn from Jesus, the **only real need** (v. 39). The rebuke that Jesus gave Martha was gentle; her heart was right; it was her priorities that were wrong. And, too, she was focusing on herself. People in counseling will evidence similar problems. Priority problems (there was nothing wrong with serving a meal to Jesus) will be a constant challenge in counseling. Always keep this passage in mind. When business, when family or even when service for Jesus becomes so much a part of one's life that he has no time to learn from Jesus (studying his Bible prayerfully), then his priorities are all wrong.

CHAPTER 11

1 Now it happened that He was in a certain place praying, and when He finished, one of His disciples said to Him, "Lord, teach us to pray as John taught his disciples."

Jesus' example of prayer occasioned one of His disciples to ask Him to teach them to pray (v. 1). Example is always a powerful teaching tool—or, as in this case, leads to the desire to learn. A good counselor, by the way he handles Scripture, the way that he teaches and applies it, and, indeed, the way he prays about problems ought to be a prime influence in the lives of his counselees. This should happen as a by-product of his actual counseling. Remember, you teach more than you intend to. There are the things that occur around the periphery of the counseling session that, often, have as much effect on the counselee as the counseling itself.

In verses 2 through 4 Jesus reiterates in somewhat condensed form the prayer that we have come to know as the Lord's prayer. Lenski (rightly) argues for this being the second giving of the prayer on a separate occasion rather than saying that the two versions are variants of the prayer given on the same occasion. There is no reason why Jesus could not have repeated this basic format whenever asked to teach others how to pray. Good counselors will find themselves using material over and over again in various cases, usually in slightly different form. That seems to be what happened here.

This **prayer** is brief, concise, to the point. It is non-repetitious, it contains no extraneous material. If Jesus is teaching us anything, that is it. It strikes all of the keynotes of prayer: prayer for God's **Name** to be sanctified in the earth, for His **empire** to spread, for one's **daily** needs, for **forgiveness** of sins and for avoidance of temptation. Counselors might do well to construct their prayers in sessions on this basic outline (you do pray in sessions, don't you?). In a time of crisis for the counselee, it is important to begin by helping him think first of God (His Name and His empire) rather than himself, thus leading the counselee beyond his own immediate problems. Then, he may pray for the regular needs of life to be met. These must not be neglected in times of crisis. Finally, he may help him ask for forgiveness, reminding him (as Jesus does) that he too must forgive and ask to be led away from temptation and sin. Try it; you might be surprised at the effects of your prayer. I am not suggesting that you

Christian Counselor's Commentary

> 2 So He said to them,
>   When you pray, say,
>   "Father, may Your name be held holy,
>   May Your empire come.
> 3   Give us each day our daily bread,
> 4   Forgive us our sins, because we ourselves forgive all our debtors;
>   And don't lead us into testing."

pray the exact prayer; or *only* this prayer; it wasn't intended for that purpose. It was an *outline* of essential items, in succinct form and in proper order. Minds focused too fully on one thing need to be transported beyond it. They also need order. To insure those things is the idea behind my suggestion.

One of the things to keep in mind is the way in which Jesus introduces the prayer: He addresses God as "Father." That was the way He prayed and that is the way you should too. In this day of feminist propaganda, there are those who would avoid calling God "Father" since, for them, it is a hated word as applied to Him. Rather, in gender-neutral language, they would prefer to call God our heavenly Parent. This is to cloud over with non-biblical jargon a word that expresses the essential nature of God with all of its important denotations and connotations. God is set forth as a Father Who protects, cares, loves as a father does. You must not lose that. God is not a father/mother god. He is not Sophia, Isis, Gaia—or some other feminine deity. He is set forth in the Bible as Male. What a counselee needs is to know is that he has a powerful, loving, heavenly Father to Whom he can turn—not some vague deity or (worse) some goddess out of paganism that feminists are trying to introduce into the Christian church.

If there is anything that some counselees need to understand, it is the importance of forgiveness. Of all the matters that Jesus might have included in the prayer, but didn't, it is significant that He did include forgiveness. All of us—at some time or other—need to seek forgiveness. At other times, we must extend it to others (cf. ch. 17). Because forgiveness is such an important matter in counseling, it is well for a counselor to have in mind the fundamental biblical facts concerning forgiveness. Here, it is *Fatherly* forgiveness. There is no more need for judicial forgiveness which was granted once for all in Christ. Parental forgiveness, however, is ongoing between sinners and their holy heavenly Father. It is also necessary between brothers and sisters in the family of God. For a full treatment of forgiveness see *From Forgiven to Forgiving*.

Luke 11

5	Then He said to them, Suppose one of you has a friend and goes to him at midnight and says to him: "Friend, lend me three pieces of bread
6	because a friend of mine who is traveling has come to stay with me, and I don't have anything to feed him."
7	From within, he answers and says, "Don't bother me. I've locked the door, and my children are in bed with me. I can't get up and give you anything."
8	I tell you, even if he won't get up and give it to him because he is his friend, yet because of his persistence, he will get up and give him whatever he needs.
9	So I tell you, ask, and it will be given to you. Seek, and you will find. Knock, and it will be opened to you.
10	Everybody who asks receives, everybody who seeks finds, and to everybody who knocks it will be opened.

Having given a basic outline for prayer, Jesus goes on to speak at length and in several distinct connections about prayer. He takes the opportunity to give us thorough instruction on the subject. We must listen.

The story in verses 5 through 8 is typically Palestinian in flavor. A brassy friend, going beyond the bounds of propriety, seeks bread from his friend at midnight. Another friend has dropped in unawares. Hospitality is an important matter in the biblical culture. He must feed his traveling friend. But the sleeping friend is unwilling to get up, wake the family and unlock the door (a troublesome activity in those days). Yet, the intruder continues. While the sleeping friend will not get up because of his friendship, he does because of the persistence of the intruding friend. Thus, the traveling friend's needs are satisfied.

What is Jesus teaching about prayer? And of what importance is that for counseling? The idea is not **persistence**, as some think. God is not a friend who doesn't want to be bothered by your counselee's prayers. That isn't to be pushed in interpreting the parable. Nor is the idea merely that God will not answer unless you are persistent. Often, He answers right away. The *fervency* of the one praying seems to stand out. That is what led to persistence. Moreover, if this sleeping friend would eventually get up and go to the trouble of responding to his intruding friend, it seems that the parable teaches that God is far more accessible. If this person could be roused to a favorable response, why should we think that God would not be? God is willing and able—indeed, *ready* to answer (we have not because we ask not!). That is why Jesus went on to encourage us to **ask**,

Christian Counselor's Commentary

> 11 Fathers, suppose one of your sons asks for a fish; you wouldn't give him a snake instead, would you?
> 12 Or if he asked for an egg, will you give him a scorpion?
> 13 So then, if you who are evil know how to give good gifts to your children, how much more will the heavenly Father give the Holy Spirit to those who ask Him?
> 14 He was casting out a demon that caused dumbness. When the demon left, the dumb man spoke and the crowds were amazed.

---

seek and **knock**. Those who do will receive, will find and will see heaven's door open (v. 9). The unwillingness is not on God's side; it is on ours. We simply don't believe what He affirms in verse 10. We doubt, and we have not. Press the facts of this parable and its explanation on your counselees. Many probably have prayed only halfheartedly (but see James Chapters 1, 4, 5).

To reinforce what He has just taught about God's willingness to answer the prayer of His children, Jesus continues with a series of dramatic questions aimed at driving His point home (vv. 11-13). If **evil** persons like us (v. 13; don't miss Jesus' description of human beings as such) are still able and willing to **give good gifts**, how much more so is God Who is holy and good? Here the argument is from the lesser to the greater (or, you could say, the worst to the best). If your counselee doubts whether God will hear his prayers and answer, ask, "Do you think He will give you a **snake** or a **scorpion**?" The goodness of God to *His* children is what is behind the argument that Jesus is making. He would no more deceive His children with His responses than an earthly father would deceive his.

In verses 14 through 26 we read about the exorcism of a **demon** and the discussion that grew out of that incident. The crowd is **amazed**. Presumably, that was enough to raise the ire of some who did not want people following Jesus. They slander Him saying, **"He casts out demons by Beelzebub, the chief of demons."** Still others, not satisfied with the works Jesus was doing asked for a **sign** to authenticate His mission (vv. 15, 16). Knowing their thoughts about these matters, Jesus spoke to them.

First, He addressed the idea that He was casting out demons by the power of Satan. His response is that the idea is absurd. If **Satan** is **divided** so as to fight **against** his own interests how can his **empire stand**? (v. 18). Even the evil one is smarter than that! And, since you have exorcists who claim to cast out demons (from the number of those who were yet pos-

Luke 11

15 But some of them said, "He casts out demons by Beelzebub, the chief of the demons."

16 Others tested Him, asking Him for a sign from the sky.

17 But He knew their thoughts and said to them,
> Every empire that is divided against itself will be devastated and a house that is against itself falls.

18 So then, if Satan also is divided against himself, how will his empire stand? I say this because you are saying that I cast out demons by Beelzebub.

19 But if I cast out demons by Beelzebub, by whom do your sons cast them out? So then, they will be your judges.

20 But if I cast out demons by God's finger, then God's empire has come upon you.

21 When a well-armed, strong man guards his own courtyard, his possessions are safe.

22 But when a stronger man attacks and overcomes him, he takes the armor on which he relied and divides the spoils.

23 Whoever isn't with Me is against Me, and whoever doesn't gather with Me scatters.

---

sessed in Jesus' day it seems they weren't very successful!), He continued, **by whom do your sons cast them out?** That is to say, if it is by Satan's power as you say, then who is to say that you don't do the same? What is good for the goose is good for the gander.

I am casting out demons by God's personal power (**God's finger**) He affirms. And that is an indication that **His empire has come upon you** (v. 20). Jesus went on to reinforce His argument with a story (a great way to do so in counseling too). In verses 21 through 23 He speaks of a **strong man** (Satan) who is **attacked** and **overcome** by a **stronger** one (Jesus); the latter **takes** the **armor** on which the former **relied and divides the spoils**. In effect, He was saying, "In casting out the demon that is precisely what I am doing."

Then, in an important statement, Jesus declares that if they were not **with Him** (on His side of the battle with the strong man and his hosts), **gathering** the lost sheep of Israel, they were **against Him, scattering** the flock. There is no neutrality. Eclectic counselors seem to have little sense of the antithetical thinking of Jesus and that is found in the Bible message as a whole. One cannot have a foot in both Jesus' camp and in that of the enemy. Whenever a counselor departs from the Bible as the source of his counseling methods, to the extent that he does so, he scatters rather than

Christian Counselor's Commentary

> 24 When the unclean spirit leaves a person, he goes through dry areas, looking for a resting place. But when he doesn't find any he says, "I'm going back to my house that I left."
> 25 When he gets there he finds it swept and tidy.
> 26 Then he goes and gets seven other spirits more wicked than himself, and they go in and live there and the last state of that man is worse than the first.
> 27 As He said this, a certain woman in the crowd raised her voice and said to Him, "Happy is the womb that bore You and the breasts that You sucked."
> 28 But He said, "Rather, happy are those who hear God's word and keep it."

gathers. His efforts have a negative effect on the church rather than a positive one. How we have seen that in our day in counseling!

Then, from the incident of the exorcism, Jesus draws another parable. That of the cleanly swept house (vv. 24-26). These Jews who were opposing His ministry were like that house. They may have been baptized by John, they may claim to have been converted and to have reformed their lives, but it was all superficial, temporary, outward only—it did not reach the heart. Consequently, when He came along, their response was a holier-than-thou one which meant that they were only deepened in their sin, hardened by their opposition. It was as if the one demon who left returned accompanied by seven more! Their seeming righteousness was mere outward reformation; there was no regeneration.

It is sad when that is all that comes out of counseling. If God is not brought into the sessions, then that is all one can expect. But even if He is prominent in all that is said and done, there is no assurance of a good effect (here Jesus was even physically present!). If one rejects God's way, he hardens himself. Some who profess faith are counterfeit Christians. Counseling will often expose this fact and thus be a **scattering** rather than a **gathering** of the church.

At this point Jesus is interrupted by a **woman** (vv. 27, 28) before He could continue to deal with the request for a sign. She extols Mary for her privileged position as Jesus' mother. Taking nothing from Mary, Jesus answers, saying that those who **hear and keep God's Word** are the **happy** ones. A spiritual relationship to Him is more important than a physical one. That is the point that He makes. It is also a point that you ought to make continually to counselees who are prone to put family before God in one way or another. For Luke to mention this interruption

Luke 11

29 As the crowds pressed upon Him, He began to say,
This generation is an evil generation. It seeks a sign. But no sign will be given to it except the sign of Jonah.

30 As Jonah became a sign to the Ninevites, so too will the Son of Man be to this generation.

31 The Queen of the South will be raised up in the judgment with the men of this generation and will condemn them because she came from the ends of the earth to hear Solomon's wisdom; but listen, Someone greater than Solomon is here.

32 The men of Nineveh will rise up in the judgment with this generation and will condemn it because they repented at Jonah's preaching; but listen, Someone greater then Jonah is here.

---

and Jesus' reply is interesting. Why did he? Well, simply because it broke the continuity of the account—just as it did in real life. It gave him, thereby, the chance to emphasize, by the very fact that it stood out and was incongruous with the flow of conversation, the reader's need for that spiritual relationship. Sometimes, to respond to a digression in counseling makes the matter all the more prominent. To do so is wise and useful, if, like Christ, you come back to the matter at hand and don't lose your train of thought.

Jesus now takes up the matter of the **sign** requested (vv. 29-36). His response is strong: He calls the **generation wicked because it seeks a sign**. Why is that? Not only had there been signs that had not been acknowledged (cf. 7:22), but now, rather than look for those God had already provided, they were insisting on something greater—perhaps something that they themselves set up as the proper sign. As Jesus will say in chapter 16, even if someone rises from the dead, many will not believe. Indeed, that is the point with counselees—they must be content with what God thought that they needed in the Bible and not endeavor to set up some sign of their own making for God to perform as a means of guidance. This is wicked because God has already given them everything that they need in the Bible (see *The Christian's Guide to Guidance*).

Jesus graciously does mention one great **sign** that will be **given**: the **sign of Jonah**. That sign would be His rising from the grave after three days as Jonah was released from the fish after the same period of time (v. 30). He goes on to tell them that a **greater** Person than **Jonah** is here; a **greater** Person than **Solomon** with all his wisdom is here. The queen of Arabia came over 1,000 miles to see Solomon and was amazed. Here is Someone far greater than he, right here—on the doorstep, so to speak—

Christian Counselor's Commentary

> 33 Nobody, after lighting a lamp, hides it or puts it under a bushel basket, but rather on a lampstand, so that those who come in may see the light.
> 34 The lamp of the body is your eye. When your eye is healthy your whole body is full of light; when it is unhealthy your body also is dark.
> 35 So see to it that the light in you isn't darkness.
> 36 Therefore, if your whole body is light, and has no dark part, it will be thoroughly lighted as when a lamp's light shines on you.
>   37 As He spoke, a Pharisee asked Him to eat with him, so He went into his house and reclined at the table.
>   38 The Pharisee was astonished to see that He didn't wash first before dinner.

and there is little amazement or faith. Truly it was a wicked generation. Solomon's wisdom was great; they were passing up Wisdom Himself! Pagans like the Ninevites repented when Jonah preached. They will rise up in judgment on this generation and condemn it. That is serious.

Then Jesus tells them another parable. When you light a lamp, you don't **hide it** or **put it under a basket**. No. You put it on a **lampstand** so that it will give **light** to everyone in the house. (v. 33). So too, the body's **lamp** is the **eye** (it lets light in so that one may see). When the eye is unhealthy the light coming in doesn't enable you to see as you might. It might as well be darkness that enters. The problem is not with what is to be seen, it is with the eye. The spiritual sight of the Pharisees, who will not see Jesus for Whom He is, is compared to eyes with a disease that will not allow one to discern an object. The light that is coming in may really be darkness (v. 35). That is to say, the ideas, the teaching, the way of life that one *thinks* is enlightening may actually be causing blindness. That is true of those who reject biblical counsel for pagan counsel. Warn counselees of the danger. If one has been regenerated (the whole body is light), he truly sees what the true light reveals to him (v. 36).

Now comes a very important episode—the meal at the **Pharisee's** house. The Pharisee wanted to get something on Him; perhaps having Him there would be the way to do so. This explains the (otherwise) rude attack Jesus made on him and his friends. Jesus begins the exchange with an evaluation of the Pharisees as a whole (v. 39). They are, He says, those who look good outwardly but like a **cup clean** on the **outside** but full of the green hairy stuff that grows inside when it isn't cleaned, so they were filthy within. Their hearts were bent on **robbery** and **wickedness** of all

Luke 11

39 Then the Lord said to him,
   Now, you Pharisees clean the outside of the cup and dish, but inside you are full of robbery and wickedness.
40   Fools! Didn't He Who made the outside also make the inside?
41   However, give as charity those things that are within and everything will be clean to you.
   42 But woe to you Pharisees, because you tithe mint and rue and all sorts of herbs, but pass over justice and the love of God. These you should have done without passing over the other.
43   Woe to you Pharisees because you love the chief seat in the synagogs and greetings in the marketplaces.

---

sorts. That is foolishness, He says. Why? Because God made both the inner and the outer man and is concerned about both. Moreover, such hypocrisy doesn't deceive Him; He knows what is in a man's heart. The danger for a counselee is to conform outwardly, with no concern about bringing his heart in line with God. That is not what biblical counseling is all about. Warn counselees that they are to "obey from the heart" (Romans 6:17). With a new heart, the motive behind charitable giving, for instance, is clean and so is the act (v. 41). And take **tithing**. They tithed even small seeds, but they **passed over justice** toward man and **love** toward **God**. While not forgetting the minor matters of the law, they should certainly not neglect the weightier ones (v. 42). A counseling dodge often is, "Well, look what I *did* do" (then, some trivial thing is mentioned). Counselors might say, O.K., but what about the larger matters of which we are speaking? If you have done those smaller things, how much more ought you do the larger? Turn the dodge around and use it to expose sin that is being covered up.

Other **woes** are listed in this paragraph. A **woe** indicates a pending serious judgment of God that will fall upon the one against whom it is pronounced unless he repents. These woes, therefore, were warnings issued in mercy and grace to these proud Pharisees. The next **woe** concerns pride. The Pharisees were given inordinate respect by the people of the day. This went to their heads. They loved it and curried this respect. Indeed, it seems that they even vied with one another for the **chief seats in the synagogs and** number of **greetings** received **in the marketplaces** (v. 43). They wore special, long robes that were supposed to signify their unusual holiness, for which others lauded them. Pride in a counselee, like the pride of these Pharisees, may keep him from hearing and heeding God's holy Word. Warn counselees about Christ's woes pronounced upon

Christian Counselor's Commentary

> 44 Woe to you because you are like unnoticed graves that people walk on without realizing it.
>
> **45** One of the teachers of the law answered and said, "Teacher, when you say this you insult us too."
>
> 46 Then He said,
>> Woe to you teachers of the law too, because you load people with burdens that are difficult to carry, but you yourselves won't lift a finger to help them with their burdens.

---

those who flaunted themselves before others.

The Pharisees needed to repent of the unholiness that they communicated to others. As teachers, they held sway over the minds of the people. Jesus describes them as **unnoticed graves that people walk on without realizing it**. When one walked on a grave, he became ceremonially unclean. Old, forgotten, unseen graves, unnoticed until it was too late, therefore, constituted a hazard. The Pharisees, like these graves, contaminated those with whom they came into contact. That is what Christ is saying. The leaven of the Pharisees (hypocrisy; cf. 12:1) permeated and spread to the people in general. Counselees must watch out for those who would spread sinful ways to them as well. The danger in this **woe** is a real one today. Associating with proud, legalistic churches, with persons who set up their own standards of holiness and look down on others who do not follow their humanly-manufactured rules, can be dangerous to one's spiritual health!

As Jesus was pronouncing these **woes**, a **teacher of the law** interrupted Him (v. 45). He got the point of Christ's words and objected, **when you say this you insult us too.** That was correct. But the **insult** was not unfounded; it was totally apropos. So, rather than apologizing (something counselors are all too ready to do these days), Jesus pronounces a **woe** on him and his fellow **teachers**. He condemns them for **loading people with burdens difficult to carry** while unwilling to **lift a finger to help them with their burdens.** It is not that Jesus thought the **burdens** that the **teachers of the law** loaded people with would be OK if they only helped them carry them. No, these **burdens** were *wrong*—they were accretions of the centuries that the elders had added to the Bible, thereby covering over its true meaning and making it ineffectual. He is condemning them for this *and* for not helping **lift** other **burdens** they had quite apart from those loaded on their backs by legalists! Sin burdens us all in this sinful world. No one needs additional burdens added to those that we accumulate as we live in this world of sin. What we need is counselors who will **lift a finger**

47	Woe to you because you build tombs for the prophets that your fathers killed.
48	So then, you are witnesses that you approve of your fathers' deeds; they killed them and you build them tombs.
49	So then, God's Wisdom said, "I will send prophets and apostles to them, and they will kill and persecute some of them,"
50	that this generation may be held responsible for the blood of all the prophets, shed from the foundation of the world,
51	from the blood of Abel to the blood of Zechariah, who was destroyed between the altar and the house. Yes, I tell you, this generation will be held responsible for it.

or two to **help** people deal with them. From one perspective, under God, that is what counseling is all about, isn't it? Ask yourself, "Am I adding burdens to my counselees or helping them deal with them?" That is an important test for every counselor to take from time to time. Never equate your suggestions about how to implement a biblical command with the command itself. And be very sure that any such suggestions are not additional **burdens** but **lifting** solutions to problems created by sin.

Jesus goes on to accuse them of being in league with those who **killed** the **prophets**. The fathers did so, and they enter into their sin by **building tombs** for them (vv. 47, 48). What He refers to is not merely the erection of physical tombs, but also their teaching by which they virtually silenced them. It was like sealing them up in tombs so that they could not be heard. That is to say, by wrongly interpreting and concealing what the prophets said under legalistic traditions, they no longer spoke to the people. They were as effectively silenced by this as they were when the fathers put them to death! Misinterpretation (willful or not) by counselors also silences the Bible writers. How important it is for them to be able to *open* the words of the prophets so that they speak anew to counselees!

In His **wisdom** (recorded in the Bible) God predicted that OT **prophets** and NT **apostles** would be sent with His life-giving message, only to be **killed** and **persecuted** for preaching it (v. 49). For this—all the murderous deeds of the Jewish people against their own preachers from the beginning until the present—judgment would come upon those living at that time. The cup of God's wrath had been filling up over the years. It was now spilling over. God would give them only a grace period before the judgment actually fell upon that **generation** in 70 AD.

There comes a time when God will no longer patiently wait for repentance. If it is not forthcoming, His judgment will fall. Many situa-

Christian Counselor's Commentary

> 52   Woe to you teachers of the law because you have taken away the key to the house of knowledge. You didn't go in yourselves, and you have hindered those who were entering.
>
> **53** When He left there, the scribes' and the Pharisees' resentment toward Him grew fierce, and they began to draw Him out on a number of issues,
>
> 54 watching carefully to see if they could catch Him in something spoken from His lips.

---

tions encountered in counseling call for making this fact known. There are people who think that God will go along suffering rebellion forever. He will not.

As His parting shot, Jesus lets the **scribes** (teachers of and "experts" in the Bible who had played a large part in covering its teachings with their own laws and ordinances) have it: **woe ... because you have taken away the key to the house of knowledge. You didn't go in yourselves, and you hindered those who were entering.** Powerful, fearful words! Here were men who were supposed to have the key to unlock the truths of the Bible for those they taught. Rather, they locked them up so that neither they themselves nor those they taught were able to enter into God's truth. What a fearful condemnation! Every counselor must take heed to this sad situation so as to be sure that he uses rightly the key that his position hands him.

Rather than repenting at these **woes,** these teachers became furious and determined to kill Jesus—just as He was saying they would. This would be the culmination of the wickedness of the fathers executed by their sons. They, therefore, tried to **draw Him out on a number of issues** in order to catch Him saying something for which they could condemn Him (vv. 53, 54).

Chapter 12

> 1 Meanwhile, as a crowd of so many thousands gathered that they were stepping on one another, He began to speak to his disciples first:
> Be on your guard against the leaven of the Pharisees, which is hypocrisy.

A large crowd began to gather, perhaps over the ruckus that the Pharisees were making. But Jesus, for the moment ignoring the crowd, had something more to say to His **disciples**. He warned them against **the leaven of the Pharisees, which is hypocrisy**. They were, first of all, to be wary of their contacts with these professed worshippers of Yahweh. Their profession was false—they were hypocrites. They might talk a good game, but they were malicious at heart. There are people to warn your counselees about too. Many counselees are gullible; Proverbs 14:15 may be apropos. Not only do counselees accept advice that purports to be biblical (but is not), but they often listen to radio and TV programs, and read books that are "religious" although anything but Christian, in their teachings. Many counselees are affected by persons who are out to make money off them—people who are not sincere in their profession of faith any more than were the Pharisees.

But secondly, the warning might also have been personal. **Leaven** works its way through a substance until it has affected all. That is the way with **hypocrisy**. Neither the disciples, nor you, nor your counselees are immune to **hypocrisy**. It has an insidious way of getting into all of our lives. We must help counselees clean the house of every scrap, as the Israelites did when preparing the unleavened bread. Dealing with hypocrisy may be a prime task of a counselor in dealing with some counselees.

"How is that?" you ask. If your counselee comes from a legalistic background, he is more than likely to have been affected by pharisaical leaven. Fear (about which Jesus will have much to say in this chapter) and hypocrisy go together, The hypocrite is a pretender who lives in constant fear of being found out—fear of exposure. Much of the lifestyle of one who lives among legalists is devoted to keeping the truth about his doubts, sins, concerns unknown to others around him (who, incidentally, have taught him how to do so by their own example). He will have developed ways and means (including his speech) of telling you that things are OK when they are far from it. He will have learned to smile when his heart is breaking. He will come to counseling only because matters have gotten so

Christian Counselor's Commentary

2	Nothing is covered that won't be uncovered or hidden that won't be known.
3	So whatever you have said in darkness will be heard in the light, and what you have whispered in private rooms will be proclaimed on the rooftops.

---

bad he can hardly maintain the farce any longer, or because someone else involved has let the cat out of the bag. But even then he will not find it easy to give up the pretense. Frequently, one of your hardest tasks will be to get him to "open up." Even in counseling, according to his regular style, he will go on pretending. He may theoretically agree that we are all sinners—his doctrine at that point may be correct—but he will carry on as if in his life it were not true. One of the best things that you can do for such a person is to warn him of the **leaven of the Pharisees**.

One of the other things you will come up against with legalistic hypocrites is the problem of seeking men's approval. In almost every legalistic context there are those who are judging the motives and the behavior of their fellows. They have a basic list of man-made rules that they apply to others and are constantly on the lookout for any violation of them. Counselees who have been looking over their shoulders for years under such a regime will have a hard time revealing the depths of their problem. They suspect that you will "land on them" as soon as you hear the truth, so they will disguise or color it. While never countenancing sin, a biblical counselor doesn't "land" on anyone. What he does is hold out the hope of forgiveness through repentance, cleansing through confession, and change through the Word and the Spirit. The problem with the legalistic church or school is that it teaches people to become liars and deceivers. Many times, when one has lived in that sort of context long enough, he has even deceived himself. Because there is so much legalism and because it is like leaven, spreading to all around, you will find many counselees who have become astute hypocrites.

Hypocrisy is essentially a cover-up. One disguises his true intents and purposes under a veneer of plausibility. It is not always possible to detect it in a counselee. But the time will come when what is in the heart of a person will be made known: **nothing is covered that won't be uncovered or hidden that won't be known** (v. 2). Of this fact you may assure a counselee who needs to be warned about the possibility of hypocrisy. Jesus explains that things said **in darkness will be heard in the light and what** was **whispered** privately will be **proclaimed** publicly. That

Luke 12

4	And I tell you, My friends, don't fear those who can kill the body but after that have nothing more that they can do.
5	But I'll show you Whom you should fear—fear Him Who, after killing, has authority to cast into Gehenna. Yes, I tell you, fear Him!
6	Aren't five sparrows sold for two pennies? Yet not one of them is forgotten by God.
7	Actually, even the hairs of your head are all numbered. Don't be afraid; you are worth more than many sparrows.

warning is important for those who think they can get away with things because no one knows or ever will. Perhaps no one will know in this life, but the day is coming when these things will be disclosed. The Pharisees will be stripped of their outer piety and shown to be what they really are within. Perhaps that is the hypocrite's greatest fear: being exposed for what he is.

Well, Jesus goes on to deal with the matter of **fear**—a very realistic problem given the hostility that was brewing in the Jewish leadership at the moment (vv. 4, 5). He tells the disciples that they ought not fear **those who can kill the body**, but can do no more; rather, they should fear Him Who not only can kill the body, but **has authority** to cast the whole person into eternal punishment. Jesus, clearly, was referring to Himself as the One to Whom the Father had given such **authority** (cf. John 5:27).

Many counselees are troubled with **fear**. They order their lives according to those actions that they think will be the safest. They never take risks. They are not concerned about doing God's will if it is likely to lead to trouble. **Fear** is a powerful motivator. It will make people say and do things that they know are quite contrary to what they ought to do. Much of what you will find yourself advising from the Bible may seem very risky to them. That is when clashes between counselor and counselee may occur. Fear will make an otherwise docile counselee turn on you with a snarl and try to bite you! Recognize the symptoms of fear. Then turn to this passage and explain what Jesus said about **fear**.

Why should we **fear**? There is no reason for the believer to do so. That is the implication of what Jesus goes on to say (vv. 6, 7). If God does not **forget** the little, insignificant **sparrow**, will He forget you? Of course not! If He knows the **number** of **hairs** on your head, will He not take care of the rest of you? Of course. These simple illustrations show the profound truth that God providentially watches over His own. Now, if they know that He does so, why would they fear? That is the point. And it is

Christian Counselor's Commentary

> 8 Now I tell you, everybody who confesses Me before people, the Son of Man also will confess before God's angels;
> 9 and everybody who denies Me before people will be denied before God's angels.
> 10 Everybody who says a word against the Son of Man will be forgiven, but whoever blasphemes against the Holy Spirit won't be forgiven.

the point to make to the counselee who is afraid to confess his sin to another, who is afraid to reveal his true opinions and beliefs, who is afraid to do something radically different from what he has ever done before.

Jesus now puts it to them in terms of **confessing** or **denying** Him (vv. 8-10). **Confess before people** and the time will come when Jesus will **confess them before God's angels**. But the converse will be true too. That is to say, what one does now, in this life, about Jesus Christ has eternal consequences. To confess Christ is to trust in Him and acknowledge Him as your Savior (Romans 10:9). For Him to confess you is for Him to acknowledge you as one of His elect for Whom He died. Before the **angels** means in God's presence since the angels attend Him and are at His service.

Fearful "Christians" may even need to be warned that if they fail to do the hard things that mean confessing Christ before people, they may be on the wrong side. They may be self-deceived. Be careful, though, not to confuse your suggestions with biblical commands. If one refuses to obey the latter out of fear, and is persistent in that refusal, even after every encouragement and help, it may be time to read him verses 8 and 9. Which is the more deadly—embarrassment and discomfort here, or abandonment in the presence of the **angels**? Some who have even done works ostensibly for Christ will hear Him say, "I never knew you." That will be a terrible day!

Verse 10 is significant. Persons who **deny** Christ before men out of fear (and many have, including some of your counselees) are not in an irretrievable position. They may repent and confess Christ anew. Thank God for that fact! But, those who, like the Pharisees, are so hardened that they attribute the work of the *Holy* Spirit to an *unclean* spirit have gone beyond the bounds. The Pharisees who did so were no longer reclaimable. Never forget to explain and offer the hope that is set forth in this verse when dealing with counselees who are grief stricken over their denial of Jesus in some situation. A good example to use in fleshing out this point is the three denials of Peter. These denials were occasioned by **fear**; not

Luke 12

> 11 Now, when they bring you before synagogs and rulers and authorities, don't worry about what you will say in defense or how to do so,
>
> 12 because the Holy Spirit will teach you in that very hour what you ought to say.
>
> 13 Someone from the crowd said to Him, "Teacher, tell my brother to divide our inheritance with me."
>
> 14 But He said to him, "Man, who appointed Me judge or divider over you?"
>
> 15 Then He said to them, "See to it that you be on guard against every kind of greed; a person's life isn't made up of the abundance of his possessions."

---

by a heart hardened against Christ. Indeed, just the opposite was true. Peter loved his Lord in spite of his weakness. The contrast between the forgivable and the unforgivable is the contrast between Peter and the Pharisees.

Verses 11 and 12 look forward to the time when Jesus' disciples will become apostles preaching His Word. What Jesus was here beginning to experience by way of hostility would be transferred to them. They would be hauled up before **rulers and authorities**. They would be persecuted and punished for their faith. But at the time when it was needed, they could count on the Holy Spirit to teach them what to do and say so as to confound those before whom they came. Unlike us, therefore, they would have no need to think through beforehand what to say, or how to say it. They would not only be writing inspired books, but would be giving inspired sermons as well (cf. Acts 2:4, 14 in which the term used for speaking indicates precisely that).

Another interruption occurs (vv. 13-15). Someone asks Christ to divide the inheritance between himself and his brother. Doubtless, he understood something of the fairness and impartiality that Jesus showed. "Here," he thought, "is the person to adjudicate between us!" But Jesus does not take kindly to such a suggestion. Not only had this man interrupted an important discourse, but it showed his lack of interest in spiritual things; his concern was only about material ones. Jesus, therefore, rebukes him (v. 14) and takes advantage of the incident to warn him and those who were around against **greed** (v. 15) saying, "**a person's life isn't made up of the abundance of his possessions.**" That is a powerful statement.

Many counselees have financial problems. You will find yourself

Christian Counselor's Commentary

> 16 And He told them a parable, saying,
> A certain rich man's land yielded a good crop.
> 17 So he thought to himself, "What shall I do? I don't have any place to store my crops."
> 18 Then he thought, "This is what I'll do—I'll pull down my barns and build bigger ones, and I'll store all my wheat and goods there.
> 19 Then I'll say to myself, 'You have many goods stored up for many years; take it easy, eat, drink and be merry.'"
> 20 But God said to him, "You fool! This very night your life will be demanded of you. Then who will get what you have stored up?"
> 21 So it will be for anybody who lays up treasure for himself but isn't rich in relation to God.
> 22 Then He said to His disciples,
> I tell you, therefore, don't worry about your life—what you are going to eat; nor about the body—what you are going to put on.
> 23 Life is more than food and the body is more than clothing.

dealing with finances from every possible angle. And, when you do, you will notice how these problems often crowd out every other thing that you are trying to do for them. The last words of verse 15 will assist you greatly in bringing this issue to a head. If fear of loss, concern over jobs, or whatever form this dominating financial problem takes, is driving all that the counselee does and says, you may have to make it crystal clear to him that this undue emphasis on money must change.

Elaborating on the question of money, Jesus now tells them a **parable** (vv. 16-21). It is the parable of the rich **fool**. The problem with this man in the parable was not that he **stored** up grain, but (like the man who was interested in money more than what Jesus was teaching) that was his only concern: he wasn't **rich in relation to God** (v. 21). Counselees with this same orientation will constantly come back to one thing in their discussions: money. They will be so concerned with the financial aspects of every problem that they will tend to hear nothing that you say about anything else. The one-sided person is always in trouble, especially when that one side is materialistic. Man does not live by bread alone!

In verses 22 through 34 Jesus continues to discuss avarice. He warns His disciples not to **worry about** what they will **eat** or wear. Then He makes this very powerful statement: **Life is more than food and the body is more than clothing** (v. 23). That is a very useful statement for counselors who, from time to time, will find themselves confronted with counselees who think otherwise. There are those who are obsessed with

Luke 12

24		Consider the ravens that neither sow nor reap, that have neither storehouse nor barn, but God feeds them. You are worth a great deal more than birds!
	25	Which of you by worrying can add one moment to his life?
26		So then, if you can't do a small thing like that, why are you worrying about other things?
27		Consider the lilies; they neither spin nor weave, but I tell you Solomon in all his glory wasn't arrayed like one of them.
28		Now, if God so clothes the grass of the field that is alive today but tomorrow is thrown into an oven, how much more will He clothe you, men of little faith?
29		Don't be intent on what you will eat and what you will drink; don't worry about these things.
30		These are the things that all the Gentiles diligently seek. But your Father knows that you need them.

---

eating and clothing themselves. The bulemic and the anorexic is the extreme example of such truncated living. He (or she) lives for food and for what people will think of his (her) looks. To help such persons see the sin of this solitary focus and bring them into a fuller life, which focuses on Jesus and His grace, will often be your task. This verse could be the very one out of which you bring such help.

The verses which follow reinforce His point. God cares for the **ravens** who do none of the things that persons obsessed with things do. Yet, there they are, having their needs met every day (v. 24). Moreover, suppose you *do* **worry**—what good will that do? Worry can't change anything (except you—for the worse): by worrying you can't add even one minute to your life. So, if you can't accomplish anything positive through worry, why worry (v. 26)? The lilies are another good example—God clothes them and the grass of the field. Don't you think that He will care for you? If God takes care of ravens, lilies, grass, surely He will take care of you. It is an argument from the lesser to the greater.

What is the problem with those who worry? Jesus nails it in verse 28^b in which he calls the worrier a person of **little faith**. It is a matter of faith. Does one believe God will care for him or not? That is it. And that is how the issue often must be put to the worrying counselee. It is a matter of whether or not he believes the Word of God and the God of the Word. The person who continually troubles himself over such matters gives evidence of little faith—that is an insight you can use in counseling in diagnosing problems.

Christian Counselor's Commentary

31		Rather, be intent on His empire, and these things will be yours as well.
	32	Don't fear, little flock, your Father is pleased to give you the empire.
33		Sell your possessions and give to charity. Make yourselves purses that won't grow old, and amass a treasure in the heavens that won't be depleted, where a thief won't come near and that a moth won't destroy.
34		Where your treasure is, there your heart will be too.
	35	Keep yourselves dressed in readiness and your lamps burning.
36		Be like people waiting for their lord to return from the wedding feast, so that when he arrives and knocks they may open the door for him at once.

The problem, in essence, is this: he is living like a pagan (**Gentile**; v. 30). That is how those who have no God to which to turn think and act. The pagan way of life is self-oriented and focuses on this life and the things that one may be able accumulate in it. In contrast, the believer must have his focus on something else: God's **empire** and then, God will add **these things** as a by-product. But those who misplace their efforts, concerns and faith upon the by-product will never know the abundant **life** about which Jesus was speaking (v. 23).

"But we are so few," some may object. Yes, the Christian is a part of a **little flock**. But look at Whose flock it is! That is what makes the difference. Don't hesitate to tell counselees that they will be in the minority, that what God requires of them will not fit standard, worldly life patterns, etc., so long as you also emphasize that *with Christ* you are in the majority!

With graphic hyperbole (v. 33) Jesus tells us to put aside all of those interests that make life one-sided and lay up a treasure in heaven where nothing can happen to destroy it. Then He makes this important statement: **Where your treasure is, there your heart will be too** (v. 34). That is another powerful counseling insight. The statement here has to do with money. But it is larger than this context in which it appears; it is a maxim that has a life of its own. One's focus of attention (**heart**), his concern, is revealed by learning where he spends his time, his money etc. What he considers of importance and value (his **treasure**) will dominate his life. It will orient him. It will consume him.

Moreover, Jesus warns about the fact that undue concern for something in this world will make persons unprepared for the **coming** of their

Luke 12

37	Those slaves will be happy whom the lord will find watching when he comes. I assure you, he will get himself dressed to serve, have them recline at the table and will come and serve them.
38	If he comes in the second or third watch and finds them so, those slaves will be happy!
39	But be aware of this: if the householder had known the hour at which the thief was coming, he wouldn't have permitted him to break into his house.
40	So you must be prepared, because at the hour when you least expect it the Son of Man is coming.

41 Then Peter said, "Lord, are you speaking this parable to us or to everybody?"

42 The Lord said,

	Who then is the faithful and wise steward whom his lord will put in charge of his servants to give them their rations at the proper time?
43	That slave will be happy whom his lord finds doing so when he returns.
44	I assure you that he will put him in charge of all his possessions.
45	But if that slave says in his heart, "My lord has delayed his coming," and begins to beat the men and women servants, and eats and gets drunk,

---

Lord. If He is their treasure, they will be ready with **lamps burning** and **dressed** for the wedding (v. 36). If they are preoccupied with other interests, they will be lost in the shuffle in the hour of His unexpected coming (vv. 37-40). How important, then, it is for the counselee to be ready, prepared at all times! When the destruction of Jerusalem came, those who had been waiting obeyed and fled to the hills near Pella; those who were not prepared, to whom things were more important (who turned back like Lot's wife), were taken away in the destruction. When our Lord comes in the future, we too must be ready for Him. Part of your work as a counselor is preparing people for Christ's return.

In verses 42 through 48 Jesus pursues the matter of readiness in terms of faithfulness. Those who work faithfully for the Lord when He is absent will receive a reward at His coming. Those who take advantage of His absence to run roughshod over others will feel His wrath. They will be exposed as unbelievers and will be apportioned a place with them where they belong (v. 46). Here is a powerful section to use with counselees who think that they are getting away with something simply because the Lord has not done anything to stop them. He will, in His time, and

Christian Counselor's Commentary

46   that slave's lord will come on the day when he least expects it and at an hour that he doesn't know about, and will hack him to pieces and will place him among the unbelievers.

47   The slave who knew what his lord wanted and didn't get ready or act according to his will is going to be beaten with many stripes,

48   while the one who didn't know, who deserved a beating, will be beaten with few stripes. Much will be demanded from the one to whom much was given, and from him to whom much was entrusted, they will ask much more.

49   I came to set fire to the earth; and I really wish it were already blazing.

50   I have a baptism to be baptized with, and I am really distressed until it is completed.

51   Do you think that I came to bring peace to the earth? On the contrary, I tell you, division!

52   From now on there will be five in one home who are divided: three against two and two against three.

53   They will be divided, father against son and son against father, mother against daughter and daughter against mother, mother-in-law against daughter-in-law and daughter-in-law against mother-in-law!

54   And He also said this to the crowds:
When you see a cloud rising in the west, right away you say, "A storm is coming," and it does.

---

they will be very sorry.

    In verses 47 and 48 we learn that there will be degrees of punishment in hell. And the principle on which those **stripes** will be administered (to use Jesus' figure) will be how much light they rejected (v. 48). Those who knew more but rejected it will receive more stripes; those who knew less, will receive less stripes.

    Then, in verse 49, Jesus makes another amazing statement: **I came to set fire to the earth; and I wish it were already blazing**. What does He mean? Simply this—He came to shake things up. He came to set fire to all that the devil had erected on earth. He came to divide and conquer the forces of the evil one and to redeem out of them the little flock that He wants for His own. And all of this will take place through the **baptism** of the cross. It was agony for Him to anticipate the wrath of God poured out on Him in that coming, all-important event. He was more than anxious to get it over with so that the fire could begin to blaze forth. He did not come to bring **peace** to the world, but **division!** The message of the cross would

Luke 12

55 And when you see a south wind blowing you say, "It's going to be hot," and it is.
56 You Hypocrites! You know how to interpret the appearance of the earth and the sky, but why is it that you don't know how to interpret the present time?
57 Why don't you judge for yourselves what is right?
58 As you go with your opponent to the magistrate, try hard to settle with him on the way. Otherwise, he may drag you to the judge, and the judge will hand you over to a policeman, and the policeman will put you in prison.
59 I tell you, you won't get out until you have paid the last cent.

---

divide members of the very same household (vv. 52, 53).

How important these verses are to the counselor. For his own orientation, he must recognize the radical antithesis of which Jesus spoke in this discourse. He must also recognize the fact that there will be **division** and conflict in homes between believers and unbelievers. None of this should take him by surprise. On the contrary, he should expect it. And, in his dealings with counselees, he should express the facts that Jesus revealed here.

Finally, there is Jesus' word to the great crowd that gathered, listening to these things (vv. 54-59). He spoke of how they could forecast the weather by the signs in the sky (**clouds, winds**), but had failed utterly to interpret the signs present to them (His miracles, teachings, etc.). They, too, had been affected (as a whole) by the hypocrisy of their religious leaders; like leaven, it had spread until it permeated the nation (v. 56). But He appealed to them to start making **right judgments** about what was happening all around them and, indeed, in front of their eyes (v. 57). A final, short parable wrapped up His discourse: don't put matters off. If you do, you will be like the man who fails to come to terms with his legal opponent on the way to court. He may lose everything because of his hesitancy (or, perhaps, false pride thinking he will win). Now is the time to believe; don't wait until God closes the door of the ark!

CHAPTER 13

1 Now at that time there were some present who told Him about the Galileans whose blood Pilate mixed with their sacrifices.
2 So He replied, saying,
> Do you think that these Galileans were worse sinners than all the other Galileans because they suffered these things?

The story picks up again with the observation of some present that Pilate had killed some Galileans while they were offering their **sacrifices** in the temple (a sacrilege). Luke puts it dramatically saying that sending soldiers to kill them in such a manner amounted to *mixing their blood* with the blood of their **sacrifices**. What they had in mind by bringing up the incident is uncertain. Perhaps they wanted Jesus to say something that would enable them to condemn Him for speaking against the government. We don't know. But what He does with their report is to take advantage of it to show those who were listening that they are **sinners** who need to be forgiven. This technique that we have seen Jesus using throughout the last couple of chapters is a useful one. As here, in the way every successful speaker handles interruptions and heckling, Jesus uses what was said to launch forth on some point that he wants to drive home.

In verse 2 He asks, "**Do you think that these Galileans were worse sinners than all the other Galileans because they suffered such things?**" The matter that He is bringing to the fore is very important to counselors. Again and again counselees will claim that what has happened to them (or others) is the result of some special sin. Now of course, in a given instance, this may be true. But the conclusion is in no way a necessary one. God brings trouble, tragedy and even death for a variety of reasons; each situation stands on its own two feet. What the reason was in this particular situation is not disclosed (it is not always possible to come up with a one-to-one answer). These facts must be clear to every counselor so that, as Jesus does, he will be able to respond to such thinking in a biblical manner.

What Jesus says is that it could have happened to any or every one of them. They were all **sinners**; *no one* deserves to live (v. 2). That is the first response to a question of this sort. His second response is that since this is true, they need to **repent** and be saved—or they too will **perish** (here, doubtless, He refers to eternal punishment; v. 3). Jesus took the opportunity that the comment gave Him to preach repentance to the crowd. Coun-

3	I tell you they weren't. But unless you repent you will all likewise perish.
4	Or, take those eighteen on whom the tower in Siloam fell and killed them—do you think they were more culpable than all the others who lived in Jerusalem?
5	I tell you they weren't. But unless you repent you will all likewise perish.
6	Then He told this parable: A certain man had a fig tree planted in his vineyard, and he went to look for fruit on it, but didn't find any.
7	So he said to the vinedresser, "For three years I have gone looking for fruit on this fig tree and haven't found any. Cut it down! Why should it take up space in the ground?"
8	But he responded, "Lord, leave it this year too, so that I can dig round it and put manure on it.
9	Then if it bears fruit in the future, good. Otherwise cut it down."

selor, take the opportunities that your counselees serve up to you to direct the conversation into the channels that are needed at the moment.

In order to drive home His point (not everyone gets it the first time) Jesus, Himself, recalls for them an additional incident about which similar interpretations might be made—the **eighteen** on whom **the tower** in **Siloam fell** and **killed**. It was, He said, not because they were more **culpable than all the others who lived in Jerusalem**. Throughout the chapters we have been considering, you will notice that Jesus uses multiple incidents, parables, etc., to drive home His teaching. That, too, is an effective technique that counselors ought to use if there is even the slightest indication that a counselee might not "get" the point. People often have a hard time relating what the Bible says to their situations. Multiple examples help by demonstrating how the teaching works out concretely in everyday life. Moreover, sometimes the incident counselees bring up that occasions the discussion is not quite as much on target as one you'd like to offer in addition so as to even more clearly demonstrate the point. That is another time when multiple examples helps. At any rate, it is often better to use overkill (saying it over and then over again) than to have anyone miss the point. If a counselee doesn't "get it" with one illustration, he may with the next.

Jesus has used the two incidents to make it clear that all must **repent** because all are guilty sinners who dare not approach God unforgiven. He is not yet through with the point. He encapsulates it in a **parable** (inciden-

Christian Counselor's Commentary

> 10 Now He was teaching in one of the synagogs on the Sabbath,
> 11 and a woman who had been ill for eighteen years with a sickness caused by a spirit appeared. She was bent in two and was unable to straighten herself at all.
> 12 So when Jesus saw her He called her and said to her, "Woman, you are free from your illness."
> 13 Then He put His hands on her and at once she was straightened and glorified God.
> 14 But the synagog ruler was furious that Jesus healed on the Sabbath and told the crowd, "There are six days when people ought to work; come to be healed on those days instead of the Sabbath day."

tally, it might be useful to compose several parables of your own to use in counseling from time to time). The parable of the unproductive **fig tree** (vv. 6-9) is a powerful one. The owner (God) tells the vinedresser (Jesus) to **cut it down** since after looking for fruit for three years he hasn't found any fruit on the tree. The vinedresser asks for a little while longer. He will give special treatment to it (**digging around it** to aerate its roots and putting **manure** on it) to see if it will then produce. Obviously, it was the Jewish people that Jesus had in mind in the **parable**. For nearly **three** years He had been ministering to them. He was not quite through. He would make a last special effort. If they failed to respond, then the nation would be destroyed (they didn't, and it happened in 70 AD). But, as He is making clear, there was yet time to **repent** and bear **fruit** that is appropriate to repentance.

We turn in verse 10 to a different occasion when Jesus **was teaching** in a **synagog**. It was a **Sabbath** day. A woman who had been **bent in two** as the result of a demon who possessed her entered (v. 11). Jesus called to her and told her that she had been **freed** from her demonic-caused **illness**. He **put His hands on her** and she **straightened** up and **glorified God**. This was a dramatic incident; the woman had been in this condition for eighteen years!

But the **ruler of the synagog** was **furious** because Jesus **healed on the Sabbath**. Reproachfully, he explained to the **crowd** that there were **six** other **days** in which this could have been done. Here was a religious official more concerned about his man-made rules than the person who had been healed. He should have been **glorifying God** along with the **woman**. Counselees who have been affected by the leaven of hypocrisy (see the last two chapters) will often think similarly. They will be so wrapped up in the rules with which others have chained them that they

15 But the Lord answered him and said,
    You hypocrites! Doesn't each of you on the Sabbath free his ox or his donkey from the stall and lead it away to water it?
16 So shouldn't this woman—a daughter of Abraham that Satan bound for eighteen years—be freed from this bond on the Sabbath day?

---

will find it hard to think of anything else. People, and their welfare, will always come second (if at all) to keeping the rules. God's true commands never cause such a problem; when followed correctly, they always honor God and bless people. Human additions to God's law split up the twofold nature of God's command to love Him and love one's neighbor.

Jesus **answered** the ruler (vv. 15, 16). Once more, He uses His favorite term in addressing such a person. Speaking to him and all who sided with him He addressed them as, "**You hypocrites.**" There are times to be just as explicit, even though most of the weak, mushy Christians around you today will disapprove, and even though it may get you in trouble. One of those times is when people need to be awakened from their stupor. Here were people who had been duped by their leaders; they needed desperately to understand that this was true, that those who had led them down the garden path were **hypocrites** who were actually leading them to hell. There are those today in Christian counseling who need to be exposed for the harm they are doing to the church. Lives are being destroyed, marriages broken up—all because they advocate some system other than that which comes from the Bible. Teachings that do not originate there do not accord with what God has written there.

How was the hypocrisy apparent? Jesus exposes it plainly. If one's **ox** or **donkey** needed water, they would do the "work" (judged by the tradition of the elders to be work) of freeing it and leading it to the water source. Why, then, would they object to a **daughter of Abraham** being released from her bondage by **Satan** after eighteen years of confinement in *his* stall! If something had a direct bearing on their own financial welfare, it was OK; if it didn't, then they could become quite firm with others even when they were fellow Jews in dire need. Here was hypocrisy personified!

This response on the part of Jesus was effective; the ruler and those who were giving assent to what he said were **put to shame** in the eyes of the people who **rejoiced over the glorious things that were being done** (v. 17). There is a need to expose error and its bondage so that the church

Christian Counselor's Commentary

> 17 When He said these things, all those who opposed Him were put to shame, and the whole crowd rejoiced over all the glorious things that were being done by Him.
> 18 Then Jesus said,
>   What is God's empire like? To what shall I compare it?
> 19   It is like a mustard seed that somebody took and threw into his garden, and it grew and became a tree, and **the birds of the sky nested in its branches.**

in general may **rejoice** in the truth and its good effects. When you have opportunities—in conversations, on radio or TV interview shows, in articles you are asked to write—take advantage of these to set the truth of God's way over against those ways that are harmful because erroneous. Where hypocrisy exists, expose it. There are far too many who claim to take a biblical stand who, when the chips are down, give in to the eclectics. Others, in order to retain their "scholarly status" in the eyes of the eclectic elite, kow-tow to them—or at least from time to time play footsie with them. There is none of this in the way Christ deals with these men. He has His eye on the crowd—He wants them to recognize the truth before it is too late. The antithesis appears once again, something that people today abhor. Yet, Jesus' approach, setting the earth afire and dividing between members of the same household, is sharply antithetical: there is God's way, and all others are unacceptable. If you call yourself a "biblical counselor," then act like one.

Jesus now sets forth two brief parables to top off what He has been saying (note, again, it is the multiple thrust method that He employs). The first is the parable of the **mustard tree** (one He used on more than one occasion). The point of the parable is that the kingdom that He was setting up (the church) was not a large entity at this point (before He had called it a **little flock**). They might dismiss it on those grounds. But, in time, this small **mustard seed** would grow into a tree large enough for **birds** to **nest** in. Nouthetic counseling, like every other manifestation of God's word, if it is to do its job, will grow slowly but eventually become large enough to command attention in the church. At present it is but a frail bush; if it is truly God's work, it will eventually become sturdy and tall enough that even some of the birds now nesting in the eclectic trees that abound might want to nest in it!

The parable of the leaven likewise speaks of the spreading of God's empire. Small though it may be, because God is in it, His empire will fill the entire world. That is the way God works—not by the earthquake, nor

20 Then He said again,
  To what shall I compare God's empire?
21   It is like leaven that a woman took and mixed into three batches of flour until the whole was leavened.
22 So He traveled throughout the cities and villages, teaching while heading on His way toward Jerusalem.
23 Somebody said to Him, "Lord, will only a few persons be saved?" And He said to them,
24 Make every effort to enter the narrow door. Many will try to enter but won't be able to.

---

by the fire, but by a quiet voice! Yet He accomplishes His goals. You can be sure of that! Be certain, counselor, that you are a part of the growth of the kingdom, a part of the permeating influence of the biblical leaven which the church so desperately needs.

The exclusiveness and the minority status of the kingdom is in the mind of the Savior throughout the material that comprises verses 22 through 30. Heading toward Jerusalem, Jesus, the divine Vinedresser, continues to dig and dung the fig tree. Again, a discourse follows a question by someone from one of the crowds that He was teaching. This may have been occasioned by teaching akin to the two parables that we have just looked at, in which the empire of God is said to be small at the outset. We do not know for sure. But we do know that someone asked whether **only a few persons will be saved** (v. 23). Jesus' reply indicates that true believers, though not necessarily only a **few**, would be in the minority. Though the empire would permeate the entire earth so that some from every tribe and kindred and nation would be saved, nevertheless, there would be no worldwide turning of the majority of the people on the earth to Christ, as some post millennialists think.

There are two **doors** (though here, Jesus mentions only the one): one wide, the other narrow. Jesus doesn't tell them to enter the wide door, but the **narrow** one. Why? Because there are **many who** enter the wide door but only **few** who enter the **narrow** one. Here, He says that there are **many who try to enter but won't be able to.** That is to say, they take a route that they think will lead to it, but it only leads into eternal death. This is the way of the proud, hypocritical Pharisee who trusts in his own works rather than coming in repentance and faith to Jesus Christ.

Like the ark door that was shut, the time will come; then the **door** to eternal life will be locked. But then it will be too late, even though those who have finally found the right door will knock and cry out for admis-

Christian Counselor's Commentary

25 When the Householder gets up and shuts the door you will begin to stand at the door and knock, saying, "Lord, open the door for us." But He will answer, saying, "I don't know where you came from."
26 Then you will begin to say, "We ate and drank with you and you taught in our streets."
27 But He will speak these words to you: "I don't know where you came from. **Leave Me, all you workers of unrighteousness!**"
28 There will be weeping and gnashing of teeth when you see Abraham and Isaac and Jacob and all of the prophets in God's empire, but yourselves thrown out.
29 People from the east and west and from the north and south will come and recline at the table in God's empire.
30 Then some who are last will be first, and some who are first will be last.

---

sion. But it will be too late. The householder will say, "**I don't know where you came from**." That is to say, they came to the door of heaven by some other road than the right one. Jesus said, "**I am the way, no one comes to the Father but by Me**." They will say, "We know You; you were with us, teaching in our streets. Why we even ate and drank with You. We are Jews." But the Householder will say, "**Leave Me, all you workers of unrighteousness**" (v. 27). The Jews, at that time, will **weep** and wail when they are separated from the faithful fathers of the nation (v. 28). But they will be **thrown out** as they clamor for entrance! And instead, Gentiles from every part of the globe will be admitted through faith. And though they were last, some will be given the first place, and visa versa (v. 30). There is no doubt that this is hard teaching, but it is vital. Warning is a large part of what Jesus is doing as He digs and dungs the fig tree to see if it will produce fruit. Counselors must not hesitate to teach and urge hard things whenever remaining true to the Word of God demands it. Warning is vital in counseling. Give it—with all the intensity that is necessary to whatever it is that you are warning the counselee about. I think that you will agree that in this passage Jesus pulls out all the stops and sounds a clear note.

At that very time some Pharisees came and said, "**Leave**, Herod is after you to kill you." They were probably trying to get rid of Christ and His teaching by relaying this message. They thought that this would frighten Jesus so that He would flee. But Jesus answers, "**Go tell that fox that I have work to do, and I will complete it. I will do as I planned, going**

31 During that very hour some Pharisees came to Him and said, "Leave here and go someplace else, because Herod wants to kill you."
32 He said to them,
>Go tell that fox, "Today and tomorrow I am going to cast out demons and do healings, and on the third day I will finish My work.
33 Nevertheless, I have to keep going today and tomorrow and on the following day, because it simply couldn't be that a prophet should perish outside of Jerusalem!"
34 Jerusalem, Jerusalem, that kills the prophets and stones those who are sent to her! How often I wanted to gather your children as a hen gathers her chicks under her wings—but you didn't want Me to.

---

from town to town where the seventy have preceded me, and on **the third day I will finish My work** (v. 33). Nothing Herod, cunning though he may be, can do will deter me. The time is short, but I will teach and heal as I have planned regardless of what he may do. After all (said sarcastically but truly), I must go to **Jerusalem** because **it simply couldn't be that a prophet should perish outside of Jerusalem**" (v. 33).

That Christ should "call names" and use sarcasm is astounding to some. Evidently, the Reformers were not appalled by it, as some wimpy Christians are today; they did too! Why shouldn't Jesus use the name of an animal to refer to Herod *if the name fits*? It is a powerful way to point out a characteristic that is outstanding in both Herod and a fox is similar. He never calls names unless it is appropriate to do so. Nor does He use sarcasm inappropriately. But used properly, sarcasm is also a powerful way of making a point.

Again Jesus uses the incident to appeal to those around Him (vv. 34, 35). Every counselor must become astute at doing the same. In this appeal Jesus bares His soul (something that the clinical counselor would never dream of doing). He expresses His dismay and grief at the response of those who live in Jerusalem. In tearful words He informs them that His ministry has been aimed at **gathering** the little **chicks** of Israel under His wings, but they refused to come to Him. And now, as a result, the temple (**house**) has been **forsaken** by the Shekinah glory; it is doomed. Over its door is now written ICHABOD ("the glory is departed").

What does Jesus mean when He goes on to say, **"you won't see Me again until you say, 'Happy is He Who comes in the Lord's name?'"** He is saying that they **would not see Him** (in the sense of see Him for

35		Now, your house is forsaken. And I tell you, you won't see Me again until you say, "**Happy is He Who comes in the Lord's name!**"

Who He is) until they, in faith, utter those words. Some would do so meaningfully at the triumphal entry; many would when Peter preached (Acts 2ff.).

The tender, wooing note of verse 34 along with the strong words earlier in the chapter show that Jesus ranged over the entire gamut of emotions in His ministry and appealed through threat, warning and entreaty. Counselors should do no less in seeking to help counselees do that which will glorify God and bless themselves.

Chapter 14

1 One Sabbath, when He went to eat at the house of one of the leaders of the Pharisees, they were carefully watching Him,
2 and right there before Him was a man with dropsy.
3 So Jesus spoke to the teachers of the law and to the Pharisees, saying, "Is it or isn't it lawful to heal on the Sabbath?"
4 But they kept quiet. So He took him, healed him, and told him to go.
5 And to them He said, "Which one of you is there who has a son or an ox that has fallen into a well, who won't pull him up on a Sabbath day?"

The chapter begins where the last left off. There is no logical reason for the division. We see Jesus going to **eat** at the home of another **Pharisee** (perhaps this one was not quite as hostile as those to which we were previously introduced). It was probably in another town that the following account took place. This Pharisee was the **ruler** of the local synagog. Those who were in attendance were **watching** Him **carefully**. Probably, there were some who followed Him from place to place hoping for some word or act by which they could condemn Him. There will be people like that who watch your every move as a Christian counselor in order to find some inconsistency, false statement, etc. You cannot avoid developing enemies who will do such things if you counsel biblically and if you oppose false systems of counseling.

Suddenly, there was standing there a man with **dropsy**. Anyone was allowed to attend these semipublic affairs to listen and to watch, if not to participate in the feast. Evidently this man just wandered in. This time, before doing anything, Jesus put the question to those He knew would object: **"Is it or isn't it lawful to heal on the Sabbath?"** It was the crucial point at which the differences between Jesus' understanding of the law and theirs erupted. **They kept quiet.** So Jesus **healed him** and told him to go.

When they had no response to make, Jesus demonstrated what He taught as the answer to His question by healing the man. When He took hold of the man, it was clear that even this physical effort put forth was not a violation of the Sabbath—as God viewed it (vv. 1-4).

Now Jesus reasons with them, putting a slightly different twist upon the illustration that He had just used on a previous occasion. He asks if any of them who had a **son** or even an **ox** that had **fallen** into the shaft of a **well** would refrain from **pulling him out** on the Sabbath. Of course, they

Christian Counselor's Commentary

6   But they couldn't reply to this.

7   Then He told a parable to those who were invited, when He noticed how they chose the chief seats, saying to them:

8   When you are invited by anyone to a marriage feast, don't recline in the chief seat, because a more distinguished person than you may have been invited,

9   and the one who invited you and him will have to say to you, "Give this guest your place." Then, humiliated, you will have to start all over by taking the last place.

10   Rather, when you are invited, go and sit in the last place, so that when the one who invited you comes he may say to you, "Friend, go up higher." Then you will be honored before all those who recline at the table with you.

11   Everybody who exalts himself will be humbled, and everybody who humbles himself will be exalted.

---

would not do so. So no one answered this question either. This time it wasn't simply that they wouldn't answer; they **couldn't** (v. 6). Having dealt with that matter in so summary a fashion, Jesus went on. Often, before an issue arises, if it seems likely that it will, it is wise to get the jump on others and deal with it. This allows you to go on to the things that you want to address.

Jesus now raises the matter of pride and position—a serious problem for many in places of leadership (vv. 7-11). He speaks of those who take the **chief seat**s at a feast (probably there had been the usual shuffle to do so at this very banquet). He makes the point that it is embarrassing to do so, if one must be told to move since someone **more distinguished** than you must have it. He made it clear that it is better to take the **last** place and have your host tell you to take a **higher** position. He was not saying that they should do this as a *technique*, in order to "set up" the honor that it would bring. Too many Christians are willing to obey God *only as a means for* obtaining some desired end—not to please Him. Rather, He meant that they would take the **last** seat sincerely willing to remain there. And then, if the host thinks they should be in a more distinguished seat, he will invite them to go forward and take it. Let others decide the question, not you yourself. That is the point.

Many counselees think more highly of themselves than they ought to think. If they would apply this story to themselves it would go a long way toward keeping them out of the sorts of difficulties into which they insert themselves by their proud attitudes. Last night at a home to which I was

Luke 14

12 Then He said to the one who had invited Him
When you give a dinner or supper, don't invite your friends or your brothers or your relatives or rich neighbors. Otherwise, they also may invite you in return and you will be repaid.
13 Instead, when you give a party, invite the poor, the maimed, the lame, the blind,
14 and you will be happy, because they can't repay you and you will be repaid in the resurrection of the just.

---

invited for a meal, along with other guests, one woman dominated the conversation, most of the time talking about matters of interest to her but to no one else. She was loud and loquacious. Presumably she was unaware of the fool that she was making of herself. One thing is for sure, she will probably get no more invitations from those who were present. She didn't have to "take the chief seat" literally; she simply assumed that wherever she sat *was* the chief seat!

In verses 12 through 14 Jesus goes on to set forth another principle that covers another matter common to many people. He is dealing with the "I'll scratch your back if you will scratch mine" principle. When you give a dinner, He says, you shouldn't invite those who can invite you in return *in order to repay* you. That is wrong. Rather, He says, with obvious but striking hyperbole, "**invite the poor, the maimed, the lame, the blind**—people who have no way of doing so. The repayment you receive will be from God when those who have been justified are raised from the dead."

Did Jesus mean that you should never invite **relatives** or **rich friends**? Did He mean that you must always invite people who fit the categories mentioned in verse 13? Of course not. He was vividly making a point—as He often did—by means of hyperbole (overstatement). While I am sure that from time to time He would want you to include such people as those mentioned in verse 13, He meant simply that your purpose in inviting and selecting guests ought not to be in order that they will invite you in return. We see this insidious principle at work in a variety of ways. Take the sending of Christmas cards. Some people keep a list of those who sent one to them the previous year and send cards only to *them*. There is the *quid pro quo* principle at work with a vengeance—even in so small a matter!

Again, in verses 15 through 24 we see Jesus giving a discourse that grows out of an interruption from someone else (see the last chapter for comments on this). The observation of the person speaking was that **The**

Christian Counselor's Commentary

15 When one of those who reclined at the table with Him heard this, he said to Him, "The one who eats bread in God's empire will be happy."
16 But He said to him,
A certain man gave a large banquet and invited many people.
17 Then he sent his slave at the time of the banquet to tell those who had been invited, "Come; everything is now ready."
18 But they all alike began to make excuses. The first said, "I have bought a farm, and I must go out to see it. I ask you to excuse me."
19 Another said, "I have bought five yoke of oxen and I am on my way to test them. I ask you to excuse me."
20 And another said, "I have just been married, so obviously I can't come."
21 The slave went back and reported this to his lord. Then the householder grew angry and told his slave, "Go out quickly into the city streets and lanes and bring in here the poor and maimed and blind and lame."
22 Then the slave said, "Lord, what you ordered has been done, but there is still room."
23 So the lord said to the slave, "Go out into the highways and hedges and compel them to come in, so that my house may be filled.

---

one who eats bread in God's empire will be happy. This gives Jesus an opening to set forth a parable (that seems to have been developed and used on the spot). He says that to do so is like a certain man who **gave a large banquet** and sent invitations to many people. According to the custom, when it was ready, he sent slaves to inform them saying, "**Come; everything is now ready**." But they all made **excuses** why they couldn't come (the fact was that they didn't *want* to come). All of the excuses were lame, full of holes (they didn't even have respect enough to come up with more convincing ones!). No one **looks** at a **farm** *after* he has purchased it! No one **proves** whether **oxen** are any good *after* he purchases them. The fellow who had just been married had the most valid excuse, but even then, it was not very good!

Hearing their replies, the host sent his slave out into the **city streets** and the **lanes** to bring in the same kinds of people as those mentioned in verse 13. He did. But there were not enough to fill the seats (v. 22). He then told the slave to go farther afield and **compel people to come in**. He was determined that his house would be **full** (not one of God's elect will be missing)! Those who made excuses would not get so much as a **taste**

Luke 14

24	I tell you, none of those men who were invited will get a taste of my banquet."
25	Large crowds accompanied Him. Turning to them He said,
26	If anybody comes to Me but doesn't hate his father and mother and wife and children and brothers and sisters, and even his own life too, he can't be My disciple.
27	Whoever doesn't carry his own cross and come after Me can't be My disciple.

---

of the banquet!

That is what it is like to be invited to eat in the empire of God. One must come and not make excuses. Excuses have been made by sinners since the garden of Eden when Adam and Eve tried to excuse their sin. Sinners have this tendency inborn as a part of their sinful natures. Even after becoming Christians, the patterns by which it is manifested persist and counselors must deal with it. They may take no excuses for failure to obey the commands of God's Word.

Here, the two groups represent the Jews and the Gentiles. Perhaps the twofold invitation to those in the streets, and later to those at a greater distance, reflect the picture in Acts where, after being given in Judea, the invitation to God's banquet of salvation is extended to Samaria and then to the uttermost parts of the earth.

A later discourse, presumably outside, concludes the chapter. Turning to the **large crowds** that followed Him, Jesus spoke of the cost involved in becoming one of His disciples (vv. 25-35). It is not merely an invitation to a banquet which is all fun and games (too often people are invited to trust Christ in that very manner). No, while there will be much joy, there also will be hardship and sacrifice involved.

In much the same vein as He spoke earlier about creating division in homes, Jesus now says that one must **hate** family, wife and himself or he can't be His disciple. This again is hyperbole. What He is getting at, by this striking word, is that one must put Him before anyone else. He must love Jesus more—even than himself. This is an emphasis rarely found in counseling rooms today. Its note needs to be sounded far more often and clearly. "So there is trouble?" the biblical counselor asks. "What did you expect? Jesus didn't promise you a rose garden, did He?"

He goes further. One must **carry his own cross** (v. 27). The cross was an instrument of death. To carry it was to take it to the place where the one doing so would be crucified on it. To follow Jesus, then, is to be willing to put to death one's own desires and **come after** Him (that is, do

Christian Counselor's Commentary

28 Which of you, wanting to build a tower, doesn't first sit down and count the cost, to determine whether he has funds to complete it?
29 Otherwise, when he has laid the foundation and isn't able to go beyond that to finish it, all who see it will make fun of him,
30 saying, "This man began but wasn't able to finish."
31 Or what king, going to battle against another king, doesn't sit down first and determine whether with 10,000 men he is able to meet the one who is coming against him with 20,000.
32 If he isn't, while the other is still far away he will send envoys to ask for terms of peace.
33 So then, every one of you who doesn't say good-bye to all of his possessions can't be My disciple.
34 Salt is fine, but even salt—if it has lost its taste—how can it be seasoned?
35 It isn't fit for the ground or for the manure pile; so people throw it away. Whoever has ears to hear, let him listen.

His will rather than one's own; follow His lead). In verses 28 through 30 Jesus uses the first of two examples to illustrate His point (note, once more, the use of multiple example). No one builds a **tower** until after he has calculated the **cost**. Otherwise he might run out of funds and have to quit after laying the **foundation**, and people will **make fun of him**. The second makes a similar point. A **king** first determines the odds in terms of troops, supplies, etc., before going to **war**. If his figuring has misfired, and he discovers so, when he and his enemy are yet **far** apart he **sends envoys** who sue for **peace**. In other words, understand that to become a member of the empire of God will cost. It is freely entered but, once having done so by faith, the believer begins to see that it costs everything (cf. v. 33). One must be willing to surrender all to Christ and to His use.

Finally, a motivational word about salt is appended. **Salt is fine.** But if it loses its tang by mixture with other things, it is useless since there is nothing with which to **season** it. People throw it away. If someone comes to Christ (outwardly) and that is all, his profession of faith isn't genuine. Soon it becomes clear that he is not **salt** at all, but a mixture of everything else. The saltiness with which he previously seemed to be endued was not real, so he will be cast off. He never was a true believer.

CHAPTER 15

1 Now the tax collectors and sinners were coming near to listen to Him.
2 But the Pharisees and the scribes grumbled, saying, "This person welcomes sinners and eats with them."
3 So He told them this parable:
4 Which one of you people, if he has a hundred sheep and has lost one of them, wouldn't leave the ninety-nine in the desert and search for the lost sheep until he finds it?
5 Then when he finds it, he puts it on his shoulders, rejoicing.
6 When he comes home he calls his friends and neighbors together and says to them, "Rejoice with me! I have found my sheep that was lost."
7 I tell you that in just that way there will be more joy in heaven over one sinner who repents than over ninety-nine righteous persons who have no need for repentance.
8 Or what woman who has ten silver coins, if she loses one, doesn't light a lamp and sweep the house and carefully look for it until she finds it?
9 Then when she finds it, she calls together those women who are her friends and neighbors and says "Rejoice with me! I found the silver coin that I lost."

The fifteenth chapter of Luke is commonly known as "The Lost and Found Chapter." That, of course, is because of the three things lost that were found (the lost sheep, coin and son). It has also been a prime passage for Gospel preachers who have not only preached about how to be saved from each of these stories but have also been known to preach a series of sermons on the third. Unfortunately, both of these assumptions about the purpose and use of the passage are false.

First, it is not the lost and found chapter. Certainly, things lost are found. But to emphasize that fact as primary is to miss the Savior's point. The chapter rather is the Lost SOUGHT FOR, Found and REJOICED OVER Chapter. The thrust is not to emphasize that Christ saves (though that is implicit in the background) but that He SEEKS the lost who, when they are found are REJOICED OVER by heaven, and ought to be by earth.

The Pharisees and scribes **grumbled** because Jesus welcomed and **ate** with sinners (v. 2). In other words, they were unwilling to receive

Christian Counselor's Commentary

10   I tell you that in just that way there is joy in the presence of God's angels over one sinner who repents.
11   And He continued,
       A certain man had two sons.
12   The younger said to his father, "Father, give me my share of the property that is coming to me." So he divided his possessions between them.
13   Now it wasn't long before the younger son gathered together everything he owned and left for a country far away. And there he squandered his possessions in wild living.
14   When he had spent everything, there was a bad famine throughout that country, and he began to be in need.
15   So he went out and got a job with a citizen of that country, who sent him into his fields to feed pigs.
16   And he longed to fill his stomach with the pods that the pigs were eating, but nobody gave him anything.
17   But when he came to himself, he said, "How many of my father's hired servants have more than enough bread, while I am perishing here in this famine!
18   I'm going to get up and go to my father and say to him, 'Father, I sinned against heaven and before you.
19   I'm no longer worthy to be called your son. Treat me as one of your hired servants.'"

---

those who had led lives of open sin—they snubbed such persons (as legalists generally do) and thought anyone who preached to them and tried to win them was to be disdained too. It was to expose and denounce that attitude that Jesus told these three stories.

The second error in the understanding of the chapter is that too often the three stories are presented as if they were three separate parables. That is not so. In verse 3 we read, **So He told them this parable**. Get that clearly fixed in mind—*this* **parable**—there is only one. It is a three-part parable with a twist at the end. Three times Jesus says the same thing from different perspectives. First a **shepherd** loses a sheep, he searches for and finds it, and then he gathers his fellow shepherds together and they rejoice. The same is true of the **woman** who loses and finds her coin. She too gathers her female friends and they hold a hen party. Finally, the same is true of the **father** who also looks for his son and one day, seeing him afar off, runs to him. He then throws a huge party to rejoice over the son who was lost but now is found. At the conclusion of each of these stories

Luke 15

20	So he got up and went away to his father.
	Now while he was still at a distance his father saw him and was moved with compassion for him. So he ran to him and hugged and kissed him.
21	But the son said to him, "Father, I have sinned against heaven and before you. I am no longer worthy to be called your son...."
22	But the father said to his slaves, "Quickly, bring out the best robe and clothe him. And put a ring on his hand and sandals on his feet,
23	and bring the fattened calf and slaughter it, and let us eat and celebrate.
24	This son of mine was dead and is alive again; he was lost and is found." So they began to celebrate.
25	Now his older son was in the field, and as he came in and drew near to the house he heard music and dancing.
26	So he called one of the servants and asked him what was happening.
27	So he said to him, "Your brother has come, and your father killed the fattened calf because he has returned safe and sound."
28	Then he grew angry and didn't want to go in. So his father went out and begged him.

---

the listener could do little more than shake his head in assent. "Yes, that's what shepherds do. Yes, that's what women do. Yes, that's what fathers do." But suddenly, as a jarring interruption to the rhythm that has been set up by the three stories, the elder brother enters. He, like the scribes and Pharisees, grumbles and grouses about the treatment his brother is getting. He is sullen and unwilling to **rejoice**. That is the point of the three-part parable with the kicker at the end. The elder brother is out of sync with reality. He is self-centered and cares nothing for his brother. There is no love in his heart for him or for his father. He is like the Pharisees and the scribes.

Jesus had come to seek and to save that which was lost. Publicans and sinners flocked to hear the life saving message He preached. They were being saved. Jesus was rejoicing over this. Even the **angels** in heaven **rejoiced**. This rejoicing was the only proper thing to do—but the religious leaders complained rather than rejoiced. *They* were the elder brother. And Jesus condemned them for their attitude toward Him, toward God and toward poor sinners who were repenting.

Counselors will meet the very same attitude today. If someone

Christian Counselor's Commentary

29 But he answered, "Think of it! For so many years I have served you like a slave and never disobeyed a command of yours, but you never even gave me a goat so that I could celebrate with my friends.

30 But when this son of yours, who has devoured your possessions with prostitutes, returned, you killed the fattened calf for him!"

31 Then he replied, "Son, you are always with me; so everything that I have is yours.

32 It was right for us to celebrate and rejoice, because this brother of yours was dead and is alive again; he was lost and is found."

---

repents, there will be those who will stand off from them. There will be those who will question their sincerity. There will be some who will evidence a sour grapes attitude about it all. They will refuse to accept them into their fellowship, look down on them and, in some cases, even regret that any such thing has taken place. Such persons need to hear the real message of the passage which, if it is not denuded by a misapplication of its purpose, is powerful in exposing such bitterness. Counselor, use it for that purpose. Don't weaken the chapter by merely making it present the gospel. The gospel is there, surely, but there is more. The gospel and how people respond to its converts is the subject. Tell counselees who act like the elder brother that they must get in sync with the angels of heaven!

CHAPTER 16

1 Then He also said this to His disciples:
There was a certain rich man who had a steward, and a complaint that he was wasting his goods was made against him.
2 So he called him and said to him, "What is this I hear about you? Give an account of your stewardship. You can't be my steward any longer."
3 Then the steward said to himself, "What am I going to do, now that my lord is taking away the position of steward from me? I'm not physically up to digging; I'm ashamed to beg. . . .
4 I know what I'll do, so that when I am removed from my position as steward others will welcome me into their houses."
5 So he called in his lord's debtors one by one. He said to the first, "How much do you owe my lord?"
6 He replied, "One hundred barrels of oil.'" Then he told him, "Take your bill and sit down quickly and make it fifty."
7 Then, to another he said, "How much do you owe?" And he replied, "One hundred sacks of wheat." He told him, "Take your bill and write eighty."
8 The lord commended the dishonest steward because of his shrewd action. The sons of this age are more shrewd with people of their own kind than are the sons of light.

There are many items of interest to counselors in this chapter. I shall attempt to mention, if not discuss, all of them. The chapter opens with Jesus talking to His disciples. It would be interesting to locate all such places in order to discover what matters Jesus considered to be of importance to the apostles, part of whose task it was to counsel new converts in the churches that they founded. Having done so, it would be of value, perhaps, to concentrate on those items from the list that pertained directly to counseling. Having done so, a book detailing the results of such a study might be published with profit. Anyone reading want to take on the task?

At any rate, in verses 1 through 9 Jesus tells the parable of the shrewd **steward** (the emphasis isn't on his **dishonesty**, but on his **shrewdness**, cf. v. 8). Those who stress the former err. The only reason for the mention of the **dishonesty** is to set up the story.

What is Jesus teaching you and me as He teaches His disciples? Simply this: believers are to use **money** for the purpose of winning people into the faith and blessing those who are won. The *steward knew how to*

Christian Counselor's Commentary

> 9 So I tell you, make friends for yourselves with the mammon of dishonesty, so that when it fails they will welcome you into the eternal dwellings.
> 10 Whoever is trustworthy about smaller things is trustworthy about larger ones, but the one who is dishonest about smaller things is dishonest about larger ones.
> 11 So then, if you haven't been trustworthy about dishonest mammon, who will entrust the true riches to you?

---

use money for his advantage. His idea was by it to place others in his debt so that they would care for him when he was fired. Now, although that isn't the purpose for using money as a Christian, it makes the point that if one spends his money rightly, to help others and bless them, he will find that when he gets to heaven he will be heartily welcomed by them. Thus, that which is so often used for evil purposes, if used discreetly according to biblical principles, may be turned to good use. **Mammon** (that "pile" is the meaning of the term; it is akin to our expression, "He made a pile.") is a problem. Money, *per se*, is not the problem; it is one's attitude toward and consequent use of it.

Few passages could be of more help in dealing with selfish, money hoarding or (on the other hand) money squandering Christians. You will want to turn to this passage frequently. You can also echo the shaming observation that it is a pity unbelievers know how to use money better than believers (v. 8). One thing—when you use this passage, don't get bogged down in the details of the steward's sin. Make it clear that this is simply the supporting material for the story (there would be none without it). Rather, as we have tried to do here, having said so much, go on to the point of the parable.

In verses 10 through 13 Jesus continues His observations about money, setting forth both principles for its use and warnings about its misuse. First a principle: those who prove themselves **trustworthy** in **smaller** matters will be **trustworthy** about **larger** ones and visa versa (v. 10). If one will take risks and put himself in jeopardy about small matters (which will profit him little) he is altogether likely to risk being caught taking risks about larger ones. If a Christian can't be proven trustworthy in his use of money (the smaller thing) then who will entrust the ministry of the Word (true riches) to him (v. 11). On this point refer to the qualifications for church officers in Timothy and Titus. The principle in verse 10, however, is larger than the context. It does not refer to money alone. It is an aphorism which has a life of its own and which may be applied to any

Luke 16

12   If you haven't been trustworthy about somebody else's things, who will give you anything for yourself?

13   No servant can serve two lords; he is going to hate one and love the other or be devoted to one and despise the other. You can't serve both God and mammon.

14 The Pharisees, who were money-lovers, heard these words and they made fun of Him.

---

number of circumstances. You might find yourself applying it as Jesus did in verse 11 when He spoke of the ministry of the true riches of God. Here, also, is a self-examining passage that should be of great importance to every counselor. How do you handle money? How do you handle small matters of all sorts? If not well, should you be doing counseling until you are sure that you have learned the lesson of this passage? It is so easy to take advantage of helpless, needy, trusting counselees! There is little question that many have misused counseling for their own benefit. If you traced their history back to a time prior to their counseling you would find them untrustworthy in smaller things.

Moreover, Jesus goes on to apply the principle, with a twist, to one's use of other's things (v. 12). People will soon find you out, and you will lose out! The same is true of serving God. If you wish to serve Him, you must use what He lends you as a steward in His ways.

Finally, the concluding word (v. 13). A counselor may not **serve** God and **mammon**. What you live for is your God. If you live for money, money is your God. You are not living for the true God. This is a warning apropos to counselor and to counselee. For instance, the minute you find yourself prolonging a counseling case for the sake of money you should judge yourself unfit for such ministry. You must repent and put God first. Power, as well as money, can take the place of God.

Often there is a choice to be made in the counseling room; you must call yourself and your counselees to choose God rather than mammon. **You cannot serve two masters.** One will take the uppermost place over the other. When anyone comes to the place where he tries to serve God and money as his masters, inevitably, he ends up serving money and despising God. This is serious business.

In verse 14, we encounter another interruption from **Pharisees** who must have been listening in to Jesus' words to His disciples. Being **money-lovers** who would cheat an orphan or widow if they could squeeze money out of her, they **made fun of Him**. So, in one blistering word, Jesus sets them straight (v. 15). He tells them that they may have their way

Christian Counselor's Commentary

> 15 So He said to them,
>> You are those who justify yourselves before people; but God knows your hearts. That which is highly valued by people is an abomination before God.
>> **16** The Law and the Prophets were preached until John; from his time on, God's empire has been preached, and everybody has been pressing into it.
> 17 But it is easier for heaven and earth to pass away than for one dot of the law to fall from it.

---

of **justifying** their greed and thieving hypocrisy before others in order to look good, but that they cannot fool God. He knows their **hearts**. And He makes it clear that the judgment of sinful people is not the standard God uses to judge what is good and evil. He judges the thoughts and the intents of the heart, not outward words and actions. And what sinful hypocrites **highly value**, He counts an **abomination**. Frequently counselors must challenge the value systems of their counselees. It is all too often that they will find that the acquisition of money is driving them. This is wrong—and an abominable way to live—says Jesus. That kind of strong word may best be leveled by quoting this section of Scripture to them. On the subject of the use and abuse of money, it is wise to have an exposition and application of I Timothy 6 ready at hand as well.

The transition from the discussion of money to the two verses that follow (vv. 16, 17) is not obvious. For all of their touted reverence for God's **law**, the Pharisees had invented ways of getting around its provisions. They thought up ways of **justifying** their greed and lust. Thus, they adopted a standard of conduct that, while purporting to show respect for the law, was a way of violating it. Now, the Old Testament order, and the order they had built on top of it, was passing away, and they could do nothing to stop it. Since the coming of John the Baptist, people were **pressing** to get into God's **empire**, which was Daniel's fifth empire. The Pharisees were losing their grip on the people—and their money! Yet, the preaching of this new empire that Jesus had come to bring, and of which He would as the God-man become the Emperor, would not mean an overthrowing of the Old Testament revelation; it would be the renewal of a proper understanding of it that scraped away all the pharisaical additions that now covered it like barnacles. It would be easier for the universe to disappear than for one small jot of God's Word to do so.

How important this is for those counselees who want to discard this or that commandment of the Bible because it disagrees with their thinking

Luke 16

18 Whoever divorces his wife and marries another commits adultery, and the one who marries a divorced woman commits adultery.
19 Now there was a certain rich man who used to put on a purple robe and fine linen and celebrate in style every day.
20 And a certain poor man named Lazarus, covered with sores, was laid at his gate every day.
21 He longed to be filled with the scraps that fell from the rich man's table. The dogs even came and licked his sores.
22 Now it came about that the poor man died, and he was carried away by the angels to recline at the place closest to Abraham. And the rich man died and was buried.
23 And in the unseen world, where he was suffering torment, he raised his eyes and saw Abraham far off and Lazarus close to him.
24 So he called out, saying, "Father Abraham, show mercy toward me and send Lazarus to dip the tip of his finger in water and cool my tongue with it. I'm suffering in this flame."

---

or it hampers their sinful actions. Verse 17, therefore, is a good one to use for those who would attempt to do so by some specious justification of their own making. Misuse and misapplication of Scripture is rife in the church, and among counselees it may be even more prevalent.

Then, in verse 18, which seems to come out of nowhere, Jesus gives an example of what He has just said. The teachings of the Scriptures about **divorce** still hold—even though the Pharisees had many ways to weaken them. Failure to interpret and follow biblical teaching about divorce and remarriage in Deuteronomy 24 correctly is an instance in which the accretions of the elders had made God's word "of no effect." It needed to be scraped clean of all such barnacles and understood aright. What it taught is that **marriage** after **divorce** for improper reasons is **adultery**. For more on this see my book, *Marriage, Divorce and Remarriage in the Bible*. Counselors must be ready to deal with all aspects of marriage and divorce. This is not a day in which they can hide their heads in the sand and hope that such problems will go away. The problems connected with these issues are everywhere—in the church as well as without.

The chapter closes with the story of **the rich man and Lazarus** (vv. 19-31). The fact that it does makes it abundantly plain that Jesus has not yet finished His discussion of money and the evils of making it one's God. The rich man had become the **slave** of money. **Lazarus**, without riches, had put his trust in the true God. The **rich man**, then, was like the Pharisees who laughed at the notion that money wasn't to be highly valued.

25	But Abraham said, "Son, remember that you received your good things in your lifetime, and in the same way Lazarus received bad things. But now he is comforted, and you are suffering.
26	Moreover, between us and you a great gulf has been firmly fixed, so that those who want to pass from here can't, nor those who want to cross over from there to us."
27	He said, "I ask you then, father, to send him to my father's house,
28	because I have five brothers. Send him to warn them, so that they won't come to this place of torment too."
29	But Abraham said, "They have Moses and the Prophets; let them listen to them."
30	But he said, "No, father Abraham. But if somebody from the dead goes to them, they will repent."
31	Then he replied, "If they won't listen to Moses and the Prophets, they won't be persuaded even if somebody rises from the dead."

They both die. They enter into the eternal state consciously existing after death in the **unseen world,** the one in **torment**, the other reclining next to **Abraham**, in bliss. The separation between them is permanent and impassable; Lazarus cannot reach the sufferer in order to come to his aid. The rich man pleads with Abraham to send Lazarus to warn his five brothers about the torment so that they won't end up in the same way he has. Abraham says that they won't believe even though one rises from the dead (they didn't when Jesus did!). And then he reminds him that they have the Scriptures—God has given them all they need to know to be saved—and says, **"Let them listen to Moses and the Prophets."**

When counselees seek to find God's will from sources outside the Bible, turn them to verse 29. All they need for life and godliness may be found there. Experience—even of a miraculous sort—would be of no additional value if they reject the Bible. The Pharisees were justifying their love of riches; they could not be talked out of such greed even by a risen Lazarus! They had all that God had told them in the Bible about loving Him rather than money, but they refused to listen to Moses and the Prophets.

Chapter 17

> **1** Then He said to His disciples,
> Stumbling blocks are sure to come, but woe to the one through whom they come!
> **2** It would be better for him if a millstone were hung around his neck and he were thrown into the sea than that he should be the occasion for one of these little ones to stumble.
> **3** Be on your guard. If your brother sins, rebuke him; if he repents, forgive him.

Jesus now speaks to His disciples (a larger group than the twelve, who are addressed in v. 5ff.). He is incensed at the attitudes of the Pharisees expressed in the preceding chapters. Doubtless, temptations to sin (**stumbling blocks**) would **come**; His disciples would be tempted to believe the criticisms directed at those who seek to promote the truth. And criticisms would come. Of that, there is no question. Counselors must mention this fact to counselees and warn them about those who would like to stop them from doing as God requires.

"But," says He, "**woe to the one through whom they come!**" That is a strong statement. Keep it in mind to use whenever dealing with those who would lead your counselees away from the way, the truth and the life. This strong statement had to do with the Pharisees who would do anything they could to estrange these weak, young disciples from the Lord Jesus Christ. The statement is even further strengthened by the words of verse 2. Anyone who gives occasion for a new convert to stumble and fall into disbelief or some other sin is treading on exceedingly dangerous ground! Don't hesitate to tell him so whenever necessary.

But because offenses will come, it is necessary for the brothers in Christ to know how to deal with them whenever they occur. The discussions of forgiveness that follow outline what the Lord wants them to know about this.

Jesus begins His discussion with a word of warning: "**be on your guard**" (v. 3^a). Not only must one guard himself from the temptations that unbelievers will pose, but he must guard from too hasty an understanding of what to do about them. Jesus is about to say some very difficult things—not difficult to understand, but difficult to do. You will find many counselees ready to balk when they understand what God requires of them. Persist; don't take "no" for an answer. We are dealing here with

Christian Counselor's Commentary

> 4   And if he sins against you seven times a day and returns to you seven times, saying, "I repent," forgive him.

commands. These are not optional matters.

In verse 3 Jesus goes on to say, "**If your brother sins, rebuke him; if he repents forgive him**." Here is the beginning salvo He shot in the all-important war Jesus waged against confusion, bitterness and the like among Christian brothers. Forgiveness is the oil that keeps the church, the home, the Christian school running smoothly. Lack of it means grit in the machinery. Forgiveness is so important a matter in counseling that it is rare when a case does not involve the need for it in some manner or other. It is absolutely essential, therefore, to understand and teach biblical principles of forgiveness in counseling. Most counselees fail to understand these and you will find that, instead, they have been taught all sorts of non-biblical ideas. They will have notions that bear little resemblance to the biblical data (like forgive persons whether they repent or not). That is one reason why this chapter is so vital.

If one has been sinned against, that obligates *him*. That is the first thing that makes forgiveness difficult. A counselee asks, "Why does that obligate me? I didn't do anything wrong." Well, to begin with, you are obligated because Jesus says so. That, in itself, ought to be sufficient. He says *you* are to respond by **rebuking** the one who wronged you. You cannot simply stand there in all your self-righteous anger saying, "Well, let him come to me!" No, you must go to him. "Why?" Well, think about it. It is possible that he may have not understood that you were offended. And indeed, you may have misunderstood the action. Then, it would be important to iron out that misunderstanding by going. If you don't, he may never know that you took offense. But even if the offense against you is obviously such that both of you know it is an offense and is taken that way, he needs to be brought to repentance. Unless you go and confront him about the matter, the two of you may simply drift apart carrying bitterness on the one hand and a self-assured smugness on the other. That will not do. You must go to him and gently rebuke him in love. Direct counselees to do so whenever it is necessary.

But then, there is the rest of the verse: **if he repents, forgive him**. That is even harder to do. "Harder?" you ask. Yes. "It seems that it would be easier than rebuking him." Well, let's continue: **If he sins against you seven times a day and returns to you seven times, saying, "I repent," forgive him**. That's hard! That means that if he hits you on the nose seven

Luke 17

5   Then the apostles said to the Lord, "Increase our faith!"
6   But the Lord said,
> If you have faith like a mustard seed, you could say to this mulberry tree, "Be uprooted and be planted in the sea," and it would obey you.

---

times and returns seven times the same day asking for forgiveness, you *must* grant it. Your tendency will be to say, "Once, yes. Twice, maybe. Three times—unh unh!" Jesus says, however, that that attitude is unacceptable.

"But if he keeps on doing it, how can he be repentant? Shouldn't we wait to see if there is evidence of the repentance before forgiving? Surely there ought to be fruit."

The point is that Jesus says you must do so **seven** times in the *same* day. That doesn't allow time enough for fruit to grow. It takes time to change, and it may take extensive help in counseling. You can't give that in one day. Moreover, note how Jesus puts it, *saying* **"I repent."** That means that at this point you must take his naked word for it. After three or four months of help and counsel, if there is no difference, you may rightly concern yourself with the matter of fruit. But not this soon. So, it is not possible to slide out of the obligation to forgive by saying "When I see the fruit, I will forgive." Teach counselees that!

No wonder the apostles, who caught on to what Jesus was saying, then replied, **"Increase our faith!"** That was a pretty good response, wasn't it? No! It certainly wasn't. Jesus had told them to do something and they reply "No, not until you give us more faith." That is wrong—dead wrong. And Jesus won't allow counselees today to get out of their obligation to forgive by any similar excuse.

"Are you sure they were wrong?"

Yes. Look at what follows (v. 6). Jesus says, that they did not need more faith, that obedience to His command doesn't require some certain amount of faith. Any faith at all will do. He says this in declaring that if they had faith like the teeny mustard seed they could do wonders! So, just as He allows no one to slide out of his obligation to forgive by saying, "When I see the fruit I'll forgive," here He says that it won't do to protest that "when I get more faith, I'll forgive." Jesus is closing all of the doors of escape and throwing away the key.

Then he tells a story that anticipates a third possible excuse. A slave comes in who has been working all day under a hot Palestinian sun. He is

Christian Counselor's Commentary

7   Which of you, if he had a slave plowing or tending sheep, would say to him when he comes in from the field, "Come, recline at the table right away"?
8   Wouldn't he say to him, "Prepare something for me to eat, and when you are dressed, serve me until I have finished eating and drinking, and then you can eat and drink"?
9   Does he thank the slave because he did what he was commanded?
10 So you too, when you do everything that you are commanded, say, "We are unprofitable slaves; we have simply done what we ought to have done."

11 On His way to Jerusalem He was passing through the area between Galilee and Samaria.

12 Now as He entered into a certain village ten lepers met Him. They stood their distance

13 and raised their voices, saying, "Jesus, Master, show mercy to us."

14 When He saw them, He said to them, "Go, show yourselves to the priests." As they went they were cleansed.

---

sweaty, tired and thirsty. Jesus observes that his master doesn't say, "Sit down and rest and get yourself a meal." No. Rather, he requires him to make and serve his meal even though he has eaten nothing. That is against all his feelings. What is Jesus teaching? Simply this—that there is no excuse for not forgiving the one who says "I repent." He cannot plead when I see fruit, when I get more faith or when I *feel* like it. Since forgiveness is a promise, the promise not to bring up a matter to the offender or anyone else, one can make that promise *whether he feels like it or not*. And he can keep that promise against all his feelings. Forgiveness is a promise—not a feeling.

This teaching about forgiveness is essential to all effective counseling. This chapter is essential to the teaching. Mark it, understand it, use it—frequently—in counseling. For further data on forgiveness, see my book *From Forgiven to Forgiving*.

In verses 11 through 19 there is record of an important healing that contains valuable information for the biblical counselor. Jesus is met by ten lepers as He travels. They plead for healing. Jesus does not heal them. Instead, He tells them, "**Go, show yourselves to the priests**." The priests were the ones who must declare them clean after examination. But they had not been healed. We read that they went—and that **as they went they were cleansed** from their leprosy (v. 14). Often, Jesus gives us what we desire not before we need it, but in the doing. Were they cleansed by

15 But one of them, when he saw that he had been healed, turned back and praised God in a loud voice.
16 Then he fell on his face at His feet and thanked Him, and he was a Samaritan.
17 Then Jesus said, "Weren't ten cleansed? Where are the nine?
18 Is this foreigner the only one who turned back to praise God?"
19 Then He said to him, "Get up and go. Your faith has saved you."
20 When He was questioned by the Pharisees about the time God's empire would come, He responded,
>God's empire doesn't come in a way that you can see.
21 People won't say, "See, here it is," or "There it is," because, as a matter of fact, God's empire is in your midst!

---

works? No, they were **cleansed** by faith (cf. v. 19). It was faith that led them to obey. If they had not believed, they would not have gone.

Now comes the point of the story for which Luke recorded it. Only **one** came back to give **thanks**—and he was a **Samaritan** (v. 16). That last comment, about the Samaritan, was rubbing it in since the Jews despised the Samaritans. Ingratitude—even among Christians—often is pronounced. Helped the most, they often seem to take it for granted. They are thankful neither to God nor to you for being used as an instrument in His hands to counsel them. Don't expect gratitude. When it happens spontaneously (without prompting) it will doubtless happen in the lesser number of instances (here the ratio was 1 to 10). And often, it will come from the one from whom it is least expected. Having read this account, it is perhaps important to teach thankfulness in counseling regularly along with everything else that you teach. In fact, it might be important to devote a part of the last session of a case to giving thanks. The use of example, in that way, may be the very best way to elicit and teach gratitude.

Verses 20 through 37 record the response of Jesus to another Pharisaical interruption, this time about **the time when God's empire would come**. It is interesting to study how frequently the teaching of Jesus grows out of a question from others. He knew how to use those questions (which at least showed some sort of interest) to teach what He wanted others to learn. Counselors must not think that responding to questions that may seem irrelevant is worthless. Use those questions as opportunities to teach what it is that you want the counselee to learn.

First, Jesus made it clear that the **empire** of God (Daniel's fifth kingdom) would not come in a way that they could **see**. They were expecting Him to perform a military spectacle. It would come as nothing of the sort.

Christian Counselor's Commentary

> 22   Then He said to His disciples,
>   The days will come when you will long to see one of the days of the Son of Man, but you won't see it.
> 23   People will tell you, "See, there it is; see, here it is." Don't go after them or follow them.

Jesus had said, "**My empire is not from this world. If My empire were from this world, My servants would have fought . . . My empire isn't from here**" (John 18:36). He went on to say that it was an empire composed of those who believe the **truth** to which He had come to **bear witness** (v. 37). In other words, this empire that the Father gave to the Son (Daniel 7:13, 14) is one in which one enters by believing in Him as his Savior and Lord. The great commission likewise tells us that it is a matter of baptizing those who enter by faith in the message preached, **teaching them to observe everything that I have commanded you** (Matthew 28:19, 20). In other words, it was an empire into which persons could come while remaining citizens of their respective countries. That was because they would acquire dual citizenship (cf. Philippians 3:20). Indeed, the Emperor of this new empire, at that very moment was **in their midst**. In Him, it was already present. That is why people won't go about saying, "**Here it is**" or "**There it is**." It will not come as various kingdoms had come in the past—through taking over kingdoms by means of physical destruction and warfare. It would come quietly, as one here and another there believes.

Jesus was teaching about the empire from the heavens that John and He had proclaimed was "at hand." But He was also correcting mistaken ideas about what it was like and how it would appear. While the Romans would have much to do with destroying the city of Jerusalem and the temple, thus bringing down the old order of things, Jesus (personally) would gather no earthly forces of His own to do so. Nor would He take over in some earthly way; the new order would come as it did on the day of Pentecost.

Turning to His disciples, He continued that discussion telling them that the days would come when they would like to go back to the "good old times" when they were being instructed by and were ministering with Jesus, **the Son of Man** (v. 22). But those days are gone forever. You can never go back. Many counselees long for former seemingly "better" times (cf. the argument in the book of Hebrews against just such an idea). But the better days are always ahead—so long as they are lived in the light of

24	In His day¹ the Son of Man will be like lightning that flashes and lights up the sky from one end to the other.
25	But first He must suffer much and be rejected by this generation.
26	As it was in the days of Noah, that is also how it will be in the days of the Son of Man.
27	People were eating, drinking, marrying, being given in marriage until the day when Noah entered the ark, and the flood came and destroyed them all.

---

[1] Some MSS omit these three words.

---

what Jesus commands and in anticipation of His Word at work in one's life. While there may be a place for nostalgia, if it leads to inertia, to regrets, to complaining—or anything of the sort—then it is sin. Keep counselees looking forward.

The day will come, however, when there will be no question that the empire from the heavens has arrived. That **day** of the **Son of Man** will have visible manifestations, so that one will not have to wonder about what it is that has happened. These will be as visible as lightning that flashes from one end of the sky to the other, lighting up the whole (v. 24). So there will be no need to go about questioning one another about whether this event or that is the one looked for. The disciples must not follow false teachers who claim that they have a corner on the fulfillment of Christ's prediction (v. 23). There are always plenty of these from which you must help counselees to withdraw.

There are previous events that must come before the empire will be present in all its fullness. Preeminently, Jesus must **suffer much and be rejected by this generation** (v. 25). The day would **come** when people least expect it. It would come as the destruction came in **Noah's** day, in **Lot's** day. It would be when people were going about their normal activities (v. 27). The **days of the Son of Man** would be those days when vengeance would come in 70 AD upon the **generation** that **rejected** Him and crucified Him—destruction to the uttermost. In those **days** when the Roman armies were making havoc of the city and temple, the truth about Jesus would become apparent: He would be **revealed** as Daniel's **Son of Man** (Daniel 7:13). That is, He would be shown to be the One Who was to receive the empire from the Ancient of Days.

Those on the housetops should not go down to retrieve anything from their houses; Christians should run from house to house until they were outside the city and should head for the hills on the other side of Jordan

28	The same was true in the days of Lot. They were eating, drinking, buying, selling, planting, building,
29	but on the day that Lot left Sodom it rained fire and brimstone from heaven and destroyed them all.
30	This is just how it will be on the day when the Son of Man is revealed.
31	On that day whoever is on the roof, with his belongings in the house, must not go to get them, and whoever is in the field likewise must not turn back to the things behind.
32	Remember Lot's wife!
33	Whoever tries to preserve his life will lose it, but whoever loses his life will preserve it.
34	I tell you, on that night there will be two people in one bed. One will be taken away and the other will be left.
35	There will be two women grinding together. One will be taken away and the other will be left.
36	[1]

---

[1] Some MSS add vs. 36: *Two men will be in the field. One will be taken away and the other will be left.*

(vv. 30-32; they were to **Remember Lot's wife**, who looked back, reluctant to leave). There is a time in counseling to warn people to flee, to place no importance on things, and to get out of a situation before it is too late. It would be interesting for you to make a list of such situations (they probably will not be as dramatic as the destruction of Jerusalem, but they can be as deadly to an individual).

We know from Josephus that when the Romans laid siege to the city, that they withdrew once, and only once, for a brief time. Christians who obeyed Christ's words of warning fled to Pella and were saved. Then the army encircled the city once more, never to leave again until the destruction was complete. One who attempted to **preserve** his life in the city or by his own ways and means, rather than follow Christ's directions, would fail to do so, whereas those who appeared to be losing all that was important by obeying, actually were **saving** their lives (v. 33). When the destruction would come, there would be separation between those who were the closest, depending on whether they would obey or not. One would be swept away (as in the **flood**) and another would be preserved.

The disciples asked, "**Where, Lord?**" That is, where will this take place? Jesus answered. The **vultures** will gather together where the **corpse** is. Jerusalem, with regard to the faith, after forty more years of

Luke 17

37 "Where, Lord?" they asked Him. He said to them, "Wherever the corpse is the vultures will gather."

---

mercy He would extend to her, would become nothing more than a rotting carcass, fit only to be eaten up by the Roman vultures! What vivid language Jesus uses! Why? To warn of the horror of what was to come. Vivid language is remembered when it is needed. Counselor, take heed!

CHAPTER 18

> 1 Then He told them a parable illustrating the need to keep on praying and not to give up.
> 2 He said,
>> in a certain city there was a judge who didn't fear God or respect people.
> 3 And in that city was a widow who kept coming to him and saying to him, "Give justice to me against my adversary."
> 4 But for some time he refused. Then, afterwards, he said to himself, "Even though I don't fear God or respect people,
> 5 I'm going to see that she gets justice, or, at length, coming, she will hit me."

The eighteenth chapter begins with a parable that the Lord Jesus told to His disciples (**them**). Helpfully, Luke tells us the purpose of the parable: it is to illustrate **the need to keep on praying and not to give up**. That is plain and simple, but it is a message that many counselees, despairing over things as they are, need to hear. Certainly, every biblical counselor deals with counselees who are about to or have **given up**. Here then, is a parable to use with persons in such a condition.

Once more, like the parable of the shrewd steward (whose shrewdness, and not his dishonesty, is emphasized) we come to a parable in which by the very name usually given to it, and the emphasis made, is misunderstood. It is *not* the parable of the Unjust Judge; it is the parable of the Persistent Widow. By her persistence, the widow impressed upon the judge that she meant to get justice, whether he was anxious to mete it out or not. Indeed, though he feared neither God nor man, at length he acted out of fear of the widow (v. 5).

Now, clearly, it is not to be inferred from this parable that one must threaten God to get a hearing for his cause. Again, that is to miss the point. Nor is God to be likened to this judge in that it is difficult to obtain satisfaction from Him. No! Exactly not that. Well, then, what is the point? Verses 6 through 8 indicate that just the opposite is true. God will not make His suffering saints **wait** a single day longer than it is necessary for His purposes to be fulfilled. He is not uninterested in their cry for justice, as was the judge. He will give them justice quickly. They will never have to wait so long that they must **give up** on God and cease praying. Therefore, they must patiently and persistently continue their regular prayers

Luke 18

6 Then the Lord said,
   Listen to what the unrighteous judge is saying.
7 Now won't God give justice to His chosen people who cry to Him day and night? Will He make them wait?
8 I tell you He will give justice to them quickly. Nevertheless, when the Son of Man comes, will He find faith on the earth?

9 Then He also told this parable to some who were depending upon their own righteousness and despised others:

---

for help and mercy and understand that at exactly the right time God will answer. From the eternal perspective—not your counselee's, who may want everything yesterday—he will receive justice **quickly**. So, what do you tell the counselee who maintains that he cries out day and night (v. 7) and yet receives no answer to his prayers? Simple. You tell him two things. First, the promises of I Corinthians 10:13 have not been removed from the Bible. Secondly, that he must keep on praying and not give up. You can assure him that *at the right time* God will answer. It is not because He is unable or uninterested in His child, but He answers when and how and where He sees fit. We see only a part of the whole picture—a very meager part at that. God sees it all in relation to all of time past and time future. That means that when He answers your prayer, He fits that answer into the *whole* picture; not merely into the part of which you are somewhat aware. Tell counselees that too.

In something bordering on despair itself, the Lord Jesus (doubtless with a sigh) asks whether **when He comes** He will find any **faith** that persists in prayer. So many tend to **give up**. It was true then; it is true now. They are unwilling to wait for God to move in His time when He is ready to do so. Jesus is preparing His own for the difficult times ahead. He wants them to persist and not give up—even though they would find themselves in the midst of severe persecution. It might be well for counselors to tell counselees something along these lines before sending them off from counseling. There will be times when they all are tempted to **give up** on God, when it may even come to their minds that God doesn't care, or is like an unjust judge. In such times they must remember this parable.

In verse 9, Luke introduces another parable, again replete with an explanation as to its purpose. The parable of the Pharisee and the Tax Collector is a familiar one. Its purpose? To urge none to **depend** on **their own righteousness** (their good works) which leads to **despising others**. The story is that the Pharisee didn't pray at all (Jesus says, that he **prayed to himself**). That is to say, his prayer never reached God because it wasn't a

Christian Counselor's Commentary

> 10 Two men went up to the temple to pray. The one was a Pharisee and the other was a tax collector.
> 11 The Pharisee stood and prayed to himself like this: "I thank You, God, that I am not like other people—robbers, unjust, adulterers, or even like this tax collector.
> 12 I fast twice every week, I tithe everything I get."
> 13 But the tax collector, standing at a distance, wouldn't even raise his eyes to heaven, but beat the breast, saying, "God, show mercy to me, the sinner."
> 14 I tell you that the latter went down to his house justified, rather than the former. Everybody who exalts himself will be humbled, but whoever humbles himself will be exalted.
>
> **15** Now people started bringing babies for Him to touch. But when the disciples saw this, they rebuked them.

---

prayer at all. It was a recital of all the good things that he had done, hoping thus to commend himself to God. He is the perfect example of what Paul mentioned in Romans 10:3. On the other hand, the tax collector recognized his sin, confessed it to God and asked for His forgiveness. Jesus says that the latter went away **justified** rather than the former. **Exalting** self leads to abasement; **humbling** self to exaltation.

There is an emphasis for our self-righteous age if there ever was one! Not for unbelievers alone. The whole self-esteem, self-image movement exalts self. Children are told to pat themselves on the back. People of every stripe are encouraged to think of themselves as "somebody," God's gift to mankind! This teaching is bound to produce a crop of little Pharisees who, in time, apart from God's grace, will grow into very large ones. When you counsel those who have been growing up under such teaching, look for the pharisaical streak in what they say. You may need to use the concluding verse of this parable (v. 14) to shock them out of their self-exaltation. Again, here is a parable that helps a counselor understand people. The dynamic is clear: they trusted in their own righteousness *and despised others*. When you counsel one who you discover despises others, you can be sure that it is because he is trusting in his own righteousness. He thinks that he is pretty hot stuff. Others can't begin to measure up. When he speaks about them, it is like the Pharisee saying **or even like this tax collector**. You can hear him say it; you can see him look down upon this despised creature. Self-righteousness and the despising of others always go together.

In verse 15, we read how people began to bring babies to Jesus **for**

16 But Jesus called them to Him, saying,
> Let the children come to Me. Don't stop them; after all, God's empire belongs to people who are like them.

17 > Truly I tell you, whoever doesn't welcome God's empire like a child certainly won't enter it.

18 Then a certain ruler questioned Him, saying, "Good teacher, what shall I do to inherit eternal life?"

19 Jesus replied,
> Why do you call Me good? Nobody is good except God Himself.

20 > You know the commandments—**Do not commit adultery, Do not kill, Do not steal, Do not bear false witness, Honor your father and mother**.

21 Then he said, "I have kept them all since I was a boy."

Him to touch. What they had in mind exactly is not said. But the **disciples**, who thought He had more important things to do, **rebuked** them for it. Jesus took the occasion to teach (as we have seen Him do over and over again). He told the disciples to let them come. "**After all**," He said, "**God's empire belongs to people like them**" (v. 16). "As a matter of fact," He went on to say, "**whoever doesn't welcome God's empire like a child certainly won't enter into it**" (v. 17). Now there is a powerful statement. What is there about a child that is indicative of those who faithfully come to Him? At least two things are apparent. First, a child is helpless, dependent on others for all that he has. That is the way people must come to Christ (the opposite of the Pharisee who focused on self). Secondly, a child is believing, trusting. Those are the two traits of childlikeness that stand out. They are essential, as He says here, for entrance into His empire. But they are also essential to the change and the growth that many Christian counselees need to make. Until a counselee becomes childlike in his attitude toward God and His Word, you probably can do little for him. On the other hand, a childlike counselee, in the hands of one who takes advantage of him, is in danger. You must be one to whom it is possible to come in childlikeness without the risk of spiritual danger.

In verse 18 the story of the rich young ruler is recounted. He questions Jesus, addressing Him in the words **Good teacher**. Jesus picks up on the word **good**, saying, "**Why do you call Me good? Nobody is good but God Himself**" (v. 19). Could Jesus be saying that He was a sinner? Of course not. What He was saying is that the standard that this ruler used to determine what constituted goodness was far different from the one He used. The ruler thought he himself was **good** because he had outwardly

Christian Counselor's Commentary

> 22 When Jesus heard this, He said to him, "You still lack one thing. Sell everything you have, give the money to the poor, and you will have treasure in heaven. Then come, follow Me."
> 23 But when he heard this, he became quite upset, because he was very rich.
> 24 When Jesus saw his reaction, He said,
> How hard it is for those who have riches to enter God's empire!

---

kept the **commandments** (v. 21). But obviously, he had failed to keep them in his heart. Jesus will get at this point. Jesus is saying also that unless you are calling Me **God** when you call me **good**, you haven't the faintest idea of what is good according to My standard. I will not be called **good** on the same basis on which you think that you are **good**. People in counseling will also need to be faced with the matter of standards. Often, what behavior they justify in themselves or others, the values they espouse, the evaluations they make, and the like, are determined according to a standard very different from the canons of biblical truth. At times, then, they too must be challenged as Jesus challenges the ruler to rethink these matters. How does He do so?

First, as we have seen, he challenges his definition of **goodness**. Then, in response to the ruler's reply about the commandments, Jesus tells him that he **lacks one thing**—that one thing is true goodness. He now demonstrates that the mere outward keeping of the commandments is not what God requires; it is the inner meaning of them in one's life that counts. Jesus puts him to the test to demonstrate to him that what he **lacks** is this essential factor. He tells him to **sell all** he has, **give** the money to the **poor**, and look for **treasure in heaven** instead. And then He says, "**follow Me.**" Those are not commands that Jesus gives to everyone; why to this man? Well, as Jesus elsewhere summed up the law, he said it meant loving God and loving one's neighbor. In selling out everything and giving to the poor, he could demonstrate that he really did keep the second great commandment. In following Jesus, he could demonstrate that the really did love God, the first great commandment. The fact is, he was willing to do neither. He **became quite upset** instead because, Luke says, **he was very rich** (v. 23). This man loved Mammon rather than God. He was not good at all.

In response to what Jesus saw in **his reaction** (v. 24) he remarked about how **difficult** it is for those who have **riches to enter God's empire**. Indeed, in a statement famous for its powerful imagery, He went on to compare that difficulty with the trouble a **camel** would have passing

Luke 18

25 It is easier for a camel to go through the eye of a needle than for a rich man to enter God's empire.
26 Those who heard this said, "Then who can be saved?"
27 Jesus answered, "What is impossible for human beings is possible for God."
28 Then Peter said, "See, we have left our possessions to follow you."
29 He said to them,
Truly I tell you that there is no one who has left house or wife or brothers or parents or children for the sake of God's empire
30 who will fail to receive many times as much in this age, and in the coming age, eternal life.

---

through the **eye of a needle** (vv. 24, 25). He did not say that a rich person could never do so, but the struggle he would have in putting God and His empire first (before riches) would be huge.

A question arose from His remarks: **Then who can be saved** (v. 26)? **Jesus answered, "What is impossible for human beings is possible for God"** (v. 27). It is **impossible** for a camel to pass through the eye of a needle. That is clear. Jesus was using hyperbole (as He frequently did) to make His point that it was very difficult for a rich men to be saved. But, as usual, some misunderstood Him. They took Him literally, noting that it is **impossible**. So Jesus has to make the point that God can get hold of a rich man's heart and so transform him that he *can* respond to the message of Christ as he ought. The regenerating and sanctifying Spirit can turn worshippers of gold into worshippers of God. The word of Jesus in verse 27, therefore, holds much hope for you as a counselor. God can and does *change* people. You must believe that, and you must affirm that truth to counselees every opportunity that you get to do so. It is a most encouraging word!

Reflecting on Jesus' words to the rich young ruler, Peter now chimes in saying that he and the other disciples had done what the ruler would not—they had **left** their **possessions** to **follow** the Lord (v. 28). We are not told what he had in mind in making this statement—perhaps, he was attempting to reinforce what Jesus had just said, indicating that there were those who had done exactly what He asked. At any rate, Jesus responds to the remark in a kindly and helpful way. He says no one does so without receiving **many times as much in this age,** and **in the coming age eternal life**. He points not only to the treasures in heaven mentioned previously (v. 22), but also to what a follower of His would receive **in *this* age**. Those who have entered the ministry, who have had to travel to places

Christian Counselor's Commentary

> 31 Then He took the Twelve aside and said to them,
> Notice, we are going up to Jerusalem, where everything that the prophets wrote about the Son of Man will be fulfilled.
> 32 He will be turned over to the Gentiles, mocked, insulted, spit at.
> 33 When they have whipped Him, they will kill Him. But on the third day He will rise again.
> 34 But they didn't understand any of this. This saying was hidden from them, and they didn't understand what He said.

away from family, can verify the fact. They have had "mothers" and "fathers" and "brothers" and "sisters" and "children" abundantly in the churches of Christ. The Christian family is large, and from it God can provide more of what the disciple has left behind than if he had never gone. Your counselee needs to know that one cannot ever give up anything for God. He may attempt to do so, but God will fill the gap with something far greater.

Now, Jesus has a word for the ears of His disciples alone. He takes them aside and begins to tell them how the prophetic word about His **death** and **resurrection** would soon be fulfilled at **Jerusalem** (vv. 31-33). Here is a prophecy as clear and plain as anyone ever could wish of His ministry to seek and to save the lost through His death. But, at this time, they didn't **understand** (v. 34). It was part of the plan of God that they would not do so yet. God has His time schedule, as I have commented before, and it even reaches to one's ability to understand. It took the events of the cross and the resurrection to make this (and other statements like it) clear to them. A rejected, crucified Savior was counter to all their hopes and beliefs. It took men like that, who didn't want to believe, to become valid witnesses. Clearly, people with this mind-set would never have invented a myth of vicarious sacrifice and bodily resurrection. Only the very facts themselves, striking them in the face, could turn such dyed-in-the-wool skeptics and selective hearers into passionate believers who would give their lives for the faith they once refused to believe. There are times when people will not respond to all you have to say. You seem unable to make a difference in their lives. Because of this, when at length that difference does come, they may be used to show others that the change in their lives and in their thinking could not have occurred apart from an act of God. Don't give up or lose heart about apparent, present failure. Look forward to what God will do in the lives of counselees in the future.

In verses 35 through 43, we encounter the final story of the chapter,

Luke 18

35 It so happened that as He drew near to Jericho, a certain blind man sat by the road, begging.
36 When he heard the crowd passing by, he asked what was going on.
37 They told him, "Jesus the Nazarene is passing by."
38 So he shouted, "Jesus, Son of David, show mercy to me!"
39 Those who were in front rebuked him, telling him to be quiet, but he shouted all the louder, "Son of David, show mercy to me!"
40 But Jesus stopped and commanded them to bring him to Him. When he came near, He asked him,
41 "What do you want Me to do?" He replied, "Lord, let me see again!"
42 Then Jesus said to him, "See again. Your faith has saved you."
43 Instantly he could see again, and he followed Him, praising God. Then all the people, when they saw this, praised God.

---

the healing of a **blind man**. This event occurred when nearing Jerusalem (v. 35). Evidently, the blind man had heard of Jesus because as soon as he learned that Jesus was there, he cried out for **mercy** (v. 38). People told him to be quiet, but he shouted all the louder (v. 39). Interestingly, he properly called Jesus the **Son of David**. This indicates that he had made inquiries about Jesus and believed in Him. Jesus stopped and asked him **What do you want Me to do** (v. 41). In asking this question Jesus was not seeking information. He was giving the man an opportunity to express his **faith**, which, indeed, he did. He asked for healing so that he could **see again**. Jesus recognized **his** faith (v. 42), commanded him to **see**, and indicated that it was this **faith** that not only healed but also **saved** him. The man, and the people together with him, all praised God for what had happened (v. 43). The response, so lacking in the nine who did not return to give thinks, in this case was gratifying.

Christian Counselor's Commentary

CHAPTER 19

1 Jesus entered Jericho and was passing through.
2 Now there was a man named Zacchaeus, who was a head tax collector and rich man.
3 He tried to see who Jesus was, but, since he was short, he couldn't see because of the crowd.
4 So he ran on ahead and climbed up into a sycamore tree to see Him, because He was going that way.
5 Now when He came to that place, Jesus looked up and said to him, "Zacchaeus, hurry and come down; today I must stay at your house."
6 So he hurried down and welcomed Him happily.
7 But when they saw this, they all grumbled, saying, "He's gone to stay with a sinner!"
8 But Zacchaeus stood up and said to the Lord, "Here and now, Lord, I give half of my possessions to the poor. And if I have cheated anybody out of anything, I will repay it four times over."

The chapter opens with the story of **Zacchaeus**. This story is topped off at the end with the words, **The Son of Man came to seek and to save the lost** (v. 10). The story is well-known. It shows how Jesus made no distinction between the rich and the poor, the "righteous" and the unrighteous. He saw them all as needy people. And, in contrast to comments in the previous chapter about the difficulty of the rich entering into the empire, it shows that it was not impossible for God to bring such a person down to his knees in repentance and faith. The unfortunate man-made separation of the chapter here makes it difficult to see this story in its bold contrast to the idea that it is impossible for a rich person to be saved. The point is made at the outset that Zacchaeus was **a *head* tax collector and a *rich* man** (v. 2). Not only does the placing of this story here in juxtaposition to the previous discussion show that though difficult for a rich man to be saved, it is possible, but it shows *how* this may take place. Zacchaeus not only went to great effort to come into contact with Jesus, climbing the tree, but when converted, he gave freely of his riches to the poor in restitution for his past misdeeds. Divinely-wrought faith and salvation radically changed the man. Notice, too, how he gives to the **poor**—something the rich young ruler refused to do (v. 8). Keep these things in mind in working with such persons.

There is one more underlying thread that needs to be extracted. Notice how Jesus' enemies complain that He went to stay at the house of

Luke 19

9 Jesus said to him,
> Today salvation has come to this house, because even he is Abraham's son.

10 > The Son of Man came to seek and to save the lost.

11 While they were listening to this, He went on to tell them a parable, because He was near Jerusalem, and they thought that God's empire would appear at once.

12 He said, therefore,
> A certain nobleman went to a distant country to receive a kingdom for himself and then to return.

13 > So he called ten of his slaves and gave them ten minas and said to them, "Trade with these till I get back."

14 > But his citizens hated him and sent a delegation after him saying, "We don't want this man to reign over us."

---

a **sinner** (v. 7). Tax collectors, because they were traitors to the community who collaborated with the Romans, had been "put out of the church." He was no longer to be counted a member of the covenant community. But Jesus thinks otherwise; He calls Him a true son of **Abraham**. That is to say, he was one who was saved, and whose heart was circumcised (v. 9).

Things are not always what they seem on the surface. The religious leaders would proclaim that the rich young ruler was a fine, upstanding child of Abraham. After all, he had been made a **ruler** of the synagog. They, in turn, called people like Zacchaeus **sinners**, persons no longer acknowledged even as *members* of the synagog. You must be careful to look beyond the surface. You may not be able to read hearts, that is true, because that is God's prerogative. But you can look at the actions of people which often give evidence of what is beneath the surface. Here, look at the lack of repentance of the ruler and the restitution of the tax collector. These two contrasting responses to Jesus' message were the sort of evidence that a counselor seeks.

In verses 11 through 27 Jesus tells another **parable**. The purpose of this parable was to confront error in their thinking that had to do with the appearance of God's empire (v. 11). While they thought it might appear **at once**, Jesus wants to let them know that this was wrong. He has the **nobleman** going away to a **distant** kingdom to receive a **kingdom** (this actually happened when Archelaus went to Rome to get a mini kingdom in Palestine). But he did not return at once; after all, the trip took him to a **distant country**. The people who **hated** him sent a delegation to attempt to try to

Christian Counselor's Commentary

15   When he returned, having received the kingdom, he called his slaves to whom he had given the money to appear before him to learn what they had earned by trading.
16   The first came and said, "Your mina gained ten minas."
17   So he said, "Well done, good slave! Because you were faithful in this small thing, I give you authority over ten cities."
18   Then the second came, saying, "Lord, your mina has earned five minas."
19   So he said to him, "And you are over five cities."
20   Then another came, saying, "Lord, see, here is your mina, that I wrapped up and put away in safekeeping.
21   I was afraid of you, because you are a strict person; you pick up what you didn't lay down, and you reap what you didn't sow."
22   He said to him, "I will judge you by your own words, you wicked slave! You knew that I was a strict person, picking up what I didn't lay down and reaping what I didn't sow, did you?
23   Then why didn't you put my money in the bank, so that when I returned, it would have drawn interest?"
24   Then he said to those who stood by, "Take the mina from him and give it to the one who has ten minas."

---

keep him from realizing his purpose. They would plead with those who were to confer the kingdom on him not to do so (v. 14). But they were unsuccessful and he was successful. This ultimately led to their death (v. 27).

Now, in this underlying theme, Jesus was speaking about Himself and the Jews who rejected Him. He would go away to heaven **to receive the kingdom** (cf. Daniel 2, 7). And after a while (70 AD) He would come back in judgment on those who did not want Him to reign over them.

Then, there was the other side of the parable which has to do with His servants. He gave ten **minas** each (about $200) to ten **slaves** and told them to **trade** with it till he returned. The apostles and the other followers of Christ who persevered would be represented by these slaves. Then, when he came back, the king asked them what they had been able to do with the money. The first had doubled his money, the second had a fifty percent return. But a third came saying that he had been **afraid** to **trade**, knowing that the Lord was **strict** and wanted a sure return on his money. So he wrapped it up and put it away for safekeeping. Jesus doesn't sympathize with him. He doesn't say, "I know, fear is so debilitating. Well done!" Not on your life. He was commanded to trade with the money he had been given. He disobeyed. If he was afraid, he could have made a safe

Luke 19

25   But they said to him, "Lord, he has ten minas."
26   "I tell you, to everyone who has, more will be given, but from the one who doesn't have, even what he has will be taken away.
27   But as for these enemies of mine who didn't want me to reign over them, bring them here and slaughter them before me."

28 Now after He said this, He took the lead as He went up to Jerusalem.
29 As He drew near to Bethphage and Bethany, at what is called the Mount of Olives, He sent off two of His disciples, saying,
30   Go to the village over there and as you enter you will find a colt that nobody has ever ridden tied up. Untie it and bring it here.
31   If anybody asks you, "Why are you untying it?" tell him this, "The Lord needs it."
32 So those who were sent went and found things just as He had told them.
33 But as they were untying the colt, its owners said to them, "Why are you untying the colt?"
34 So they said, "Because the Lord needs it."
35 Then they led it to Jesus, threw their clothes over the colt and helped Jesus get on it.
36 As He rode along, they strewed their clothes in the road.

---

investment at the bank (v. 23). But he didn't do anything. So he took the money he had retained and gave it to the one who had doubled his money. Some objected (v. 25). Then Jesus said, **"to everyone who has, more will be given, but from the one who doesn't have, even what he has will be taken away**." There is a principle that a counselor must learn to teach his counselees who, out of fear, will not move ahead in furthering the Lord's work. It is not only a powerful aphorism but it is found embedded in a memorable parable.

If Jesus refuses to accept the excuse, what judgment does He place on the non-action of the slave? He calls him **wicked** (v. 22). It is wickedness to accuse Jesus of being **strict**, etc. and not to have obeyed him. Some so-called followers of Christ will have none of His strictness. They want an easier Christianity that doesn't put them on the spot. They, in effect, invent their own form of Christianity. The modern idea is that if a person is fearful he can do nothing about it. Jesus puts the lie to that by suggesting that a safe investment might have been made. Those who are entrusted with a little and demonstrate proficiency and industry in their use of it will, at length, be entrusted with a great deal more. That, again, is a principle to inculcate in counselees.

Now, in verses 28 through 40 we read of the "triumphal entry" into

37 Then, as He drew near the point where the Mount of Olives descends, the whole crowd of the disciples began to rejoice and praise God in loud voices for all the miracles that they had seen, saying,
38 **"Blessed is the King Who comes in the Lord's name**! Peace in heaven and glory in the highest!"
39 Then some of the Pharisees who were in the crowd said to Him, "Teacher, rebuke your disciples!"
40 But in reply He said, "If they are quiet, the stones will shout."

  41 Now as He drew near, He saw the city and wept over it, saying,
42   If even today you knew what would bring peace! But now it is hidden from your eyes.
43   The days will come upon you when your enemies will throw up a bank around you and will surround you and will hem you in on all sides.
44   They will dash you to the ground, you and your children within you, and they won't leave one of your stones upon another—because you didn't know the time of your visitation.

Jerusalem. Because Jesus came **riding** into **Jerusalem** (as Zechariah had predicted; see Zechariah 9:9) on a **colt**, an ass, He was proclaiming that He was not coming to bring a military victory. If He had wanted to do so, He would have used a stallion (cf. Revelation 6:2). But the animal He rode was an animal that signified peace, not war. He staged the event (see vv. 29-34). Presumably, there had been some previous preparations on His part. This was clearly not a spur-of-the-moment action. He was making a statement. The acclaim that He received, however, indicated that the people did not understand. The people were interested in His **miracles**, not in Him (v. 37). They said the right things, but with the wrong meanings (cf. v. 38). Jesus refused to stop the shouting and the acclaim (vv. 39, 40). From the beginning to the end, Jesus and His words and actions were misunderstood. Don't be surprised if what you say from the Bible is misunderstood also.

    Now, in verses 41 through 44, the thoughts that were on Jesus' mind are recorded as He formed them into tearful words. How He longed for the people and the city to be preserved from the coming wrath they were bringing on themselves! His heart went out to them, foolish men and women that they were, people from whose eyes were **hidden** the truths about Him that would bring them **peace** of heart and life. Looking down the forty odd years to come, Jesus predicts the terrible onslaught of 70 AD (vv. 43, 44). He shows how the very temple, in which they delighted,

45 Then He went into the temple and began to drive out those who were selling, telling them,
46 "It is written, **and My house shall be a house of prayer**. But you have made it a den of thieves."
47 Now He was teaching daily in the temple. So the chief priests, the scribes and the leaders of the people were trying to find a way to destroy Him,
48 but they couldn't find a way to do it, because all the people hung on His words.

---

would be destroyed along with so many of the people. You will find yourself in similar situations as you grieve over those who will not hear the truths that would bring peace to their lives and homes. People have not changed all that much throughout the years. Technology changes at a rapid pace. Minds do not.

Then Luke records the second cleansing of the temple from the moneychangers and merchants (vv. 45, 46). His concern is how they had profaned God's **house** (the temple) by their money-making activities. There are many today who will do the same. They will use the church as a platform to get rich. They will do all that they can to solicit funds for themselves in the name of Christianity. Counselors sometimes have been guilty of doing so. Many others—televangelists, etc.—have done the same. You must take a stand with your Lord against all such activities. While the laborer is worthy of his hire, and while you must not muzzle the ox that treads out the grain, it is possible to make money one's goal rather than service and ministry.

The religious leaders, against whom Jesus had acted and spoken so forcefully, were enraged with Him. They sought ways to **destroy Him** (v. 47), but couldn't do so out in the open where He was surrounded by so many followers who, at this juncture, supported Him wholeheartedly (though out of ignorance and misunderstanding). To attempt it would have been to turn the people against them. They would have to find another way. Which, in time, they did.

Christian Counselor's Commentary

CHAPTER 20

1 One day, as He was teaching the people in the temple and announcing the good news, the chief priests and the scribes, together with the elders, came up to Him and said to Him,
2 "Tell us by what authority you are doing these things," and "Who gave you this authority?"
3 He responded,
   I too will ask you a question. Now tell Me:
4 John's baptism—was it from heaven or from men?
5 Then they discussed it among themselves, saying,
   If we say, "From heaven," then he'll say, "Why didn't you believe him?"
6 but if we say, "From men," all the people will stone us, since they are convinced that John was a prophet.
7 So they answered, "We don't know where he got it."
8 Then Jesus said to them, "Neither will I tell you by what authority I am doing these things."
9 Then He began to tell the people this parable:

Jesus took up a teaching ministry in the temple at Jerusalem. One day, while teaching, He was confronted by a delegation of religious leaders (v. 1). They demanded, **"Tell us by what authority you are doing these things,"** and they wanted to know, **"Who gave you this authority?"** His rapid rejoinder was, as it often was, to answer with a question: **John's baptism—was it from heaven or from men?** This question was significant. It put them on the spot. So they huddled (v. 5). They reasoned that if they said **from heaven**, He'd ask, **"Why didn't you believe him?"** If they said, **"from men"** the people would **stone** them because they were all convinced that John was a **prophet**. So they refused to answer (v. 7). Jesus then replied, **"Neither will I tell you by what authority I am doing these things"** (v. 8). They were momentarily stymied. But the issues at last were being joined.

It is not always necessary to tell a counselee everything he wants to know. It is possible to counter question him. How can you know when to use this technique? Well, it ought to be used at a time when the counselee's questions are insincere, when he is simply fishing for information that he can use against someone. Then the counter question would be appropriate.

In verses 9 through 16 we read the words of Jesus' last **parable**. It is the parable of the **servants** and the **son**. A man planted a vineyard, rented

Luke 20

A man planted a vineyard and rented it to farmers and went away for a long while.

10 At the proper time he sent a slave to the farmers to collect some of the fruit of the vineyard from them. But the farmers beat him and sent him away with nothing.

11 So he sent another slave, but they also beat and insulted him and sent him away with nothing.

12 Then he sent yet a third, but they also wounded him and threw him out.

13 So the vineyard owner said, "What should I do? I'll send my dear son; perhaps they'll respect him."

14 But when they saw him, the farmers debated with one another, saying, "This is the heir. Let's kill him so that the inheritance will be ours."

15 So they threw him out of the vineyard and killed him. What, then, will the vineyard owner do to them?

16 He will go and kill those farmers and give the vineyard to others.
When they heard this, they said, "May it never happen!

17 But Jesus looked straight at them and said,
What does this Scripture mean:
The Stone that the builders rejected
has become the Head of the corner?

18 Everybody who trips over that Stone will be broken to pieces, and whoever it falls on, it will crush to powder.

19 Now the scribes and chief priests tried to arrest Him right away, but they were afraid of the people. They wanted to do this because they knew that He had spoken this parable about them.

20 So they watched Him carefully and sent spies who pretended to be sincere, to try to catch Him in something that He said, so that they could turn Him over to the governor's authority and jurisdiction.

---

it to farmers and went away for a long time. He sent a servant to obtain some of the fruit of the vineyard (v. 10). But the farmers beat him and sent him back empty-handed. This he did two more times, with equal or worse results. So He said, "I'll send My **dear son**; they'll respect him" (v. 13). Instead, they decided to **kill** him since he was the **heir**. By their greedy thinking, they concluded they, instead, could inherit the vineyard. The owner then killed the farmers and handed over the vineyard to others. The interpretation of the parable is easy. Jesus is the Father's Son Who would be killed by the Jews. They didn't hear the prophets; they killed the Heir. As a result, God would destroy them, (once more a prediction of 70 AD). And the vineyard (church) would be handed over to the Gentiles. But **some of the scribes** seemed impressed with what Jesus had said (v. 39). It

Christian Counselor's Commentary

21 They asked Him, "Teacher, we know that you speak and teach correctly and aren't influenced by people, but teach God's way on the basis of truth,
22 so tell us, is it or is it not lawful for us to pay taxes to Caesar?"
23 He detected their trickery and said to them,
24 "Show Me a denarius. Whose image and inscription is on it?" They said, "Caesar's."
25 And He said to them, "Then pay to Caesar what is his and to God what is His."
26 So they weren't able to catch Him in His words in the presence of the people. And, amazed at His answer, they were silent.

27 Then some of the Sadducees approached Him (They are the ones who say that there won't be a resurrection). They questioned Him, saying,
28 Teacher, Moses wrote for us that **if a man's brother, who has a wife but no children, dies, the man must take his brother's wife and raise up children for him**.
29 Now then, there were seven brothers, and the first took a wife and died childless;
30 and the second;
31 and then the third took her, and similarly all seven who died childless.
32 Finally, the woman died too.
33 Therefore, in the resurrection whose wife will she be? All seven had her as a wife.
34 Jesus said to them,
The sons of this age marry and are given in marriage,
35 but those who are considered worthy of enjoying that age and the resurrection of the dead neither marry nor are given in marriage.
36 They can't even die any more. They are the same as the angels. They are God's sons, because they are sons of the resurrection.

---

seems that He had gotten through to some of them at least. There is always hope that someone would be moved by the truth, even when most are furious at it. Keep that in mind.

In response, Jesus continued, putting a Bible passage before them that they could not refute. He reasoned that if the Psalm says the Christ, Who is called the **Son of David**, is addressed as **Lord**, there must be something stated here that they were missing. Of course, it was the fact that Jesus had been asserting in one way or another all along the way (cf. His words to the rich young ruler), that He was God manifest in the flesh. Scripture must be used in counseling, but so must the counselor reason from that Scripture.

37	But that the dead are raised even Moses pointed out in the passage concerning the bush, when he called the Lord the **God of Abraham, the God of Isaac and the God of Jacob**.
38	God isn't the God of the dead, but of the living; to Him they are all alive.
39	Then some of the scribes answered, "Teacher, you have spoken well."
40	So they no longer dared to question Him about anything.
41	But He said to them, How can they say that the Christ is David's Son?
42	David himself says in the Book of Psalms, **The Lord said to my Lord, Sit at My right hand**
43	**till I put Your enemies beneath Your feet like a footstool**.
44	So then, if David calls Him lord, how is He his Son?
45	Then, as all the people listened, He said to His disciples,
46	Beware of the scribes, who want to walk about in long robes and like to be greeted in the marketplaces, and take the chief seats in the synagogs and the places at the head table during banquets,
47	who devour widows' houses and under pretense pray at length. They will receive more severe punishment.

It seems that some of the people were also beginning to catch on (v. 46) but that the rest of the scribes needed watching. Jesus makes this clear. Their actions and words are hypocritical. While looking pious outwardly, they devour widows' houses—a most disreputable thing! Jesus warns them that they would receive all the more severe punishment for their hypocrisy. Pretense in the ministry is reprehensible. The greater the privilege, the greater the responsibility, and in turn, the greater the punishment. Those concepts have never been set aside. They apply to you and to all who are in positions of leadership in Christ's church.

This short chapter is important to counselors. It shows how, at times, things must be brought to a head. By this encounter, Jesus was precipitating the final conflict that would lead to the cross. But it was done naturally, properly and in a way that was calculated to bring people to a point of decision. Counselors also must do this sort of thing whenever it is necessary. They must never shy away from controversy when it is necessary to engage in it. To divide the scribes and the people was natural; His words merely exposed the division that already existed. Rarely will the counselor himself incite such confrontation. But when he sees it coming, as Jesus did, he must stand firmly and encounter it biblically.

Chapter 21

> 1 Then He looked up and saw some rich people putting their gifts into the treasury chest;
> 2 and He saw a certain poor widow putting in two copper coins.
> 3 So He said,
> Truly I tell you, this poor widow has put in more than all of them.
> 4 All of them put in gifts that were part of their abundance, but this woman out of her poverty put in her whole livelihood.
> 5 And as some spoke about the temple—how it was adorned with beautiful stones and offerings—He said,
> 6 "As for these stones you are looking at, the days will come when there won't be a stone left on another that won't be thrown down."

Jesus was standing in the **temple** environs. Looking up, He saw people putting **money** into the **chest** in which it was to be deposited for the work of the Lord. Noticing both **rich** and **poor**, He commented that the poor **widow's two copper coins** were, in fact, a greater amount than the lavish gifts of the **rich**. How is that? Well, as Jesus explained, the **rich** gave out of the **abundance** of riches that they possessed; that is, they still had much left over. But the **widow** gave **all** that she had. That is to say, proportionally, she gave far more.

God expects people to give as they are able. That is true of funds, time, gifts they have been loaned, etc. He does not expect all to give the same. Obviously, He looks at the portion of what one has that he gives; not at the sum itself. That is why *any* believer may give lavishly to the Lord, if he *will*. Make that point clear to those who protest that they "have so little to give that it will make no difference." The lack of money, things and abilities can become an excuse for doing nothing. Those who *truly* give lavishly, like this **poor widow**, can make a *vast* difference. Ultimately, it is not the money that the Lord wants (He needs none); it is the devotion of His children that He desires and that He blesses richly. Money given to the Lord is used by Him as He sees fit. The one who multiplies the loaves and the fishes can do so with a widow's mite—or your counselee's seemingly meager gift. Many counselees fail to see this. Make it clear that what happens as the result of Christians' giving is what *God* does—not how much is given to Him. The power lies in God, not in money.

There were those who **spoke about the temple** (v. 5). They were

Luke 21

7 They asked Him, "Teacher, when will this be? And what will be the sign that this is about to happen?"
8 Then He said,
>   Beware that no one leads you astray. Many will come in My name, saying, "I am He," and "The time is at hand." Don't follow them.
9 >   When you hear about wars and disturbances, don't be afraid. These things must happen first, but the end will not follow at once.

---

taken with its beauty and with all the gifts that had been brought into it over the years. Jesus thrusts a sword into their reveries. In stark realism He says, **"the days will come when there won't be a stone left on another that won't be thrown down"** (v. 6). This startled them so that all they could say was, **"When?"** and **"What is the sign that this is about to happen"** (v. 7)? In the following discourse, in response, Jesus predicts the fall of Jerusalem in 70 AD, precisely as it happened.

It is always encouraging to those who doubt and wonder about the Bible to be able to point to prophesies that have been fulfilled. In His providence, God planned that Josephus, an unconverted Jew, would take part in this event in such a way that he could write up the siege and destruction from both the vantage point of the Jews inside and the Romans outside the city. During the war, he was in both places. What he says in his book *The Wars of the Jews* accords perfectly with the prediction.

First, Jesus warns about false prophets who would say that the event was about to occur when it was not yet time. **Wars and disturbances**, contrary to what many teach, are not the sign of the event. Though they would happen, Jesus explicitly said that they would *not* be the sign that the destruction of Jerusalem and the temple was **at hand**. (vv. 8, 9). It is surprising that after Jesus said this so clearly, some still think that these things are the sign. This only goes to show that Jesus' warning was needed. It also shows you how carelessly some counselees will interpret God's Word. You will find it necessary, as Jesus did, to warn about many wrong interpretations that you have found prevalent among others. You will find yourself (as He did) saying things like, "Now, remember, when someone tells you that you are to do so-and-so, this passage forbids it," or "Don't believe those who will tell you such-and-such." Take the time (as Jesus did) to warn about false interpretations that your counselee is likely to encounter.

Christian Counselor's Commentary

10   Then He said to them,
     Nation will rise against nation and kingdom against kingdom;
11   there will be great earthquakes and famines and pestilences from place to place; there will be terrors and great signs from heaven.
12   But before all these things they will lay their hands on you and persecute you, delivering you to synagogs and prisons, and you will be led before kings and governors for the sake of My name.
13   This will provide an opportunity for you to bear witness to them.
14   Get it settled in your hearts not to practice your defense beforehand,
15   because I will give you words and wisdom that none of your opponents will be able to withstand or contradict.
16   You will be betrayed even by parents, brothers, relatives and friends. They will put some of you to death.
17   You will be hated by all sorts of people for the sake of My name.
18   But not a hair of your head will perish;
19   by your perseverance, you will save your lives.
20   Now when you see Jerusalem surrounded by armies, then you know that its desolation has drawn near.
21   At that time those who are in Judea must flee to the mountains, those who are in the city must leave and those who are in the country must not enter the city,

---

Indeed, in this passage, Jesus goes on to describe all sorts of things that must occur in the 40-odd years yet to come. There would be wars (v. 10), natural disasters (v. 11), **persecution** in **synagogs** and elsewhere as the disciples preached the Word (vv. 12-15). During such times, there would be **opportunities** to preach inerrant, divinely-inspired sermons before kings and others (so there would be no need for normal preparation; vv. 13-15). Even family members would **betray** them to the officials, and some would **die** (v. 16). But until the time came for them to go to be with the Lord, though **hated by all sorts of people**, no one could harm them (vv. 17-18). As they **persevered** in doing what Jesus commanded, they would be thus preserved for the work (v. 19). The same is true today: no one can stop a counselee from doing what God has determined he must do. His task is to persevere and depend on God to do the protecting.

Now, at last, Jesus gives the sign: **Jerusalem surrounded by armies** (v. 20). That is when they would know that the destruction was **near**. Those in Judea should **flee** to the **mountains**, those in the **city** must leave and those in the **country** must not enter the city (v. 21). They would have but a very brief time to get out before the blow fell. The **armies sur-**

Luke 21

22	because these are the days of vengeance, in which everything that is written will be fulfilled.
23	Woe to pregnant women and to those who are nursing babies in those days! There is going to be great distress upon the land and wrath for this people.
24	They will be cut down by the edge of the sword and will be led as captives into all sorts of lands, and Jerusalem will be trodden down by the Gentiles until the times of the Gentiles are fulfilled.
25	There will be signs in the sun, the moon and the stars, and on the land nations will be tense and in perplexity at the roaring of the sea and the waves.
26	People will collapse from fear and foreboding of what is coming upon the world, because the powers of the heavens will be shaken.
27	Then at that time they will see the Son of Man coming on a cloud with power and great glory.

---

rounded Jerusalem, but Josephus tells us that for some unknown reason, they withdrew briefly. At that time, those who obeyed this prophetic command were saved. The armies then once more **surrounded** the city, never more to leave until the destruction was complete with incredible loss of life. This destruction was so horrible because it was the culmination of the sins of all of the past; it was the time of **vengeance** in which all the prophecies of that destruction would be fulfilled (v. 22; cf. Deuteronomy 28!). Verses 23 and 24 detail some of the sad occurrences that would take place. Josephus says that 1,100,000 Jews perished and 97,000 were taken captive. This destruction took place at a time when Jews were present from all over the Mediterranean world. The **treading down** of the **land** by **Gentiles** would then take place and it would persist until the **times of the Gentiles** is fulfilled. There may be, in this, the hope that Jews will someday come to faith in Christ in larger numbers. That would be when the natural branch would once more be grafted in. It would correspond to the little period when, following the millennium, the devil is released from the pit and goes out to deceive the Gentiles once more (cf. Revelation 20:7, 8). Verses 25 and 26 give evidence of the **fearful** times that these days of destruction will be. The **shaking of the heavens** was an Old Testament figure for the downfall of a powerful nation or order that had seemed as permanent as the heavenly bodies themselves (here, the contemporary apostate Jewish system and nation). At that time, they would see happen what Jesus had predicted: He would **come** in judgment on the people and the city (v. 28).

Christian Counselor's Commentary

28   So when these things begin to happen, straighten yourselves and raise your heads, because your redemption is drawing near.
29 Then He told them a parable:
Look at the fig tree and all the trees.
30   When they put forth leaves you can see and know yourselves that summer is already near.
31   So too, when you see these things happening, you can know that God's empire is near.
32   Truly I tell you that this generation won't pass away until all this happens.
33   Heaven and earth will pass away, but My words won't pass away.
34 Beware that your hearts don't become burdened with dissipation, drunkenness and the worries of life, and that day suddenly spring upon you like a trap.
35   It is going to come upon everyone who lives on the earth.
36   But watch always, praying that you may be able to escape all these things that are going to happen and that you may be able to stand in the presence of the Son of Man.

Fear, mentioned here, is altogether appropriate, as it is in all those who stand against God. It is important not to let eclectic views that decry anything that might lead to fear erase the proper instilling of the fear of God in counselees. It is, therefore, important for every counselor to study the matter of fear in the Bible. Unless he does so and is ready to discuss the matter clearly from a truly biblical perspective, he is likely to buy into current psychological views that all fear must be dispelled. God has placed fear in man as an important motivating factor to be used under the proper biblical conditions.

In verses 29 and following, Jesus told them the **parable of the fig and other trees**. When they would see these things happen, they could know that **God's empire** (the fifth empire of Daniel 2, 7) was about to supersede all previous ones. And He went on to say that all of this would happen to some of those living at that time (*this* **generation**). These words would surely be fulfilled (v. 32). They would have to be vigilant and not be overtaken by the judgment because of the lack thereof (v. 34). No one in the **land** would be exempt from the ravages that were to come. Everyone would have to face them. Believers, obedient to the Lord, however, could escape the worst of it through **prayer** and careful watching (with, perhaps, little more than the loss of possessions and property), but in order to escape with their lives, they would have to do as He said. In that day, if they do obey, they will be able to **stand** before the Lord as faithful

37 During the day He taught in the temple, and at night He left and lodged outside on what is called the Mount of Olives.
38 Then early in the morning all the people came to Him in the temple to listen to Him.

---

servants.

The last two verses indicate something of the order of Jesus' routine in **teaching**. They are, however, probably introductory to the next chapter (q.v.).

Christian Counselor's Commentary

CHAPTER 22

1 Now the feast of Unleavened Bread, which is called the Passover, drew near.
2 And the chief priests and the scribes were trying to find the best way to destroy Him, because they were afraid of the people.
3 Then Satan entered into Judas who was called Iscariot, who was one of the Twelve,
4 and he went off to confer with the chief priests and officers about how he might betray Him.
5 They were delighted and agreed to give him money.

Chapter twenty two begins with the **Passover drawing near** and the religious leaders plotting to kill the true Passover Lamb of God (vv. 1, 2). This was not so easy a task because, at this time, there was still a large following that attached itself to Jesus (cf. 21:38 which is probably the proper prelude to chapter 22). This fear, exhibited by the religious leaders, indicates the amount of interest and support that Jesus had elicited by His "triumphal entry" after the raising of Lazarus.

The way in which they finally accomplished their purposes was **Satan**-driven (v. 3). Unknown to him, the devil was bringing about his own defeat by his actions. Presumably, the devil was not a good exegete of Genesis 3:15 where his own crushing defeat is predicted. **Judas**—and there seems to be one who finds his way into every work of God that is successful—was the arch traitor of history. If you are doing a work for the Lord, you can almost count on one or more such persons undermining the work as best he can. But the insightful counselor will make the point (and remember it himself) that God has a way of turning Satan's activity into blessing in the long run as surely as he turned Balaam's curses into blessings. To discover that there is a traitor in the midst, one who is working to destroy the work of Christ, then, is not necessarily a tragedy. It is important to understand that if nothing worthwhile is happening, the devil will probably leave the work alone. It is when something significant is occurring that he acts. He is not God; he cannot be everywhere all at once. He must choose the places where he will try to intervene.

The religious leaders were **delighted** at Judas' proposals (v. 5) and agreed to give him money for his efforts. Often, the evil one carries on his work that way—by the promise of wealth, fortune, popularity, etc. He is willing to pay his way. Judas, therefore, **looked for** the right time to **turn**

6 So he agreed, and looked for the right time, when there was no crowd, to turn Him over to them.

7 Then the day of Unleavened Bread came on which the Passover lamb had to be sacrificed.

8 So He sent Peter and John, telling them, "Go prepare the Passover for us, so that we can eat it."

9 So they said to Him, "Where do you want us to prepare it?"

10 He said to them,
> Notice when you enter the city; a man carrying a jug of water will meet you. Follow him into the house that he enters,
11 and tell the householder, "The Teacher says: 'Where is the guest room, where I can eat the Passover with My disciples?'"
12 And he will show you a large upper room, all furnished. Prepare it there.

13 When they went, they found things as He had told them, and they prepared the Passover.

Jesus **over** to them—a time when the **crowd** was not present (v. 6). The Passover day, on which the lamb was sacrificed came (v. 7). Jesus asked two of His trusted disciples (in contrast to Judas) to prepare the Passover. They asked Him where? Presumably, Jesus had kept the place secret until the last moment so that Judas and his crowd could not interrupt the Passover meal. He then gave them the signs that were arranged to find the place (vv. 9-12). They followed His directions and found everything to be just as He had ordered (v. 13).

The wisdom of Jesus is seen even in such details as these. Somehow, on the side, He had arranged all beforehand so that Judas would not know where **Passover** would be observed by them. Sometimes it takes such care to arrange things in a way that will keep the enemy from finding out your plans. One does not always have to reveal all that he is doing to the world in general. Here, Jesus even kept His disciples ignorant of the time and place because they were all too prone to talk carelessly, and the information would probably have seeped back to Judas in one way or another. While the biblical *message* must always be up front, the activities of God's people do not necessarily require such exposure. One is to be harmless as doves, but *wise as serpents*.

In verses 14 through 38, we read of the events that transpired thereafter at the feast. Jesus began the proceedings with the statement of His **great desire to eat the Passover** meal with His disciples. After all, it was a feast that typologically predicted the death that He soon would die. In

14 Then, when the hour came, He reclined at the table and the apostles with Him.

15 And He said to them,

> I have had a great desire to eat this Passover with you before I suffer.

16 I tell you I shall not eat it again until it is fulfilled in God's empire.

17 After taking a cup, He gave thanks and said,

> "Take this and divide it among yourselves.

18 I tell you, I shall not drink again from the fruit of the vine until God's empire comes."

19 Then He took bread, and when He had given thanks He broke it and gave it to them, saying,

> "This is My body [that is given for you. Do this in remembrance of Me."

20 And in the same way after the supper He took the cup, saying,

> This cup is the new covenant in My blood that is shed for you].[1]

21 However, the hand of the one who is going to betray Me is with Me on the table.

---

[1] Some MSS omit the portion in brackets.

---

verse 15, He ties in the meal and His **suffering**. It would be the last meal He would have with them before the new **empire** from the heavens would replace the old, until the new order of things would **fulfill** the old. That would be the time when the types and the shadows would disappear. Even now, at the conclusion of the supper, Jesus would introduce the new supper that would replace the old.

From verse 17 on, we hear the words of institution of the Lord's supper. He distributed the cup among them and, once more, alluded to the coming **empire** that was about to appear (v. 18). Taking the bread, breaking it and giving it to them, He said, "**This is My body that is given for you. Do this in remembrance of Me**" (v. 19). He did the same with the cup, declaring that it is **the new covenant in** His **blood** that was to be shed for them (v. 20). The word **in** might possibly be better translated instrumentally as **by**. At any rate, what Jesus meant is that His death for sinners constituted the institution of the **new covenant**. Sad though it may be, on this solemn occasion, Jesus knew it was necessary to reveal the traitorous actions of Judas (v. 21). Counselees living in a world of sin must recognize that even the most sacred moments may be crassly marred

Luke 22

22   The Son of Man, of course, will go as it has been determined; nevertheless, woe to that person by whom He is going to be betrayed.

23 Then they began to question one another about which one of them was going to do this.

24 Then there arose a dispute among them about which one of them seemed to be the greatest.

25 So He said to them,

      The kings of the nations lord it over them, and those who have authority over them are called benefactors.

26   But not so with you. Instead, the greatest among you must be like the youngest, and the one who governs must be like the one who serves.

---

by the presence of sinners bent on doing evil. We do not live in a sinless world; sin manifests itself and must be dealt with in the most inappropriate situations.

In verse 22 Jesus taught a very important principle: God has determined all things (here, how He would be betrayed and put to death) and yet, even though all was previously planned, that does not free those by whose hand evil is perpetrated from responsibility. Counselees are always getting tangled up in the problems of God's sovereignty and man's responsibility. While you may be able to avoid long discussions with them about the matter, it is well to satisfy their troubled minds. One way to do so is to use this verse where you may show them both predestination and human responsibility in absolute juxtaposition. If they press you further, you may make it clear that the way in which God carries out His will is not apart from but through the responsible actions of human beings. Here, clearly, Jesus did not let Judas off the hook because he was fulfilling prophecy; rather, He holds him fully responsible, pronouncing **woe** upon him as the result of his traitorous deed.

Talk about sordid things blemishing somber moments? Well, look at what follows. Growing out of a discussion about who might betray Jesus, the discussion took a new turn: the disciples began to **dispute about which one of them seemed to be the greatest** (v. 24). Not only did Judas, the son of perdition who never was saved, destroy the joy of the holy time with Jesus, but the very disciples He had chosen to be with Him as He ate this last Passover now begin to squabble over who is number one!

Nevertheless, Jesus turns the **dispute** into an opportunity to teach them further principles about His service. This was an excellent counsel-

Christian Counselor's Commentary

27 Who is greater, the one who reclines at the table or the one who serves him? Isn't it the one who reclines? But I am like one serving among you.
28 You are those who persevered with Me through My trials.
29 As My Father appointed Me to have an empire, so too I appoint you
30 to eat and drink at My table in My empire, and you will sit on thrones, judging the twelve tribes of Israel.
31 Satan has begged to sift you all like flour,
32 but Simon, Simon, I have prayed for you that your faith might not fail; so when you have turned around, strengthen your brothers.
33 And he replied, "Lord, I am ready to go to prison and to death with you."

---

ing move. They were not to be like lordly rulers who asserted their **authority** over others. Rather, **greatness** is in not asserting it, but in taking the humble place of **service** to others (v. 26). How important for counselors to use this passage with those who, like the disciples, have it all backwards! In verse 27, Jesus shows how He, himself, has come to serve others and not Himself. Then, in a powerful statement to all Christian workers (as well as to the disciples) He says, what is true of Me must be true of you (v. 28). They would be rulers in an **Empire**, but would act differently from the **kings of the nations** (v. 25). Like their Lord Who rules, they too would rule through service. In that way, they too, would rule from **thrones, judging Israel**.

Now, drawing on His omnipotence, He explains to them about Satan's desire to **sift them all like flour** (v. 31), but (He says) He has **prayed for** Peter that He might retain his faith throughout the sifting, which in his case would be extreme. And He instructs him that when he has repented from his sin (**turned around**) he should **strengthen** his **brothers** (v. 32).

There is in this a hope that many Counselees need to hear. Even though they have failed, upon genuine repentance they may be able to pray for and encourage many others who are undergoing trials similar to those they experienced. Just because one has failed and fallen does not mean he must remain frustrated. Peter was restored to his ministry (cf. John 21).

But Peter, misunderstanding, boasts that he is ready to be imprisoned and die with the Lord if necessary (v. 33). Jesus then tells him that the **rooster** will not crow until he has **denied** Him three times. That is, before

Luke 22

34 But He said, "Peter, I tell you, the rooster won't crow today until you deny that you know Me three times!"

35 Then He said to them, "When I sent you off without a purse or wallet or sandals, you didn't lack anything, did you?" They said, "Nothing."

36 He continued,
> This time, however, take not only a purse but a wallet also. And the one who doesn't have a sword should sell his coat and buy one.

37 I tell you that this Scripture must be completed by Me: **He was numbered with transgressors**. What is written about Me has a fulfillment.

38 Then they said, "Lord, see, here are two swords." And He said to them, "That will do."

39 Then He left and, according to His custom, He went to the Mount of Olives. And His disciples followed Him.

40 And when He came to the place, He said to them, "Pray that you may not enter into temptation."

41 Then He withdrew from them about a stone's throw and knelt down and prayed, saying,

---

morning breaks (v. 34).

In verse 35, Jesus contrasts the previous preaching tour of the disciples with their future mission. What He told them before met every exigency. Now, the new mission would require much that the old did not (v. 36). The situation would be very different. People can often be stuck in one mode and not want to change with changing conditions. Here Jesus shows that something far different lay ahead that would require different preparation.

Again, Jesus alluded to His death. He refers to Isaiah 53, quoting from it (v. 37) and assuring them that the prediction will be fulfilled. When they showed Him two swords, Jesus said, **"That will do."** They were going to need protection from brigands along the road as they traveled in distant lands.

After this, He left and, **according to His custom, went to the Mount of Olives** to pray. The disciples followed (v. 39). Jesus told them to **pray that they enter not into temptation**. He knew how sorely they soon would be tested. That none of us obeys this command as we should explains why we so often fall into sin in times of temptation. He withdrew slightly from them and prayed, expressing His desire not to have to be separated from the Father because of the load of sin cast upon Him. But,

42 "Father, if You are willing, take away this cup from Me. Nevertheless, let Your will, not Mine be done."
43 [Then an angel from heaven appeared to Him and strengthened Him.
44 He was in agony as He prayed even more earnestly, and His sweat like drops of blood fell to the ground.][1]
45 When He rose from prayer and went to His disciples, He found them asleep, worn out by sorrow.
46 He said to them, "Why are you sleeping? Get up and pray, so that you won't enter into temptation."
47 While He was still speaking, a crowd appeared with the man called Judas, who was one of the Twelve, leading them. And he approached Jesus and kissed Him.
48 But Jesus said to him, "Judas, are you betraying the Son of Man with a kiss?"
49 When those who were around Him saw what was going to happen, they said, "Lord, should we strike them with our swords?"
50 But one of them struck the high priest's slave and cut off his right ear.
51 But Jesus said, "No more of this!" Then He touched the ear and healed him.

---

[1] Some MSS omit vss. 43, 44.

He also expressed His willingness to endure it if God willed (v. 42). Then an **angel** appeared and **strengthened** Him for the ordeal ahead. Because of the thought that He Who all His life had never sinned, but had always done the Father's will, would be counted as sin for others, He was in **agony**. And in great drops like blood, sweat rolled from His forehead (v. 44). Meanwhile the disciples were **sleeping** rather than praying. The stress of recent events had taken its toll (v. 45). He awakened them and urged them once more to pray (v. 46).

But now Judas and a band of ruffians approached. Judas, taking the lead, **kissed** Jesus. He asked, wondering at the audacity and hypocrisy of this traitor, "**are you betraying the Son of Man with a kiss?**" One asked, "should we protect you with our swords?" Peter struck out without waiting for Jesus to reply and cut off the High Priest slave's ear (vv. 47-51). Jesus stopped the fray and healed the ear. In all of this, He is in utter control of everything. It is taking place exactly as it was determined.

Jesus has a word for the religious leaders who committed this crime. He asks why they had to send men with swords and clubs as if apprehending a bandit (v. 52). He points out that they had to do their evil deed under

52 Then Jesus said to the chief priests, the temple officers and the elders who had come against Him,
> Have you come out with swords and clubs as you would against a bandit?
53 When I was with you daily in the temple, you didn't raise a hand against Me. But this is your hour, and darkness is in authority.

54 Then they arrested Him and led Him away and brought Him into the high priest's house, and Peter followed at some distance.
55 When they had started a fire in the center of the courtyard, they sat down together. And Peter sat among them.
56 Then a servant girl looking at him as he sat in the firelight said, "This man was with him too."
57 But he denied it, saying, "Woman, I don't know him."
58 After a short time another saw him and said, "You are one of them." But Peter said, "Man, I am not!"
59 About an hour later another insisted on it, saying, "Certainly this man was with him too; indeed, he's a Galilean."
60 But Peter said, "Man, I don't know what you are talking about." Then, just as he said this, the rooster crowed.
61 The Lord turned and looked directly at Peter, and Peter remembered what the Lord had said to him, "Before the rooster crows today, you will deny Me three times."

---

the cover of darkness. Then, with fine imagery, He declares that this dark time is their **hour** since they are in cahoots with the prince of **darkness**, who was behind all of it.

When in dire straits, remembering that God's will is being done strengthens counselees to respond, like their Lord, in powerful (and sometimes even memorable) ways. But they will not be able to do so unless they have been prepared by prayer to face them. A profitable book might some day be written with the title *Prepared by Prayer*. But the disciples had not prayed, and thus they were not prepared. The arrest took place as they stood by or fled.

Jesus was taken to **the High Priest's house, and Peter followed at a distance** (v. 54). In the **courtyard** Peter sat warming himself around a fire when a **servant girl** recognized him, identifying him as a member of Jesus' followers (vv. 55, 56). But Peter **denied** it. Afterwards, another said the same thing, and Peter denied it a second time (v. 58). Finally a third made the identification, and once more Peter denied. We read, **the rooster crowed** (vv. 59, 60). Then Jesus, Who was within his sight, **turned** and, we are told, **looked directly at Peter** (v. 61). Then comes

Christian Counselor's Commentary

62   And he went out and wept bitterly.

63 Now the men who were in charge of Him mocked Him and beat Him;

64   they blindfolded Him and commanded, "Prophesy! Who was it that struck you?"

65   And they spoke many other blasphemous things against Him.

66 When day came, the elders of the people assembled, both chief priests and scribes. And they led Him off to their Sanhedrin, saying,

67   "If you are the Christ, tell us." And He replied,

> If I tell you, you won't believe it.

68   If I ask you a question, you won't answer.

---

this significant word: **and Peter remembered**. As he did, he was struck with remorse and **went out and wept bitterly**.

When you read his second Epistle, if you compare what he says with this incident, you will understand why he wrote as he did. From II Peter 1:9 on, over and over in one way or another, Peter says that he is writing to *remind*. Peter was the man who forgot. He did not want his readers to suffer the grief and sorrow that he did. Counselees are forgetful people. It is important, therefore, as Peter discovered, to repeat facts again and again. It is even important to let people know what you are doing—as he did. It also may be helpful to read these verses in Luke to make the point. This story of Peter is powerful. But also be sure to relate it to the failure to pray.

The soldiers to whose care Jesus was assigned **mocked** Him, **beat** Him and even played blind man's bluff with Him. What was done was nothing short of **blasphemous** (vv. 63-65). And all this was done in the name of God! It has not been unusual for some of the most heinous acts to be done in the name of God. There are times when counselees may find this out. It will be difficult for them. They will need the greatest encouragement. But perhaps the very best of all is to say, simply, "Remember what they did to your Lord!"

Now, after an earlier illegal trial (they could not be held at night), Jesus was led before the **Sanhedrin** (the council of the elders and priests). This trial, after daybreak, took place in order to give their action a quasi-legal appearance (see A.T. Robertson's *Word Pictures in the New Testament*). They ordered Him to reveal whether He was the **Christ** (vv. 66, 67). He refused, rightly saying that if He told them the truth about the matter they wouldn't believe, and if He asked them a question they wouldn't answer. That is to say, there is no point to further discussion.

69   But from now on **the Son of Man will be seated at the right hand** of God's power.
70   Then they all said, "Are you God's Son, then?" And He said to them, "You correctly say that I am."
71   Then they said, "Why do we need any other witnesses; we ourselves have heard it from his mouth."

There comes a place in dealing with those who are determined to go ahead, regardless, and have their way at which one simply must cease making any attempt to reason. Unfortunately, it is not always easy to determine when one has reached that point. But every counselor will, from time to time, run across situations in which this is the only way to go. He must be sensitive to all that is going on, asking God for the wisdom to know when to continue pleading and when to cease.

Jesus brings the interview to an end by referring to the prophecy of Daniel that speaks of Him, making it clear that He is the Messiah and that He will ascend to the Father's **right hand** (v. 69). This must have startled them—as indeed, it should have. Somewhat in fear, it seems, they exclaim, **"Are you God's Son, then?"** And in a ringing affirmation, Jesus replied, **"You have correctly said so."** Using this statement, they then declared that they needed no more witnesses; he had condemned himself by it (v. 71). Surely, Jesus not only made the important confession for their sakes, so that they would know what they were doing, but for His church of all time that would read these words as you and I now do. Many have attempted to make His words say otherwise, but Jesus was declaring that Messianic rights and privileges would be His in the near future and that, yes, He was the Messiah. That they understood Him is clear. There is no honest way of interpreting the passage otherwise.

CHAPTER 23

1 Then the whole group of them got up and took Him before Pilate.
2 They began to accuse Him, saying, "We found this man misleading our nation and forbidding us to pay taxes to Caesar and saying that he himself is Christ, a king."
3 So Pilate questioned Him, saying, "Are you the King of the Jews?" And He replied, "You are correct in saying so."
4 But Pilate said to the chief priests and the crowds, "I find no grounds for holding this man."

This chapter begins with the hearing before **Pilate** (vv. 1-7). Bringing Jesus before Pilate was necessary because the Jews, who wished to kill Jesus, had the power of capital punishment taken from their hands by the Romans. They, therefore, had to seek permission to do so from Pilate, the local authority in the area. The accusations made in verse two are not those for which they actually wanted to condemn Him. But the charges, they hoped, would sound much more plausible to a Roman governor. The first charge is a matter of opinion: **misleading our nation**. At best, it pointed to someone whose activities were widespread in Palestine (as, of course, they were). The hint of an uprising—something the Romans would want to quell at all points—was in that accusation. **Forbidding to pay taxes to Caesar** was a charge without foundation. But it was crafted to cause concern to any governor. The third, saying that he is **Christ, a king**, did have a basis in fact. But, as Pilate concluded, it was not the problem that the Jews made it out to be since Jesus explained that His kingdom was a kingdom not of this world, but of truth. Having ascertained these things, and pretty well recognizing the true reasons that the Jews had taken Jesus, Pilate declared, "**I find no grounds for holding him**." That was a correct verdict (v. 4). There was really no valid reason for Jesus' arrest, let alone His conviction and death. Often, the earliest judgment made by someone is more correct than the later one. Note this and contrast each. Then look for the reasons for the change. In such cases, as we shall see here, it will be because some other extraneous pressure has intervened. If called upon to adjudicate matters between persons a counselor must not become a Pilate. He must be true to his beliefs regardless of the pressure that others attempt to place upon him. He will not always be liked for a stand of this sort.

The Jews would not take "no" for an answer (v. 5). They continue to

Luke 23

5   But they insisted, saying, "He is stirring up the people, teaching all over Judea, from Galilee all the way to here."
6   When Pilate heard this, he asked whether He were a Galilean.
7   And when he discovered that He was under Herod's jurisdiction, he sent Him over to Herod, who happened to be in Jerusalem at that time.
   8 When Herod saw Jesus, he was simply delighted, because he had wanted to see Him for a long time, since he had heard about Him and hoped to see Him do some miracle.
9   So he questioned Him thoroughly, but He didn't answer him.
10 And the chief priests and scribes stood by, vehemently accusing Him.
11 Herod and his soldiers treated Him with contempt and made fun of Him. They dressed Him in a splendid robe and sent Him back to Pilate.
12 Herod and Pilate became friends with each other that day. Prior to this they had been enemies of one another.
   13 Then Pilate called together the chief priests and leaders of the people
14 and said to them, "You brought this man to me, charging that he was misleading the people, and after examining him before you I found no grounds for the charges you have made against him.

---

agitate. When Pilate heard that Jesus was from Galilee, under Herod's jurisdiction, he was delighted to be able to send them to him, since, conveniently, Herod just **happened** (it, of course, was actually part of the providence of God) **to be in Jerusalem at that time**. Verses 8 through 12 tell of the hearing before Herod.

Herod was **delighted** with the opportunity to meet Jesus. This was something he had wanted to do for some time (v. 8). But Herod's interest was in seeing Jesus do a **miracle**. He was not interested in justice, only in amusement. So Herod received no answer to his questioning of Jesus. Jesus was not concerned to "perform." The religious mob continued to accuse (vv. 9, 10). So, not having been acknowledged by Jesus, Herod's soldiers made fun of Him, dressed Him in a **splendid robe**, and returned Him to **Pilate**. After all, of what amusement value was someone who wouldn't talk. Then Pilate and Herod (who had been enemies before) **became friends** that day over this event. This is not the only time that enemies have become friends over vilifying someone else! Indeed, you will see it frequently in counseling. It is a sad occurrence. It usually means that the two are wrong, and it calls for very careful handling on the part of the counselor whom they may seek to enmesh in some trap to get their way. I cannot tell you how many times I have labeled such a coalition "Herod and Pilate."

Verses 13 through 25 record the final disposition of the matter before

15 Neither did Herod, since he sent him back to us. He hasn't done anything that deserves death.
16 So then, I will beat him and release him."
17 ¹
18 But they all shouted together, saying, "Take this man and release Barabbas to us."
19 (He had been thrown into prison because of his part in a riot in the city, and for murder.)
20 Pilate called to them once more, because he wanted to release Jesus.
21 But they shouted out, "Crucify Him! Crucify Him!"
22 Then a third time he said to them, "But what evil did he do? I found no grounds for his death. I will beat him and release him."
23 But they insisted in loud voices, demanding His crucifixion, and their voices prevailed.
24 So Pilate decided to grant their request.

---

¹ Some MSS add vs. 17: *But he was obligated to release one person to them at the feast.*

Pilate. He called the rabble-rousers together and said, "**I found no grounds for the charges . . . Neither did Herod**" (vv. 14, 15). Then, totally against Roman justice, Pilate said, "**I will beat him and release him**" (v. 16). This he did, hoping to gain their satisfaction short of death. But they were not satisfied, they chose to have **Barabbas**, a noted criminal, released rather than Jesus (vv. 18, 19).

Pilate **wanted to release Jesus** (v. 20), so he tried once more to do so. But they shouted, "**Crucify him!**" (v. 21). That was the ultimate in deaths at the time, the most agonizing and humiliating of them all. Again, Pilate suggests his alternative to no avail (vv. 22, 23). So, yielding to the mob, he released Barabbas and turned over Jesus to them. There are other aspects of these trials mentioned in the other gospels but we are studying the story as Luke records it. All along I have been refraining from the harmonizing approach (which has its place) in order to bring out the things that Luke saw as important to mention. There is value to both approaches. But the unwillingness to seek harmonization has not often prevailed. So I chose that method of study.

The abdication of responsibility by Pilate, who turns Jesus over to the Jews, is reprehensible. But in a variety of ways, you will find it happening. There is a current expression around ("Covering my backside") which epitomizes the attitude. People would rather shift their responsibility to others instead of standing for what they know to be right—in order

Luke 23

25 He released the one they asked for, who had been thrown into prison for insurrection and murder, and he turned over Jesus for their wishes to be fulfilled.

26 Now as they led Him away, they seized Simon, a Cyrenian, who was coming in from the country, and they loaded the cross on him and made him carry it behind Jesus.

27 And a very large crowd of people and of women who mourned and lamented over Him followed Him.

28 Then Jesus turned and said to them,
> Daughters of Jerusalem, don't weep for Me. Weep for yourselves and for your children.

29 The days are coming when they will say, "The barren are the happy ones, and the wombs that wouldn't bear children, and the breasts that never nursed."

30 At that time they will begin **to call to the mountains, "Fall on us!" and to the hills, "Cover us up!"**

31 If this is what they will do when the tree is full of sap, what will they do when it is dry?

32 Now there were two others, criminals, who were led away to be put to death with Him.

---

to "protect" themselves. Watch out for this tendency in others—and in yourself!

Now we turn to the crucifixion itself (vv. 26ff.). Simon, from Cyrene, was compelled to carry Jesus' cross as they led Him out to be crucified (v. 26). It is not unusual for totally disinterested individuals to be caught up in the nefarious activities of others. Here, poor Simon was the one picked. Large numbers of Jesus' followers (especially, of the women who had followed Him) **mourned and lamented** at what was happening (v. 27). But Jesus, turning to them, warned them of the destruction to come (vv. 28-31). He described the horror of the impending doom of the nation. And He made it clear that if they were willing to do such things as this now, at the beginning of the last days of the Old Testament period, what would happen later in its extremities would be even more vicious (that is the meaning of the green tree filled with **sap**, and the **dry**). Indeed, when you read Josephus' account, you recognize the fulfillment of these words: the barren woman would be fortunate, as He said (v. 29), because, in the siege, women would be reduced to the point of boiling and eating their own children! If things are bad now—wait and see how bad they *will* become!

Two criminals were crucified with Jesus (v. 32) at the hill that looked

Christian Counselor's Commentary

33 When they came to the place called The Skull, there they crucified Him and the criminals—one on His right and one on His left.
34 [Then Jesus said, "Father, forgive them. They don't know what they are doing."][1] And they cast lots to divide His clothes.
35 Then the people stood watching, and the rulers sneered at Him, saying, "He saved others. Let him save himself if he is God's Christ, the chosen one!"
36 The soldiers mocked Him too, coming to Him and offering Him vinegar and saying,
37 "If you are the King of the Jews, save yourself!"

---

[1] Some MSS omit the words in brackets.

---

like, and so was called, "The Skull." Jesus' cross was prominently placed between the two other crosses (v. 33). Jesus prayed, **"Father, forgive them. They don't know what they are doing"** (v. 34). This statement has wrongly been adduced as evidence that Jesus forgave people who were unrepentant. But careless exegesis is behind the notion. This is not a declaration of forgiveness at all; it is a *prayer*. Was the prayer ever answered? Yes, when Peter and John preached, they addressed the very same crowd that had shouted for Jesus' death. Many of these repented and believed the message. The prayer, therefore, was answered precisely as God has always done. There was no exception in this case. It is but shoddy exegesis that understands a prayer *for* as a declaration *of* forgiveness. Yet, some are so disposed to push their viewpoints that they will construe any passage they can in ways they think will further their agendas. Here, the idea that one may forgive another without repentance on his part is linked to the modern self-centered notion that the one forgiving must do so for his own sake. The one who did the wrong is considered unimportant in the transaction. Yet, in the Bible, it is primarily the wrongdoer who is in view in forgiveness. The forgiveness occurs for his benefit. The one doing the forgiving receives benefits in the transaction only as a by-product (For a thorough discussion of this and other aspects of the self-esteem movement, see my book *Self-esteem, Self-love and Self-Image in the Bible*).

Those who were crucifying Him cast lots for Jesus' clothes (v. 34). Some sneered at Jesus. They reasoned, if he is the Christ, and if he was able to save others, then let's see if he can help himself. The soldiers joined in the mockery offering vinegar and saying, **"If you are the King of the Jews save yourself"** (vv. 36, 37). And a poster had been tacked on

Luke 23

38 There also was a poster above Him:[1] THIS IS THE KING OF THE JEWS.

39 Then one of the criminals who was hanging there blasphemed Him: "Aren't you the Christ? Save yourself and us!"

40 But the other rebuked him, saying, "Don't you fear God, since you are suffering the same punishment?

41 We are being punished justly, because we are getting what we deserve for what we have done. But this man hasn't done anything wrong."

42 Then he said, "Jesus, remember me when You come into Your empire."

43 He said to him, "Truly I say to you, today you will be with Me in Paradise."

44 It was now about noon, and darkness came over the whole land until three o'clock,

45 because the sun stopped shining. Then the temple curtain was ripped in two,

46 and in a loud voice Jesus cried out, "Father, **into Your hands I commit My spirit.**" As He said this He breathed His last.

---

[1] Some MSS add, *written in Greek, Latin and Hebrew.*

---

the cross above Jesus' head that read, **this is the king of the Jews**. The irony of this was that God had so arranged all things that even at the end, a placard would proclaim the truth!

In verses 39 through 43 an important sidelight is recorded. One of the criminals crucified with Jesus railed at Him, much as the people did (v. 39). But the other, who had come to believe in Jesus, warned him. He explained that they were being put to death justly, but Jesus wasn't, and asked Him, "**remember me when You come into Your empire**" (vv. 40-42). Jesus' answer (which contradicts all notions of soul-sleep) was, "**Today you will be with Me in Paradise.**" It also belies the modern teaching that Jesus suffered after He died. The fact is that when He said, "**It is finished,**" it was. The atonement was made on the cross—not continued into death and the afterlife. Here was a man who came to faith in Jesus Christ while hanging on a cross. He couldn't be baptized, join a church or engage in any other such activity. Yet he was saved. That must be kept in mind when dealing with those who have been influenced by some cult or sacerdotalist church to think otherwise. Moreover, Jesus represented His **Empire** as a heavenly one—**Paradise**.

In verses 44 through 46, a brief summary of the actual suffering of the cross by which we are saved is given. Darkness came across the land

Christian Counselor's Commentary

> 47 Now when the centurion saw what happened, he glorified God, saying, "This man surely was righteous!"
> 48 When all the crowds that had gathered to watch saw what had happened, they went home beating their breasts.
> 49 All those who knew Him and the women from Galilee who had accompanied Him stood at a distance watching these things.
> 50 Now there was a man named Joseph from the Jewish city of Arimathea, a member of the council, who was a good, righteous person,
> 51 who had not assented to their decision and action. And he was looking for God's empire.
> 52 He approached Pilate and asked for Jesus' body.
> 53 Then he took it down, wrapped it in linen and put it in a rock-hewn tomb in which no body had ever been laid.
> 54 It was the Day of Preparation, and the Sabbath was beginning.

---

from noon till three o'clock, and the curtain separating the holy place of the temple from the holy of holies was ripped in two. These things signified that the actual time of the atonement was present at last. God darkened the sky to signify Christ's suffering for sinners. And He ripped the veil in order to signify that the temple worship was no longer acceptable to Him. All that it symbolized had now come to pass; henceforth it was not only useless but distracting. The reality that it prefigured had occurred: Messiah, God's Lamb, had been sacrificed on Calvary. At the conclusion, Jesus **committed His spirit** into God's hands, and then expired (v. 46).

Various reactions are mentioned in verses 47 through 49. The **centurion** believed and gave God glory, the **crowds** beat their breasts in dismay and **women** who had followed Jesus stood there watching. It is always instructive to notice how people react to a nefarious deed that has been done. If you have never studied such reactions, it might be helpful to you as a counselor to do so. You will learn a lot about people that will help you deal with them in the future. To get started, why not think carefully about these reactions?

Now, in verses 50 through 56, we read of those who loved Him enough to tenderly care for the **body** of the Lord. **Joseph** is one. He was himself a high official who had not been part of the outrageous activity that had just ensued. And he was a faithful follower who looked forward to the coming of the Empire of Christ (vv. 50, 51). He took Jesus' body and laid it in a fresh, rock-hewn **tomb**. The women who followed saw where it had been laid, went back, prepared **spices** and **ointment** to

Luke 23

55 The women who had accompanied Him from Galilee followed and saw the tomb and how His body was laid in it.

56 Then they returned and prepared spices and ointment, after resting on the Sabbath according to the commandment.

---

embalm it after the **Sabbath** was over. That is the conclusion of the chapter. And if it had been the conclusion of the story, I would not be bothering to write, and you would not bother to read. Thank God that there is another chapter in the book!

CHAPTER 24

1 Now on the first day of the week, very early in the morning, they went to the tomb, carrying the spices that they had prepared.
2 They found the stone rolled away from the tomb,
3 but when they went in, they didn't find the body of the Lord Jesus.
4 As they stood there confused over this, all of a sudden two men in dazzling clothing stood with them.
5 They were terrified and bowed their faces to the ground. But the men said to them,
    Why are you looking for the Living One here with the dead?
6   He isn't here; He has risen! Remember how He told you when He was still in Galilee:
7   "The Son of Man must be turned over to sinful men and must be crucified, and must rise again on the third day."
8 Then they remembered His words.
9 So they returned from the tomb and related these things to the eleven and to all the others.
10 Now it was Mary Magdalene, Joanna and Mary (James's mother) and the other women with them who told this to the apostles.

The last chapter of Luke is most instructive as well as cheering. Counselors may learn much from it. The story begins where chapter 23 left off. The Sabbath is over, and the women with spices and ointment approach the tomb which they had identified earlier (23:55). They are startled to find the **stone rolled away** (a stone in a groove was rolled in front of the door of such a tomb). And going in, they discovered that the body of Jesus was gone (vv. 1-3).

They were **confused**. Suddenly, two angels in **dazzling white clothes** stood in their midst (v. 4). They were terrified, but the angels asked why they were **looking for the Living One among the dead**. Then they went on to remind them of the predictions of Jesus about His death and resurrection (vv. 4-7). And we read, **they remembered**. How often people forget (remember Peter?). And, how often it takes an event like this for words to sink in. People are like that; they often have to be hit by a ton of bricks (or be visited by angels!) to appreciate God's truth.

In verses 9 through 12 we read of the response of the disciples when the women related their experience to them. It seemed like **nonsense** to them and they refused to believe (v. 11). But Peter, running, went to inves-

Luke 24

11 But their story seemed like nonsense to them, and they didn't believe them.

12 [But Peter got up and ran to the tomb. He stooped down and looked in and saw the linen wrappings alone. Then he went home wondering what had happened.][1]

13 The very same day two of them were walking to a village called Emmaus that was about seven miles from Jerusalem.

14 They were talking to each other about everything that had happened.

15 As they continued to carry on their conversation and discussion, Jesus Himself drew near and walked along with them.

16 But their eyes were kept from recognizing Him.

17 He said to them, "What is this you were talking about to each other as you were walking?" And they stood still, crestfallen.

18 Then one of them, named Cleopas, answered Him, "Are you the only visitor to Jerusalem who doesn't know about the things that have happened there during the last few days?"

19 He said to them, "What things?" And they replied,
> The things concerning Jesus the Nazarene, who was a prophet whose words and works were powerful before God and all the people,

20 and how the chief priests and our rulers delivered Him up to be condemned to death and crucified Him.

---

[1] Some MSS omit vs. 12.

---

tigate. He saw the grave clothes lying in the tomb, with the body gone. It is probable that Luke indicates these were still wound up, the body having passed through them. Peter goes home wondering.

Now comes the principal incident of the chapter, the appearance of Christ to two lesser disciples on the **road to Emmaus** (vv. 13-32). They were on their way to the village, talking about everything that had happened (vv. 13, 14). As they walked, Jesus drew near and walked with them (v. 15). But He kept them from recognizing Himself (v. 16). He asked them what it was that they were discussing—as if He didn't know about it. They stopped, **crestfallen** at having to recount the death of Jesus once more (v. 17). Then, somewhat amazed that He didn't seem aware of what had taken place, Cleopas asked, "**Are you the only visitor to Jerusalem who doesn't know the things that have happened here?**" He asked, "**what things?**" So they told Him.

In their account of the death of Jesus, they name Jesus and call Him **a prophet whose works were powerful**, but they fail to recognize Him as

Christian Counselor's Commentary

21 We were hoping that He was going to redeem Israel. Now, in addition to all this, it is the third day since this happened.
22 Some of our women, indeed, startled us. They were at the tomb early this morning
23 and didn't find His body. And they came back saying that they had even seen a vision of angels who said He is alive.
24 Some of our group went to the tomb and found things there were just as the women said, but they didn't see Him.
25 Then He said to them,
O you ignorant people, who are so slow to believe in your hearts all that the prophets spoke.
26 Wasn't it necessary for the Christ to suffer these things and to enter into His glory?
27 So beginning with Moses, He went through all the prophets and explained to them in all the Scriptures the things that concerned Himself.

---

the Messiah. Indeed, that had been their hope prior to His crucifixion (vv. 19-21), but no longer. They stressed that three days had gone by since it all happened. They were aware of the words of the women, but they discounted them. And they knew that some had found the tomb empty, but they had reported that they had not located the body. In other words, here was a dispirited pair of disciples, giving up, going home. It was all over for them.

How often that is the case with Christian counselees—until you bring Jesus into the picture. He, and He alone, can brighten up the situation and bring joy out of sorrow, hope out of despair. Remember, it is He, not you, Who does so. Be sure that you make it clear to counselees that it is Jesus Christ in His Word that you ask them to trust, and not you.

Then Jesus begins to expose the ignorance and disbelief of His followers. What is it that leads to such despair? Well, one thing: they are **slow to believe . . . *all* that the prophets spoke** (v. 25). There it is. They had read the Scriptures selectively. They saw the promises of the crown and read over the prophecies of the cross. They wanted physical redemption but failed to understand Christ's concern for their spiritual redemption. Little has changed today. Counselees will have the very same difficulties. Watch for their selective use of the Bible.

Jesus showed them in **all the Scriptures** those things concerning Himself that taught His death prior to His entrance into the heavenly **glory**. Jesus is invited to go in to eat with them, and as He broke the bread and blessed it, **their eyes were opened and they recognized Him**. Then

Luke 24

28 Now as they drew near to the village to which they were going, He pretended that He was going to go on.
29 But they urged Him not to, saying, "Stay with us, since it is nearly evening and the day is almost gone." So He went in to stay with them.
30 As He reclined at the table with them, He took bread, blessed it and broke it and gave it to them.
31 Then their eyes were opened and they recognized Him, and He vanished from their sight.
32 And they said to one another, "Didn't our hearts burn within us as He spoke to us on the road, as He opened the Scriptures to us?"
33 So they got up and that very hour returned to Jerusalem. And there they found the eleven gathered together, and those who were with them, who said,
34 "The Lord has really risen; He appeared to Simon!"
35 Then they told what had happened on the road and how He was known by them in the breaking of the bread.

He **vanished** (vv. 28-31).

Notice how Jesus pretended not to know, how He **pretended** to be going on. These were ways in which He gradually brought the disciples to understanding and to faith. A counselor doesn't always have to come up with the answers. He may *gradually* lead his counselees to understanding. He may even want to have them explain things to him as Jesus did when dealing with these disciples, so that He could deal with their **ignorance** and/or **unbelief**. It is often important to get them to state how they see a situation before telling them how you believe that God would have them view it. Why? Because they are forced to think it through, thereby they are brought to see their lack of understanding and their disbelief. This may be important, as here, in order to deal with the central problem.

Notice what it was that brought warmth to their cold hearts: the **opening of the Scriptures**. Never forget it! That is your task in counseling—to open the Scriptures to counselees. You cannot warm hearts, but the Word of God, chock full of vital promises and truths, can. Sometimes in counseling, it is enough to open the Scriptures—that is to explain them in relation to a person's problem—to bring hope and direction that a counselee has been lacking. Of course, you must know the Bible well to do so. Notice, Jesus showed them from **all** the Scriptures what they needed to know. A grasp of the entire Bible is necessary to do effective counseling. Not that it is necessary to always go through all the passages relating to a problem, but to be able to do so whenever necessary; that is what is

36 As they were saying these things, He stood in their midst.
37 They were startled and frightened and thought that they saw a spirit.
38 But He said to them,
> Why are you troubled? Why do disturbing thoughts arise in your hearts?
39 See My hands and My feet that I am Myself. Touch Me and see, because a spirit doesn't have flesh and bones as you see I have.
40 [When He had said this, He showed them his hands and His feet.][1]
41 While they still disbelieved out of joy and amazement, He said to them, "Do you have any food here?"
42 They handed Him a piece of broiled fish.
43 He took it and ate it before them.
44 Then He said to them,
> These are My words that I spoke to you while I was still with you, that all the things that have been written about Me in the Law of Moses, in the Prophets and in the Psalms must be fulfilled.
45 Then He opened their minds to understand the Scriptures.
46 And He said to them,
> This is what is written: that the Christ must suffer and on the third day rise again from the dead,
47 and that repentance and forgiveness of sins must be preached in His name to all nations, beginning at Jerusalem.

---

[1] Many MSS omit vs. 40.

---

required of an effective biblical counselor.

They returned to the others in Jerusalem and declared that Jesus had risen from the dead. As they were relating the events on the road and in the house, Jesus **appeared** (vv. 32-36). Their first reaction was fear. They thought that they saw a **spirit** (they too were filled with the superstitions of their age). But Jesus disabused their minds of any such thought by bidding them **touch** Him and saying, "**A spirit doesn't have flesh and bones as you see I have**." They were ecstatic with **joy**. Then, to further prove his bodily resurrection, Jesus **ate fish**—something that clinched the matter for them, since they still found it hard to believe (vv. 41-43).

Once more, Jesus refers to His prophecies and **opened the** minds of the disciples **to understand the Scriptures**. How important it is to know that it takes the illumination of the Spirit for persons to understand Scripture believingly. Sometimes it isn't that you have failed to present the truth convincingly; it may be that your counselee has not had his mind opened. In verses 46 and 47, Jesus taught the message they were to pro-

48	You are witnesses of these things.
49	Now I will send on you what My Father promised. So stay in the city until you are clothed with power from on high.
50	Then He led them out as far as Bethany, and He lifted up His hands and blessed them.
51	As He was blessing them, He withdrew from them [and was carried up into heaven].[1]
52	Then they returned to Jerusalem with great joy,
53	and were continually in the temple, praising God.

---

[1] The bracketed words are omitted from some MSS.

---

claim throughout the world about His death and resurrection and the necessity for repentance and faith in it. The disciples then were designated by Him as **witnesses**.

Then, Jesus predicted the coming of the Holy Spirit Who would give them the **power** to proclaim the message (v. 49). Since Acts would follow, Luke lets the reader wait to read and understand about this event. Finally, we are allowed to view the ascension. Notice, it was as Jesus was **blessing** that He withdrew from them. To the end of His earthly life He concerned Himself with His own. So they returned, joyfully, to continually praise God in the temple.

Clearly, in such a powerful book as the Gospel of Luke, with its many nuances and teachings as well as its insights, we have explored only a meager amount of the facts that might be mentioned. Continue to go back to it again and again in order to find more help for counseling.

www.ingramcontent.com/pod-product-compliance
Lightning Source LLC
Chambersburg PA
CBHW060516100426
42743CB00009B/1335